Social Media Management: A Complete Guide

Social Media Management: A Complete Guide

Marcus Hart

MURPHY & MOORE
www.murphy-moorepublishing.com

Social Media Management: A Complete Guide
Marcus Hart
ISBN: 978-1-63987-804-8 (Hardback)

www.murphy-moorepublishing.com

MURPHY & MOORE
Murphy & Moore Publishing
1 Rockefeller Plaza,
New York City,
NY 10020, USA

Cataloging-in-Publication Data

Social media management : a complete guide / Marcus Hart.
p. cm.
Includes bibliographical references and index.
ISBN 978-1-63987-804-8
1. Social media--Management. 2. Social media--Management--Vocational guidance. I. Hart, Marcus.
HM851 .S63 2023
302.231--dc23

Table of Contents

Preface

Social media refers to a set of computer-mediated interactive technologies that allow the sharing and creation of ideas, information and other forms of expression, with the aid of social networks and virtual communities. Social media services are interactive Web 2.0 applications that use Internet technology. The social network revolution led to the emergence of networking sites. Some popular social networking sites include Facebook, Twitter, Instagram, Snapchat, etc. Modern youth spend a major share of their time on social networks. This is due to the widespread use of smartphones. User-generated content such as digital photos, videos, text posts and comments and the data generated is the mainstay of social media. Social media tools are used for communication, marketing and sales promotion, relationship development and organizational development, e-commerce, etc. Social media also allows a business to connect with its customers, increase awareness about the brand, and boost sales and leads. This textbook provides comprehensive insights into the field of social media management. It aims to shed light on some of the unexplored aspects of social media management. It will serve as a reference to a broad spectrum of readers.

A foreword of all chapters of the book is provided below:

Chapter 1 - Social media is a broad term that refers to a set of interactive computer-mediated technologies that allow the creation and sharing of content pertaining to ideas, information and interests via virtual networks and communities. Such content can be in the form of text, digital photos, messages, introductions, text messages, videos, etc. This chapter will introduce in brief the significant aspects of social media and includes crucial topics related to writing relevant social media content, building a social media plan and the demerits of oversharing on social media; **Chapter 2 -** Social media management is the management of online content and interactions across different social media platforms. Social media channels such as Twitter, Facebook, YouTube, LinkedIn and Pinterest are used to facilitate businesses by increasing their reach and influence. Social media management is now important for existing brands and companies to stay relevant in the market by maintaining a social media presence. This chapter has been carefully written to provide an easy understanding of social media management and the roles and responsibilities of a social media manager; **Chapter 3 -** Social media optimization (SMO) refers to the use of outlets and communities for generating publicity of a product, brand or event. RSS feeds, social networking sites, blogging sites and social news and bookmarking sites are involved in this process. Users are encouraged to use and share links to the website panning across all social media sites. The fundamentals of social media optimization and the techniques of improving and optimizing SMO have been extensively addressed in this chapter; **Chapter 4 -** Social media marketing is a modern tool for brand promotion. It uses social media platforms and websites for the promotion of a product or service. Such social media platforms have in-built analytic tools which allows brands or companies to track the success and progress of their ad campaigns. This chapter provides an insight into brand promotion using social media. It includes vital topics related to social media marketing, social media marketing campaign and promoting products in social media creatively; **Chapter 5 -** Social media platforms are used by organizations and businesses to advertise their products, services and brands, and inform about upcoming events, projects and new releases. Some popular social media platforms are Facebook, Twitter,

Pinterest, LinkedIn and Tumblr, among others. The ways in which such platforms may be used by businesses as promotional tools for creating an online presence, promoting a crowdfunding campaign, etc. have been extensively discussed in this chapter.

At the end, I would like to thank all the people associated with this book devoting their precious time and providing their valuable contributions to this book. I would also like to express my gratitude to my fellow colleagues who encouraged me throughout the process.

Marcus Hart

Understanding Social Media

1

Social media is a broad term that refers to a set of interactive computer-mediated technologies that allow the creation and sharing of content pertaining to ideas, information and interests via virtual networks and communities. Such content can be in the form of text, digital photos, messages, introductions, text messages, videos, etc. This chapter will introduce in brief the significant aspects of social media and includes crucial topics related to writing relevant social media content, building a social media plan and the demerits of oversharing on social media.

Social media is a computer-based technology that facilitates the sharing of ideas and information and the building of virtual networks and communities. By design, social media is internet based and offers users easy electronic communication of personal information and other content, such as videos and photos. Users engage with social media via computer, tablet or smartphone via web-based software or web application, often utilizing it for messaging.

Social media originated as a tool that people used to interact with friends and family but was later adopted by businesses that wanted to take advantage of a popular new communication method to reach out to customers. The power of social media is the ability to connect and share information with anyone on Earth (or multitudes of people) as long as they also use social media.

Social media can take the form of a variety of tech-enabled activities, such as photo sharing, blogging, social gaming, social networks, video sharing, business networks, virtual worlds, reviews and more.

For individuals, social media is used to keep in touch with friends and extended family, network for career opportunities, find people from all over the globe who share a common interest, share content and more. Those who engage in these activities are part of a virtual social network. For businesses, social media is an indispensable tool for finding and engaging with customers, sales, advertising and promotion, gauging trends and offering customer service. Governments and politicians utilize social media to engage with constituents and voters.

Social media's role in helping businesses is significant. It facilitates communication with customers, enabling the melding of social interactions on e-commerce sites. Its ability to collect information helps focus marketing efforts and market research. It helps in promoting products and services, as it enables the distribution of focused, timely and exclusive sales and coupons to would-be customers. And it can assist in relationship building, such as through loyalty programs linked to social media.

Importance of Social Media in Business

The importance of social media in business is growing at warp speed. With more and more people joining social media sites and using them regularly/efficiently, the social media industry is bound to become bigger in the coming years. It's booming like never before.

No, the social media wave isn't ending anytime soon. And your business should take advantage of it if you want it to survive.

With such amazing growth, every business today needs to leverage proper social media channels in the best possible way. Not because it's the "in thing", and not because it sounds simple, but because their target audience is hanging around the popular social networks. And they're engaging with their favorite brands and connecting with them on different levels.

By giving your business brand the social media touch, you not only generate more business but also connect with your customers better and serve them on a higher level. It actually makes your digital marketing easier.

According an infographic published by Ambassador, 71% of consumers are more likely to recommend a brand to others if they have a positive experience with it on social media.

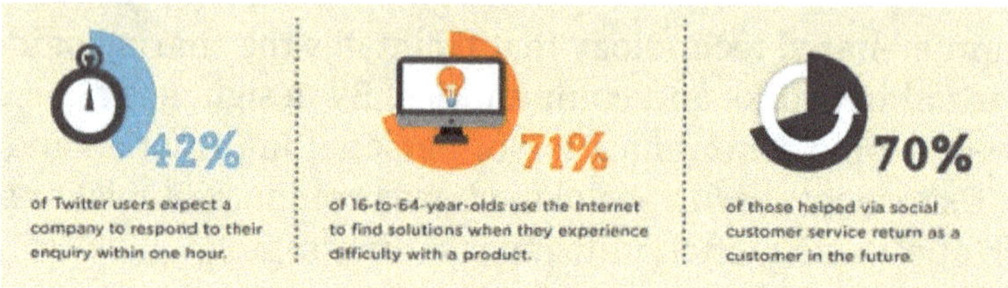

Here are some more social media statistics that prove beyond doubt the importance of social media in business. Your business needs to leverage sites like Facebook, Twitter and LinkedIn to keep up with the competition.

- The number of social media-using adults has gone from 7% in 2005 to 69% just ten years later.
- Social media use on mobile devices is seeing a 30% growth every year.
- 2 million business today use Facebook advertising for promoting their products and services.

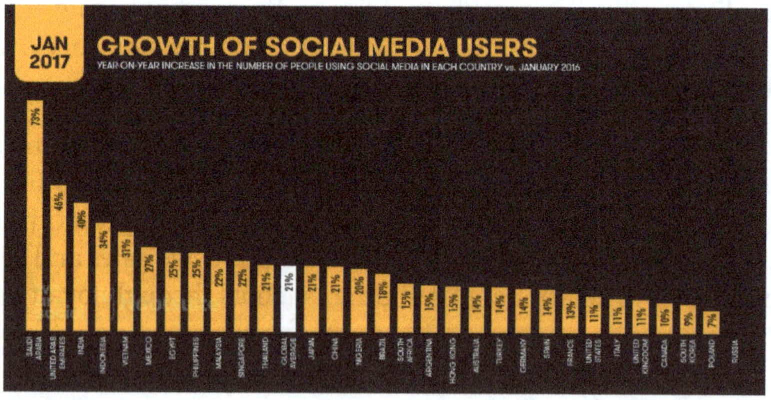

Let's now look into the importance of social media in business by analyzing its advantages.

1. Leverage Social Advertising

Social media advertising may be the new kid on the block, but it's growing faster than imagined. Take Facebook Ads for example. Even though the social network launched ads in 2005, it managed to reach 9.16B in ad revenue in the first quarter in 2017. This just goes on to show that social advertising is here to stay — for a long, long time.

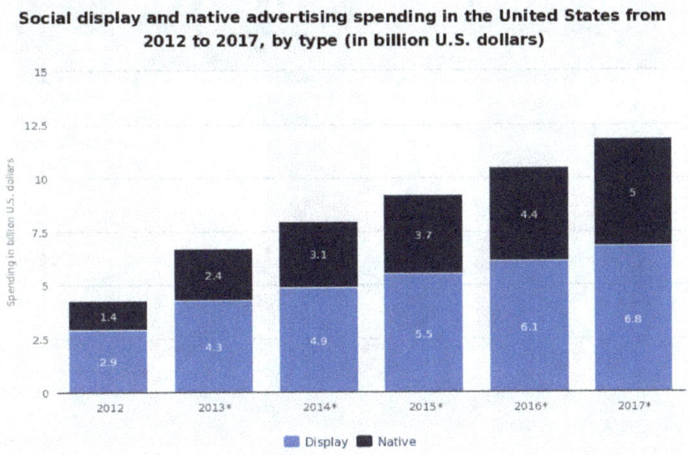

As more and more businesses successfully experiment with digital advertising, they're realizing that taking the social media advertising route makes total sense. Here's why:

- Lower ad costs: When compared to traditional advertising methods such as print media, TV and radio advertising, social ads are not only dependable, but also cheaper. What's more, you're allowed to engage on various social media channels for free before scaling with paid ads. You're free to grow on your own, at your own pace.
- Targeted reach: Traditional advertising doesn't give you the luxury to reach out to your target audience the way social media ads do. It simply doesn't work that way. When you're doing offline advertising, you're taking the blind, shotgun approach where your returns are dismal even if you're making big investments. Using social media ads you reach out to targeted prospects, increase your conversions and ultimately get a higher return on investment.
- Real-time performance analysis: Knowing if your ad is working or not is integral in order to improve it. When you're doing any type offline advertising, you're unable to analyze the performance of your ad campaign. Which cripples massively cripples your efforts. Social media ads on the other hand allow you to constantly keep track of how well (or how bad) your ad is performing. You're able to change your ad on the fly and instantaneously see the results.

Last but not the least, it's important for businesses of all types to understand that social media ads are only getting bigger and smarter. Social media advertising is where the future is headed. It's the new wave. The question is, are you a part of it?

2. Boost Brand Awareness

Social media proves to be a powerful tool when it comes to growing your brand awareness. There are businesses who dismiss it as a way to build a brand, but by doing that, they're leaving an open ground for competitors. On the other hand, many reputable chief marketing officers agree that social media has a definite impact on brand awareness.

Increasing your brand awareness via social media isn't rocket science. Here are a few tips on how you can do so.

1. Find your audience: Before you start focusing on a particular social platform, find out whether your target audience is on it. You can do this by searching for relevant conversations about your product or industry. For example, a B2B company may find their audience on LinkedIn rather than Facebook. Don't just assume or follow other brands.

2. Use visuals: Once you know where your target audience is, it's time to grab their attention by using eye-catching visuals with your content. Images and videos play a big role in helping you grow your brand awareness on social media channels. Because they not only increase engagement but also boost social shares.

3. Create conversations: Social media is all about building conversations. If you use these social platforms for one-way communication, you'll only grab so much attention. Instead, talk and listen. Get involved. Showcase your personality by conversing, tagging and mentioning others.

4. Measure your efforts: Don't just aim in the dark. Use the tracking tools provided by the platforms (eg: Facebook Page Insights) along with other external tools such as URL shorteners, Google Analytics, etc. to measure your social media activity. Use the insights you gain to understand what's working so that you can optimize your efforts and build a stronger brand with social media.

5. Build authority: If you want a higher engagement rate along with better brand awareness, then work on building your authority by sharing real value. Along with borrowed content, your content you post should also have something original, as it adds to your credibility.

Remember, every single step that you take to increase brand awareness with social media will impact the overall growth of your business in the long run.

3. Increase Inbound Traffic

Inbound marketing is one of the most effective ways to generate targeted traffic to your website.

It's the kind of traffic that actually converts because it's super relevant. However, if you leave you ignore the importance of social media in business, you will be limited to your inner circle of customers or the people that are already familiar with your market or brand.

By putting in more effort in social media promotion, you create a whole new channel to draw in laser targeted inbound traffic and get more inbound links.

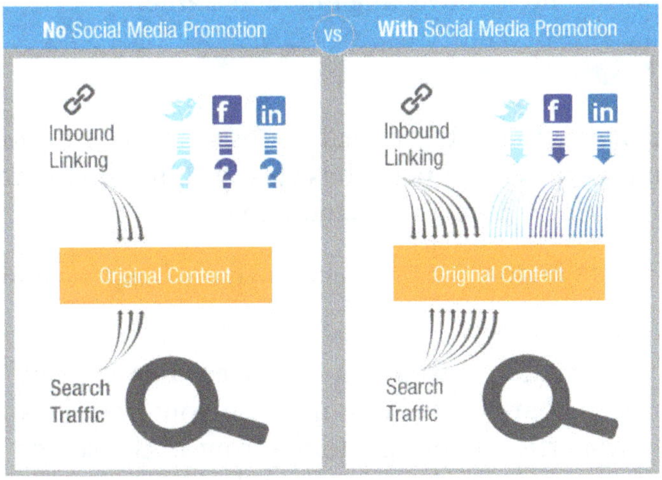

For example, having an active blog makes it easy for you to connect with your audience with the help of fresh content. But by having them share this content (on the right time) on Twitter or Facebook increases your reach 10X. You're suddenly reaching out to a bigger audience that may like plus share your content, follow your brand and ultimately become a customer.

Similarly, people that are already actively searching for keywords related to your product or service are a smaller percentage than those who aren't. Social media helps you connect to this larger, untapped segment of the market.

To help you understand, here's the amount of referral traffic social media management platform Buffer generates by creating and sharing quality content on some of the biggest social media networks:

Social Network	Sessions	Sessions
1. Twitter	79,096	56.44%
2. Facebook	35,870	25.60%
3. LinkedIn	11,449	8.17%
4. Pinterest	3,263	2.33%
5. Google+	3,204	2.29%
6. StumbleUpon	1,380	0.98%
7. Scoop.it	1,155	0.82%
8. Pocket	1,031	0.74%
9. reddit	679	0.48%
10. Hacker News	568	0.41%

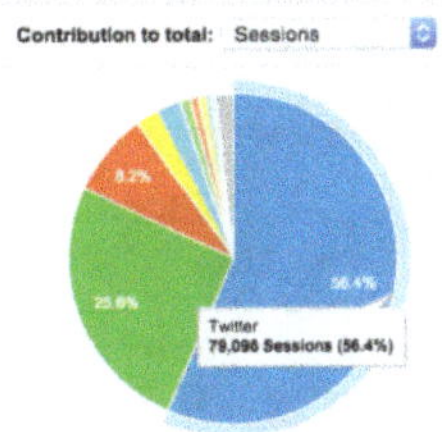

By using social media, you diversify your marketing efforts in more than one way. You don't reach out to just one type of crowd, but connect to a versatile customer base. Which is crucial to for your brand to make a mark in your niche.

For instance, serious professionals may find your website via LinkedIn while the younger crowd or the millennials may find you on Instagram. Each piece of social media content that you create is a new door for new customers to enter. It's a different opportunity for you to connect.

Ultimately, it boils down to creating enough high quality content that you can post on social media sites, and in the process attract high-converting inbound traffic.

4. Improve Search Engine Optimization

Every seasoned social media marketer knows that there is some connection between social media and search engine optimization. While Google has clearly stated that it does take "social signals" into consideration when ranking a page, there's more to it.

Here's how understanding the importance of social media in business and working on it can help improve your SEO.

1. Higher chances to be found via web search – According to Matt Cutts, the former spam head of Google, social shares have no impact on your website's ranking. But, it's a fact that social media properties do dominate the front of the search engine result pages for brand names. Which means, social media profiles indeed have the power to rank in the top 10 results. Social media profiles are a great way to connect to your prospects and customers. They work as a doorway to your business website because they show your human side. They not only inform the searcher about your business, but also help them become a part of your conversations.social media influences searchBy optimizing your social profiles and by keeping them fresh with the right content, you create a stronger presence on the web. You get more exposure. And you have multiple channels to draw people towards your business.

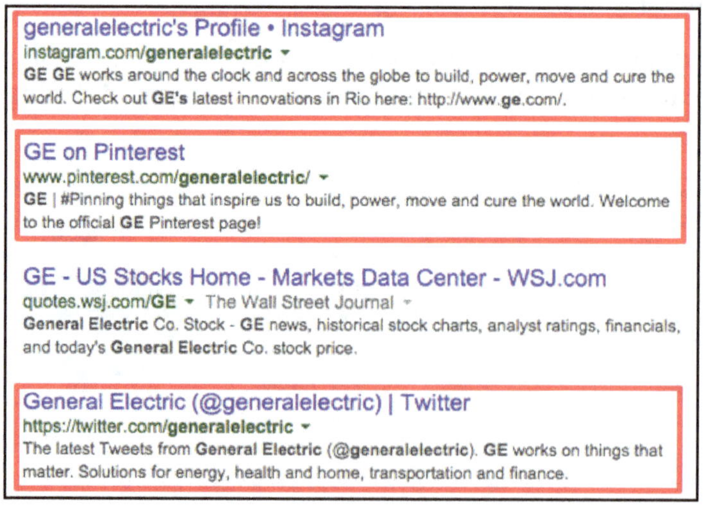

2. Ability to reach more people via social media search – People are no longer dependent on Google search when they need to connect to something or someone. Today, search is not limited to the mighty web search engines. It has moved beyond, which is why social media platforms such as Facebook and Twitter are the new search engines.

There is massive amounts of content being created and shared on the social web. This content can easily be discovered by users with the help of keyword search, hashtags, etc. When people search for the type of content you're publishing on your social media page, you may win new fans that want to follow, connect and do business with you. It's just not about the content, but also about the content producer, which is you. When people see great content being created and shared, they're curious about who's behind it. This may lead them to look you up on LinkedIn and learn more about your business. Being a business it's important that you take the necessary steps to stand out from other competing social media profiles and avoid have duplicate accounts.

The social media world is evolving and is so is the SEO arena. And there are high chances that social signals may start having affect on your rankings. So why not be prepared by building your social media presence with valuable content?

5. Increase Conversion Rates

Social media is great for capturing targeted leads for your business, but it doesn't stop there. Getting quality leads is only one part of the equation. The other part is converting those into sales.

Can social media help you increase your conversion rates? Does it have the 'x' factor when it comes to giving you the ground to achieve more sales?

The answer is a resounding yes, but only, if you do it the right way. Here are some ways you can use social media for better conversion rates.

1. Use It for social proof: Social proof, also known as informational social influence, is a psychological phenomenon where people assume the actions of others reflect correct behavior for a given situation. In simple terms, people do what others do. They like to believe what the majority likes to believe. The reason why social proof works is because it gives a sense of assurance to your prospects and lets them know about the benefits of your product, without any selling. Social media is brimming with activity that can be used for social proof. If someone commented on your Facebook post praising your company, use it. When someone tweets you about how your product changed their life, use it. When someone posts a happy Instagram picture of them enjoying your service, use it. Look at how KW Finder smartly embeds tweets from their customers on their site as social proof:

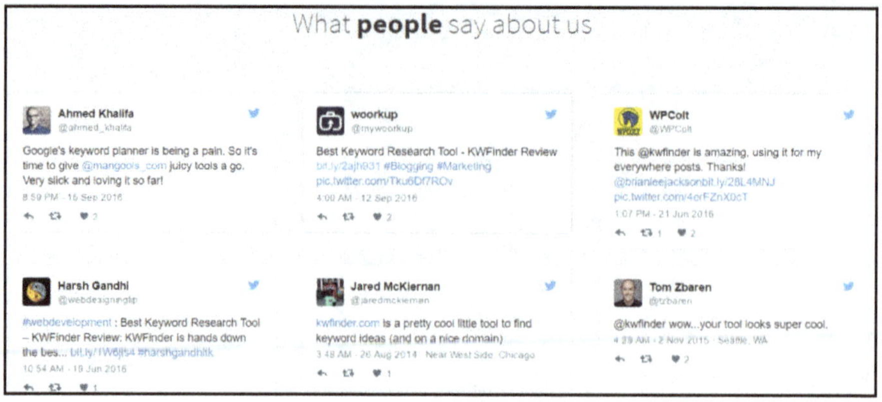

2. Use it for user-generated content creating quality content for social media is crucial. But what better way to create this content than have your loyal fans do it for you. People that follow you on social media may mention you in a positive note, which you can use to feature them on your social profile. The UGC acts like a social proof that indirectly helps you increase conversions. Also, this doesn't need to happen by chance. In fact, you can engineer it by asking people to share specific content for a chance to get featured to a wide audience. Given that you have a decent audience size, most social media users would be thrilled to have such an opportunity. You need to get creative in your approach and ask people. When Belkin did the launch for their Lego iPhone cases, they tapped into the power of their social community. They asked customers to personalize their cases in their own unique way and share the pictures on Instagram.

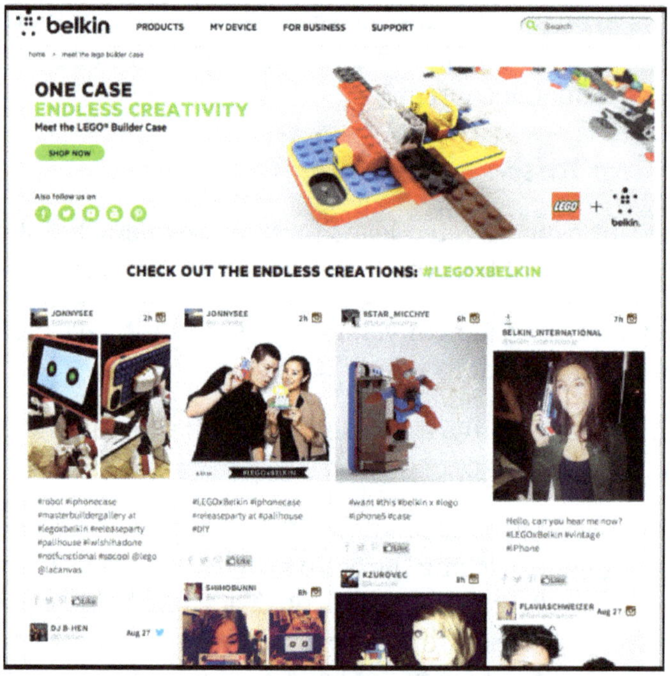

As you can see, a ton of customers were excited enough to share their personalized cases with the right hashtags. This helped Belkin gain targeted exposure and higher conversions at zero cost.

There are many ways that social media can impact conversions and help you increase sales. But for that, you need first to understand the importance of social media in business and take the necessary steps.

6. Satisfy your Customers

Losing a customer is hard, and gaining a new one is harder. But retaining an existing customer is 10 times easier. Which is why customer satisfaction should be your topmost priority.

By using social media to connect with your customers, you have the opportunity monitor what they want, the problems they're facing and how you could serve them.

In order to truly satisfy your customers and make their life easier, you need to offer them customer service that is more personalized and effective. And social media helps you do just that.

Customers these days know that social media is a lot more approachable and friendly than a call center executive, thousands of miles away, who has a hard time resolving your problem. In other words, customers want superior service without the hassle.

Increasing customer satisfaction with social media includes:

- Monitoring conversations to see if your customers are talking about your brand and in what context.
- Broadcasting important messages, announcements and offers to customers via a social media platform such as Twitter.
- Offering prompt customer service to customers who are facing genuine problems or need some help with the product or service.

> 42% of consumers complaining in social media expect a 60 minute response time.

- Holding regular question & answer sessions with customers to understand their concerns, get real feedback and see how things can be improved.
- Connect and build a relationship with power users or customer advocates so that they can help serve other customers.

Regardless of what social media platform you're using to help your customers, it's important to speak their language, give them personalized service and respond to them without much delay.

7. Enhance Brand Loyalty

A lot of businesses are stuck on their follower count, which is nothing but a vanity number. It doesn't serve a real purpose if the followers aren't loyal to your brand. There's a difference between a random follower and loyal one, because the latter adds real value.

If you want to get the most out of your social media marketing efforts, it's crucial that you focus on increasing brand loyalty. Having a loyal following means better engagement and better conversations.

Ask any loyal social media follower about their trusted brand, and they will speak positive about it without the need to push. Which leads to natural word of mouth marketing.

You can enhance brand loyalty on social media by:

1. Having a solid social media strategy – Social media platforms are evolving, and each has its own personality. Facebook is not Twitter, and Twitter is definitely not LinkedIn. Which means, you can't take the same old, outdated marketing and advertising methods and apply them to social media. You need to formulate a social media strategy that clearly aligns your goals with other areas such as content marketing, search engine optimization, etc. This should give you a fair idea of what type of value you can create for your loyal social media followers. It'll allow you to not only retain them but also help them spread the word.

2. Sharing value-oriented content – There's a reason why your followers are loyal to you. They're looking for value, which you will have to deliver at all times by sharing quality content. For example, sharing a detailed case study is much better than a 500 word article. The more useful and relevant the content you post, the better. Plan how and what type of content you would like to share with your following. By spending time on strategizing your content creation, your content will fetch you a higher ROI when you share it. So don't rush. See what sets your content apart from others. For example, visual content gets more shares than regular social media content. Which means you're free to use photos, videos, etc. as long as they add some value.

3. Being consistent – Your brand has a personality, and certain aspects that are unique to it. By identifying these personality traits and by bringing them out, it gets easier to connect to your target audience. Your aim should be to be consistent in your approach and maintain the same voice throughout your interactions. The content that you create/share along with how you converse with others should reflect your brand's personality.

4. Responding to queries – You may not be a celebrity for your social media followers, but they do look up to you for answers. So when they approach you with a relevant query, you should get back to them with the right answers. This way they will know that you are the real deal. And that your business actually cares about others. But don't limit your answering adventures to your loyal followers. Go out there and hunt for questions that have partial answers or no answers. You can search using targeted keywords and look for questions that need a response. By answering these questions, you establish yourself as an expert or an authority.

5. Show the human side –While it's okay to automate your social media posting with a tool like Buffer, it's not-so-okay to keep doing it. Personally interacting with other people and humanizing your brand will go a long way. It will keep your followers/fans keeping coming back for more.

A lot of businesses try to present themselves as big corporations, which is a mistake. People need people, not auto bots. Which is why you need to connect to them on a more personal level and engage in real conversations. Even if it's just for the sake of interacting.

How to Write Social Media Content

Social media- Internet sites designed for social interaction such as Facebook, Twitter, and Blogger- is a powerful new tool revolutionizing the advertising field. Fifteen years ago, the advertising world revolved around highly expensive TV spots designed by powerful Madison Avenue executives. Now successful advertising campaigns can be executed free of charge by some guy with a modem. In this brave new world where Facebook is the most popular form of communication, knowing how to write social media content can revolutionize the way your business interacts with customers.

Steps

1. Write for your clients at the end of the day. Whether your business caters to doctors, wine enthusiasts, or local soccer teams, most people don't log on to Facebook looking to buy something- they log on after a long day at work, beer in hand, to catch up with friends. Dinner's cooking and the kids are playing tag in the den. Your tweet, ad, or blog post must compete with this ruckus. So keep it short and sweet. Run-on sentences, technical jargon, and bloated expositions have no place in this world. A catchy tweet or Facebook post can be achieved in under ten words.

2. Aim for engagement, not exhibitionism. Customer loyalty is created not by viewing ads, but by interacting with a business. A popular Florida restaurant began tweeting diners after the meal, asking how they could improve on the experience; not surprisingly, these customers were far more likely to return. A post as simple as "How's our new Santa Fe chicken?" provides effective interaction. Just hope the chicken's good!

3. Use a fun, informal tone. Write your tweets, blogs, and posts as if you were speaking to a client in the office whom you wanted to entertain and impress.

4. Distinguish between your company's Facebook site and its website. Your company's website caters to potential clients searching for your business through industry recommendations or search engines. These clients have the necessary time to read in-depth about your company. Your Facebook site, on the other hand, caters to the guy who just got home from work but saw your post about half-price.

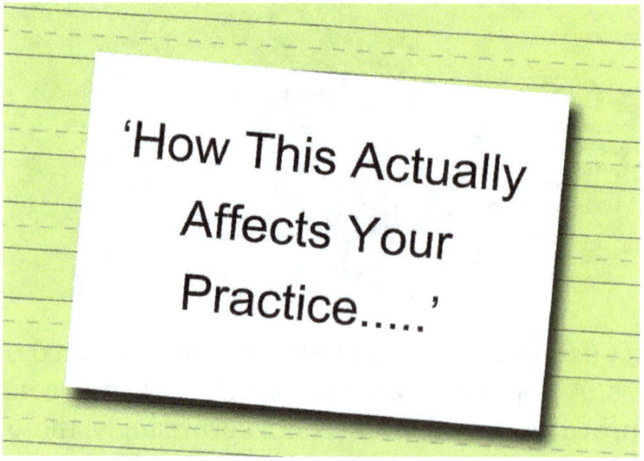

5. Educate and explain. Social media provides a great outlet for informal, explanatory pieces which

help establish your business as an expert in the field. Good examples of customer education are FAQs on a Facebook page or short, informative posts on Blogger about industry news. A successful Maryland medical technology firm distills long congressional bills into one-paragraph chunks on Blogger entitled "How This Actually Affects Your Practice." Healthcare providers turn to this firm's site for news- and increasingly, for new products.

6. Humanize your company. Social media's people-centered environment lets you put a human face on your company. Many Twitter accounts use first names such as bill@Washington electronics, etc. If your company has a story, Facebook is the appropriate place to share it. Because people are the reason that social media sites were created in the first place.

7. Re-use what you've got. Using what you've already got by reviewing all possible sources such as blogs, photos, videos and anything on your native website as well what you're sharing on other popular social sites like Pinterest, Tumblr and YouTube. Content is repackage-able. Not all of your fans or followers may have seen it when you posted it originally, so it's okay to reframe it and re-publish it occasionally.

8. Make sure the content is shareable.

How to Build a Social Media Plan

"Ready, fire, aim!" Most businesses approach social media by jumping right in and forgetting to plan. Abraham Lincoln once said, "If I had six hours to chop down a tree, I would spend the first four hours sharpening the axe!" This works just as well in launching your social media campaign. Take the time to get your strategy right. Here are the steps to build the "sharpest" social media plan on the web.

Steps

1. Know your marketing objectives. Before jumping into the heavy traffic of social media, you have to know where you want to be in the end. When working with clients, you should first establish a set of goals and what it is that they hope to achieve. How do you want to expose your business? Are you going for awareness, sales, leads? What do you hope to learn or get out of using these social mediums? You can then evaluate these set goals and have a better understanding of what to monitor and measure.

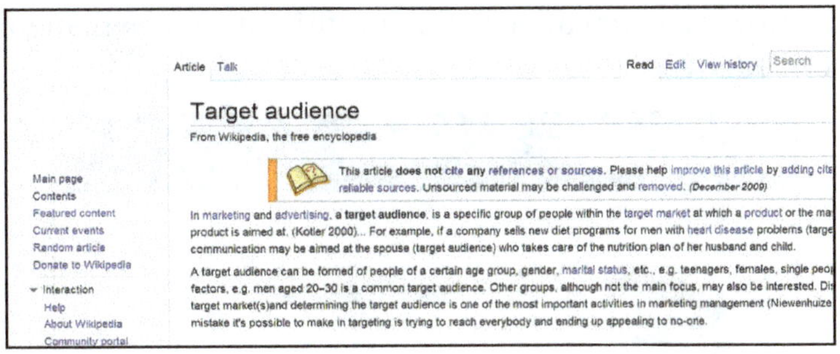

2. Know your target audience. Knowing your audience is important in creating an effective social media plan. Who are you trying to target? What are they interested in? What gets them excited? And where are they online? These are the necessary questions you need to ask yourself in developing your strategy – you need to know how to attract potential clients!

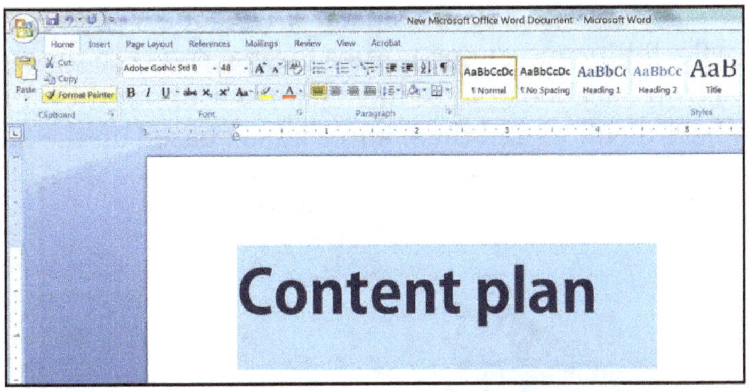

3. Develop a content strategy. If you really know your target audience you can engage with them in a way that's truly meaningful. This is where having a content strategy comes in. What do they really care about? How can you connect with them by talking about things they are interested in? What things, related to your product, are they really passionate about? Your content should be relevant to the psychographics of your audience. Answering these questions will allow you to lay the high-level approach to developing a communication style with your audience.

- After developing a content strategy, you need to develop a content plan, which is much more tactical. Your content plan outlines the actual copy in the tweets, posts, and images you intend to share to your audience.

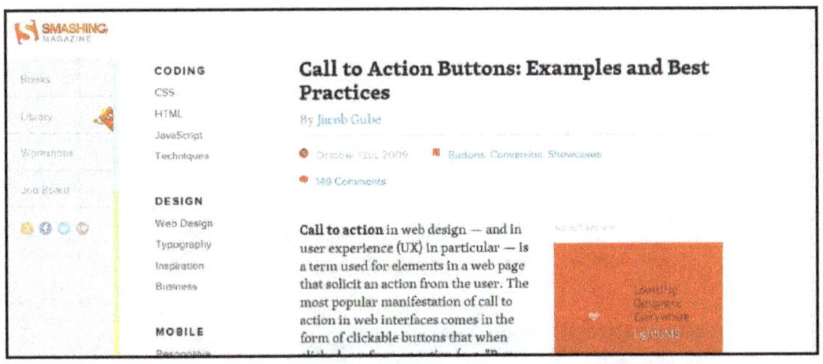

4. Determine Calls to Action. Based on your marketing objectives you should be able to develop calls to action – action that you want someone to take that will ultimately lead to business value for you. This might be getting their email address, having them call you, a direct sale online, filling

out a contact form, etc. Knowing your call to action or ultimate goal will help you really drive value from your social marketing.

5. Pick the best tools for the job. How should you go about choosing a social media to achieve your objectives. Based on the content, target and calls to action, you should look for the social media tools that will optimize your chance of objective success. The tools you pick are contingent to where your audience is and the flexibility and opportunities for marketers in the various tools. For example, your audience may be on Facebook (since most people are) but they may not be interested in "liking" you, and it may be difficult to find them and connect based on the limitations of Facebook.

6. Execute and experiment. Executing your strategy is not a walk in the park. It is important that you give yourself enough time and make resources available so you can create the best possible delivery, specific to your business. Set up different tests to evaluate different executions. For example, tweet different things, pose your questions in different ways, try different days and times and see which tweets get the most traction and clicks. This way, you can determine the best way to reach your intended audience and what strategies get the most reception.

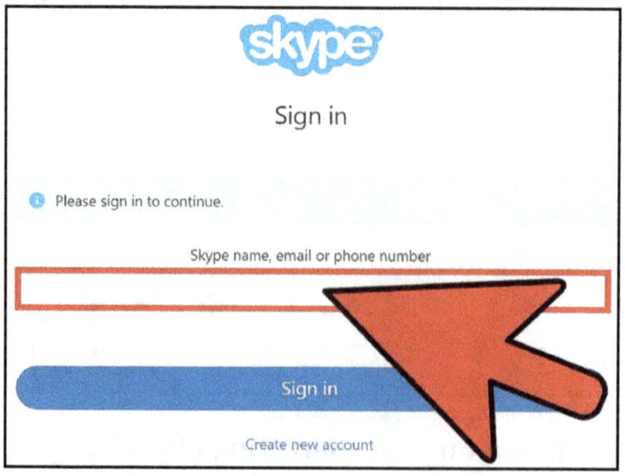

7. Engage directly with your audience. One of the opportunities that social media marketing offers

that other forms of marketing do not is the chance for an organization to have conversations with their audience in real time. Customers appreciate interactions with organizations that feel authentic and personalized; these types of interactions are much more likely to happen when you respond directly to a follower rather than solely relying on posts to your entire following. While every organization's content strategy should be uniquely tailored, it's always worth looking for opportunities to engage directly with your audience.

8. Measure the results of your work. Measure, measure, measure. Measuring Social Media is one of the most vital and beneficial pieces of advice. During the experimentation stage it is vital to test, experiment and measure your social media execution. Your measures should help you decide if what you are doing is working. Measuring can include mentions in blogs, tags, tweets, news articles and other forms of exposure for your business. Be cautious in your measures though and be sure to assess the real problem. For example, if you were given a screwdriver and asked to put a nail into a piece of wood, you probably couldn't. It doesn't mean that the screwdriver is broken, it just means that it isn't the right tool for the task. It would be wrong to conclude that 1) The screwdriver doesn't work 2) The nail can't be put into the wood. Keep your options open when it comes to the different social media engines – setting up boundaries is contradicting the limitlessness of social media.

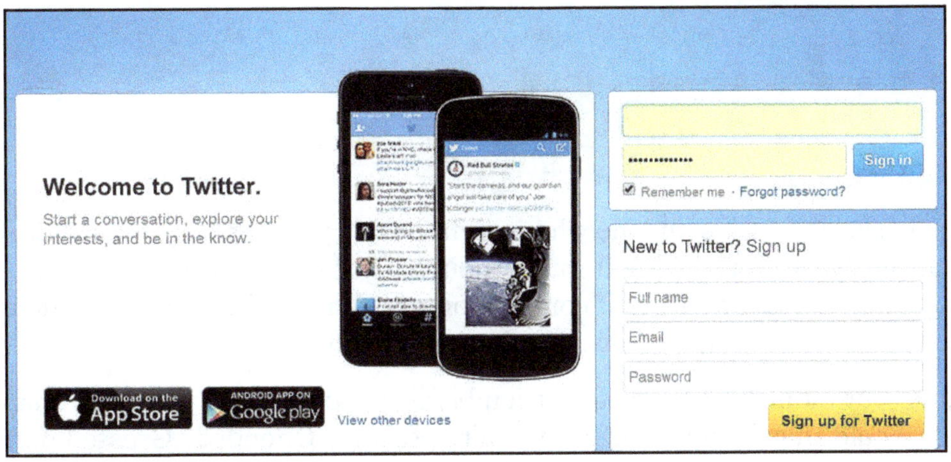

9. Adapt to the insights of your results. Do more of what works and less of what doesn't. Don't be afraid to abandon a strategy if it doesn't work. One word of caution – beware of your measures. For

example, you may have started using Twitter to build awareness, but find that it is actually really effective for customer service. If you only measure awareness you may miss the boat. So, while your measures might be specific, be sure to look at tools and success in a comprehensive way.

How to Avoid Oversharing on Social Media

Most people agree that oversharing is a problem. Fortunately, there are several ways to avoid oversharing on social media. Choose what you post wisely, and avoid posting anything that your employer, friends, or family might not appreciate. Be mindful of your security when using social media, and avoid using check-in and automatic location functions, or posting any personally identifying information that an identity thief might use against you. Finally, take some time off of social media at least once each week, and post responses to news articles and friends' posts that don't require you to offer much information about your own life.

Method 1. Choosing your Content Wisely

1. Avoid sharing about controversial topics. Certain topics like politics, religion, and polarizing issues can cause heated arguments and may alienate some of your followers. If you don't want to engage in arguments or lose followers, avoid posting about these topics or post neutral comments.

2. Act like you're sharing with someone who is right beside you. It's easy to post or reblog something instantaneously, without giving it much thought. But is the story, image, or other content you're posting really necessary? Does it contain content you'd feel was appropriate to communicate to someone in person? If not, reconsider sharing it at all.

- Imagine your mom, brother, or best friend is sitting beside you while you share something online. Would they be upset by what you're posting? Offended? Grossed out? If so, don't post it.
- Use your judgement and try to imagine how you would feel if you randomly stumbled across the content you intend to post.

3. Keep your sharing positive. Instead of posting about negative interactions with others, post only information about your positive interactions. For instance, don't post content related to your child's misbehavior or a conflict you got into with your spouse. Instead, post content related to your child's good grades, or a pleasant date you went on with your spouse.

- Posting negative content is quite personal and could make others uncomfortable – even if they are not referenced directly in your post.

4. Consider who is going to see your posts. If you're using strong language in a post, you might want to limit it to only certain people, or adjust the settings on the post so that certain individuals cannot see your post. Or out of respect for your parents, for instance, you might choose to prohibit them from seeing your posts regarding a certain sensitive topic. Think carefully about your audience before sharing to social media.

- In other cases, you might want to share an inside joke with friends. Instead of opening the post up to all your social media followers, you might instead just send the joke as a group message directly to your friends.

5. Avoid sharing information about bodily functions and changes. Nobody wants to know about your most recent bowel movement. Likewise, avoid sharing information (including imagery) about menstruation, colonoscopies, and urination. Unless you're pregnant, losing weight, or have a cold, avoid sharing details about your physical condition and bodily habits.

- You can tastefully share some physical states or events. For instance, you might post that you gave birth to a child on social media. You could even post an image of the newborn wrapped snugly in a blanket. But it would be inappropriate to post an image of your child being born.

Method 2. Staying Safe on Social Media

1. Keep personal information to yourself. Sharing the names of your pets, your grandmother's name, or your favorite movie could lead to problems later on. This unique identifying information often composes the security questions for banks, credit cards, and other financial information. Oversharing personal info, therefore, can lead to identity theft.

- Remember that anything you post on the internet is in the public domain, even if you use privacy settings. While social media is a great way to stay in touch with friends and family, other people may also be able to see what you post.

2. Keep your social media profiles private. If possible, only post information privately. On social media platforms that do not allow private posting, post as little as possible. Try to limit yourself to reposts of existing material – links to articles or songs you liked, for instance.

- Keeping your social media profile private means that you'll only be sharing with a select few people (your friends or approved followers).

3. Turn off automatic location functions. Many apps have automatic check-in options to let people know where you are. This can be very dangerous for you and your family because it tells people where you are at the moment. Someone who has bad intentions can use that information to rob your home while you're away. By turning your location function off on your phone or tablet, you'll be better able to control who knows where you are, what you're doing, and when you're doing it.

- If you need to use your GPS, just turn the location function back on.
- Consult your user guide for your phone or tablet for more information about how you can turn off location sharing features.

4. Don't check in everywhere you go. Most people neither need nor want to know where you went grocery shopping, or what dog groomer you took your pet too. You can easily avoid oversharing these superfluous details of your day by turning off automatic location functions.

- Additionally, think carefully about where you check-in. Limit check-ins to special events and trips. Don't check-in when visiting your friends, the laundromat, or other places that do not hold special interest. Additionally, don't check-in from places far from home, since this will alert potential criminals that you won't be returning to your home any time soon.

Method 3. Keeping Out of Trouble

1. Don't share pictures of others without consent. If you're taking pictures of friends or even family members, they might not like the pictures. And if they don't like the pictures, they probably won't want them available for the whole world to see on social media. Ask friends and others in the images you take if it is alright to post them on social media.

- In some places, posting images of children – even your own children – without their approval is illegal.
- If your child is old enough to ask whether you're posting a photo of them online, you should ask them if it is okay for you to do so.

- Even if others approve you posting the photo, think twice before doing so. Oversharing images of yourself with your friends or your children might grow tiresome for people consuming your social media.

2. Don't share incriminating information. There are a number of things you could say on social media that might damage your reputation or even get you in legal trouble. For instance, if you post how drunk you were last night (or drunk you are currently), the post might give a future employer or college application evaluator the wrong impression about who you are.

- Employers and colleges often check social media accounts, so your controversial posts could cost you your job or education.
- Likewise, if you are an illegal immigrant, you should not post information about how you came to be in your current country, or mention your current legal status.

3. Don't post anything related to your work. Posting critical comments about your coworkers, employer, or employees could land you in hot water. Even posting something good, though, might get you in trouble. For instance, if your employer sees you were using social media instead of working, they might be upset. Avoid sharing anything about your work experiences on social media.

- If you want, you could share where you work, but never relate stories about your workday on social media.
- Assume your employer will see all your social media posts.

Method 4. Adopting Methods to Limit Sharing

1. Talk to your friends outside of social media. Instead of sharing everything you want to say to your friends on social media, catch up with them later and strike up a conversation about whatever it is you want to communicate. You can communicate with your friends about both online content and real-world situations or ideas. For instance, if you have a funny video you want your friends to see, arrange to meet them and say, "I have a funny video I think you'd like to see. Let's watch it together."

- That way, you will ensure that they see it, since many people have so much information coming through their social media that they don't have time to check it all.
- You'll also avoid oversharing since you're adding one less post to social media.
- Don't forget the importance of face-to-face and phone conversations.

2. Respond to other posts. There's more to social media than just posting your own content about

your own life. Limit your risk of oversharing by browsing news articles and commenting on friends' pages. Try to put the "social" in social media.

- It's especially important to respond to your friends' posts regarding sincere emotional pain. It's even better if you call or visit them as well.
- Responding to other posts on some social media platforms is best done through built-in approval indicators or by rebroadcasting the post you identified with, enjoyed, or found amusing.

3. Unplug for a while. Spend at least a day or two each week where you don't use social media at all. This will give you time to decompress from the information overload that can take hold of even seasoned web users. Taking time away from social media will reduce the pressure you might sometimes feel to contribute new content to your social media streams, which can lead to oversharing.

- If you find you're checking social media so much that it interferes with your work, academic, or real social life, implement a steeper cut in your social media usage.
- There are many things you can do instead of oversharing on social media. For instance, you could play baseball with your friends. You could invite your family for a hike in the woods.
- If you prefer spending time alone off of social media, you could catch up on your reading or learn how to bake a new recipe.
- Think about some of your favorite hobbies and spend time doing them instead of oversharing on social media.

4. Watch for signs of social media or internet addiction. Social media and the internet can reward your brain in the same way that drugs do, and they can cause you to become overstimulated if you use them throughout the day. You need to make sure that you have a life and interests outside of social media. If you find yourself constantly checking your accounts or struggling with oversharing, look for the symptoms of addiction:

- Feelings of guilt
- Anxiety

- Depression
- Dishonesty
- Euphoric feelings when in front of the computer
- Unable to keep schedules
- No sense of time
- Isolation.

Social Media Management 2

Social media management is the management of online content and interactions across different social media platforms. Social media channels such as Twitter, Facebook, YouTube, LinkedIn and Pinterest are used to facilitate businesses by increasing their reach and influence. Social media management is now important for existing brands and companies to stay relevant in the market by maintaining a social media presence. This chapter has been carefully written to provide an easy understanding of social media management and the roles and responsibilities of a social media manager.

Social media management refers to the use of a wide range of tools, software, and services that make sharing content on social media easier for businesses of all sizes. By scheduling social media posts in advance, engaging with your target audience, and managing your responses quickly, you can make social media a priority. And at this point in the game, if you aren't making social media a priority, you're in trouble.

Social media has an integral part in the business landscape. With 3.2 billion people using social media around the world, and 11 new users every second, it's safe to say the fad has turned into a global standard. Social media management tools and services can help you reach this huge audience and make running a social media campaign decidedly simpler.

Engaging with your audience through social media is more important than ever. Customers interact with brands via Twitter, Facebook, Snapchat and more, and they expect fast responses and professional outputs.

However, with limited resources and little know-how, small businesses may not always have the time or knowledge to make an impact on platforms like Facebook, Instagram, and Twitter.

That's where social media management comes in.

Social Media Management Tools

If you're just dipping your toe in the social media marketing waters, do-it-yourself tools are a great way to get started. These platforms can help you manage your own campaigns with simple, comprehensive interfaces designed for the most novice of social media manager.

Plus, social media management tools are often very affordable, and many offer free versions to test out before you buy. However, if you want to really make a difference on social media, you're going to need a bigger boat.

Social Media Management Services

While social media management tools can help your company increase the quantity of your content, improving the quality of your content is just as important when it comes to engaging your target audience.

Fortunately, social media management services are equipped with the knowledge and resources to manage your social media presence right. Through targeted posting, sponsored ads, and a wide range of social media tactics that are far beyond common knowledge, these services can bring your social media game to the next level.

Importance of Social Media Management

Whether you hire a social media marketing service or take advantage of a wide range of tools, you'll be able to transform your strategy from drab to fab without spending too much or wasting too much time. You'll be able to:

- Manage multiple accounts across various platforms
- Analyze social engagement
- Schedule posts in advance
- Receive comprehensive reports of analytics
- Monitor comments and respond efficiently
- Collaborate with team members on content

As with any additional software or service your company takes advantage of, the ultimate goal of social media management is to save time and improve profits. So how does social media management create specific benefits for your company?

Benefits

Social media management tools and services are designed to make marketing easier, which ultimately increases profits. After all, what's the point of paying for new software or services if they aren't going to improve your bottom line? Social media management tools and services come with a bevy of helpful benefits that will reinvigorate your marketing efforts and put your company in front of your target audience.

Social media management can help you:

- Save time

By scheduling posts in advance, rather than burdening yourself with remembering to post at peak hours during the day.

- Increase authority

  By posting multiple times a day on a wide range of platforms.

- Understand your audience

  By providing in-depth analytics that explain who is following you, where they're coming from, and what they want from your business.

- Improve customer support

  By creating a simple pathway for customers to inquire about your company through social media and making it simple for you to respond.

- Take control

  Of your brand's reputation by allowing you to monitor comments and feedback more closely, and respond as quickly as possible.

- Foster innovation

  By encouraging collaboration through a platform where multiple team members can discuss strategy for a social media campaign.

Clearly, social media management has benefits. But, understanding how it works is only the first step in deciding whether or not you should purchase one of these tools or services for your own business. So, what's the next step? Cost.

Social media management tools and services vary in costs, which is why it's so important to get a tailored quote before you make a decision. Above all, you'll want an accurate estimate of how much social media management tools and services will cost for the particular scale and needs of your business.

Cost of Social Media Management Tools

Most social media management tools charge by two important factors: the number of accounts you plan on managing and the number of posts you plan on scheduling in advance.

Social Media Accounts

The beauty of social media management tools is your ability to schedule posts for Facebook, Instagram, Twitter, and even LinkedIn from a single platform. However, depending on how many accounts you're looking to manage, the price could go up.

Whether you're popular on a wide range of platforms, or just have six different Twitter accounts that you want to manage, make sure you know exactly how much it costs to add extra accounts to your service, as it could cost you a pretty penny.

Social Media Posts

The primary purpose of social media management tools is to schedule posts in advance so you don't need to perfectly time out your day to hit those peak hours. However, if you're trying to take the "quantity over quality" approach, you might need to pay a little extra.

Even if you only have one account, some social media management tools will put a limit on the number of posts you can schedule in advance. The more posts you want to schedule, the higher the price, so make sure you take that into account when picking your tool.

Cost of Social Media Management Services

If you're looking to truly break open the potential of a social media campaign, social media management services are the best way to go. The price is understandably a bit higher, but the results you'll see from such social media marketing specialists will be more than worth it.

Unlike social media management tools, these services offer everything from marketing strategy to paid advertising to improve your overall strategy on social media. Because of this, social media management services vary greatly in cost depending on a wide range of factors, including:

- The size of your company
- How often you plan on posting
- The type of services you require
- Which platforms you want to share content on
- The level of analytics you need
- Whether or not you'll provide customer service through social media.

When it comes to social media management services, the varying costs make it imperative to get a customized quote before you make a decision. To get a good idea of what's out there, take a look at a few tools and services we dug up just for you, below.

Social Media Management Tools you can run yourself

If you'd prefer to be hands-on with your brand's social media, then there are some brilliant tools you can choose, to manage how you go about this. Social media for business shouldn't involve logging into a standard Facebook or Twitter account, just like you would with a personal page. Businesses need to be smarter.

Social media management tools can let you schedule updates, manage customer service comments efficiently and learn about trends in how your customers interact with your brand.

Some of the best social media management tools include:

Buffer – a great, simple to use interface.

Hootsuite – lets you schedule an unlimited amount of posts.

Sprout Social – ideal for growing businesses.

Hubspot – marketing tools included, and a free trial available.

IFTTT – a super, free service to try.

TweetDeck – for Twitter only, but with lots of handy features.

The question remains, is it smarter to attempt to tackle the social media feeds for your business yourself, or to trust this vital service to an expert? Done right, social media management can transform the way you interact with customers.

Components of Social Media Management

Marketers need a simple, clear way to think about deploying a social media strategy that does not start with technology. The four main components of social media management for marketers are mention below.

Monitor

Monitoring is finding and tracking the conversations that are occurring about your company in social media and online. Even companies that have no intention of pursuing a social media marketing strategy must monitor what's being said about them. It's important to know who is saying good things about your company but it's even more important to know who is saying bad things. Negative comments-especially those that expose a legitimate flaw in a company's products or services-can snowball and be picked up by the trade and business press.

Monitoring is also the foundation of a social media marketing strategy. Before companies begin talking, they have to listen. They need to identify the most important influencers in their markets and track those conversations. Understanding the tone and subject matter of the most popular conversations in the market will help companies develop and fine tune their own social media voices.

Engage

Engaging occurs when companies decide to take an active role in social media by engaging with customers and influencers in the various forums where conversations are taking place. Examples include public blogs, social networks, and industry communities. The goal in social media engagement is to influence participants to have a positive impression of the company through factual, verifiable contributions from company employees and subject matter experts.

Marketing should monitor social media carefully and assign subject matter experts to track particular blogs and influencers. There should be an escalation process for pushing issues around the company to the people most qualified to respond to them (all practitioners, not marketing or PR people).The key to engagement is that providers do not try to control the conversation, as in traditional marketing, but that they influence the conversation in the following ways:

- Find relevant online communities and blogs and build relationships with discussion leaders and members.
- Become regular contributors to influential blogs and be willing to weigh in on issues not directly related to the company's products and services.
- Respond to customer complaints.
- Link customers to more information and offer to follow up directly.

Manage

Managing means that companies take an active role in creating conversations about the company. Examples include:

- Corporate blogs. If companies can break their traditional habits of trying to control the conversation and squashing criticism, corporate blogs can help improve perception and awareness. Corporate blogs can be managed by marketing, but shouldn't be written by marketing. Customers want to hear from subject matter experts and influencers.
- Public and private online communities. Besides creating online communities in business-oriented third-party hosted social media venues like LinkedIn, companies can start their own communities, both public and private. For example, Indian outsourcing and consulting company Infosys developed points of view about four emerging trends in global business: the growing impact of emerging economies such as India and China, demographic shifts in age and working populations around the world, technology ubiquity, and increased regulations. It then created multiple hosted forums, both public and private (C-level executives often prefer private communities because they fear speaking up about their companies in uncontrolled public communities). These communities have both online and offline components, and Infosys' marketing group works to build participation by publicizing the communities and inviting key customers and influencers to participate.

Integrate

Social media efforts need to be integrated into a company's more traditional marketing channels such as conferences, events, reference programs, and websites. Social media is notoriously difficult to measure and ROI is unclear. Therefore, social media should be used as a platform to drive traffic to the channels that are easier to measure and have proven ROI. There should also be a way to get customers and prospects from social media into systems for tracking and managing interactions (e.g., CRM).

Social Media Marketing Strategy

Essential Elements of a Social Media Marketing Strategy

1. Identify Business Goals

Every piece of your social media strategy serves the goals you set. You simply can't move forward without knowing what you're working toward.

Look closely at your company's overall needs and decide how you want to use social media to contribute to reaching them.

You'll undoubtedly come up with several personalized goals, but there are a few that all companies should include in their strategy—increasing brand awareness, retaining customers and reducing marketing costs are relevant to everyone.

First, set your goals and objectives.

It is suggested to choose two primary goals and two secondary goals to focus on. Having too many goals distracts you and you'll end up achieving none.

2. Set Marketing Objectives

Goals aren't terribly useful if you don't have specific parameters that define when each is achieved. For example, if one of your primary goals is generating leads and sales, how many leads and sales do you have to generate before you consider that goal a success?

Marketing objectives define how you get from Point A (an unfulfilled goal) to Point B (a successfully fulfilled goal). You can determine your objectives with the S-M-A-R-T approach: Make your objectives specific, measurable, achievable, relevant and time-bound.

Measurement is important to your strategy.

Using our previous example, if your goal is to generate leads and sales, a specific marketing objective may be to increase leads by 50%. In order to measure your progress, choose which analytics and tracking tools you need to have in place.

Setting yourself up for failure is never a good idea. If you set an objective of increasing sales by 1,000%, it's doubtful you'll meet it. Choose objectives you can achieve, given the resources you have.

You've taken the time to refine your goals so they're relevant to your company, so extend that same consideration to your objectives. If you want to get support from your C-level executives, ensure your objectives are relevant to the company's overall vision.

Attaching a timeframe to your efforts is imperative. When do you intend to achieve your goal(s)? Next month? By the end of this year?

Your objective of increasing leads by 50% may be specific, measurable, achievable and relevant, but if you don't set a deadline for achieving the goal, your efforts, resources and attention may be pulled in other directions.

3. Identify Ideal Customers

If a business is suffering from low engagement on their social profiles, it's usually because they don't have an accurate ideal customer profile.

Buyer personas help you define and target the right people, in the right places, at the right times with the right messages.

When you know your target audience's age, occupation, income, interests, pains, problems, obstacles, habits, likes, dislikes, motivations and objections, then it's easier and cheaper to target them on social or any other media.

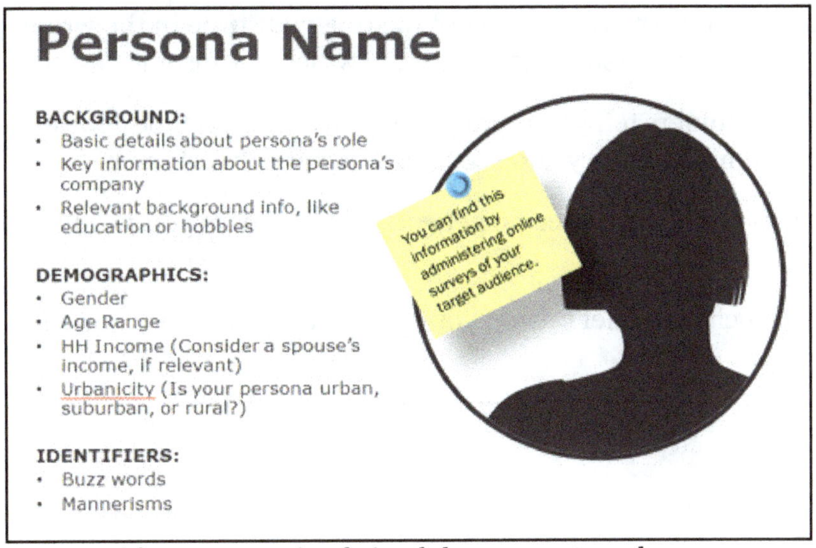

A buyer persona is a fictional character, not a real one.

The more specific you are, the more conversions you're going to get out of every channel you use to promote your business.

4. Research Competition

When it comes to social media marketing, researching your competition not only keeps you apprised of their activity, it gives you an idea of what's working so you can integrate those successful tactics into your own efforts.

Start by compiling a list of at least 3-5 main competitors. Search which social networks they're using and analyze their content strategy. Look at their number of fans or followers, posting frequency and time of day.

Also pay attention to the type of content they're posting and its context (humorous, promotional, etc.) and how they're responding to their fans.

The most important activity to look at is engagement. Even though page admins are the only ones who can calculate engagement rate on a particular update, you can get a good idea of what they're seeing.

For example, let's say you're looking at a competitor's last 20-30 Facebook updates. Take the total number of engagement activities for those posts and divide it by the page's total number of fans. (Engagement activity includes likes, comments, shares, etc.)

You can use that formula on all of your competitors' social profiles (e.g., on Twitter you can calculate retweets and favorites).

Keep in mind that the calculation is meant to give you a general picture of how the competition is doing so you can compare how you stack up against each other.

5. Choose Channels and Tactics

Many businesses create accounts on every popular social network without researching which platform will bring the most return. You can avoid wasting your time in the wrong place by using the information from your buyer personas to determine which platform is best for you.

If your prospects or customers tell you they spend 40% of their online time on Facebook and 20% on Twitter, you know which primary and secondary social networks you should focus on.

When your customers are using a specific network, that's where you need to be—not everywhere else.

Your tactics for each social channel rely on your goals and objectives, as well as the best practices of each platform.

HubSpot's effective use of Facebook for lead generation

For example, if your goal is increasing leads and your primary social network is Facebook, some effective tactics are investing in Facebook advertising or promotion campaigns to draw more attention to your lead magnets.

6. Create a Content Strategy

Content and social media have a symbiotic relationship: Without great content social media is meaningless and without social media nobody will know about your content. Use them together to reach and convert your prospects.

There are three main components to any successful social media content strategy: type of content, time of posting and frequency of posting.

The type of content you should post on each social network relies on form and context. Form is how you present that information—text only, images, links, video, etc.

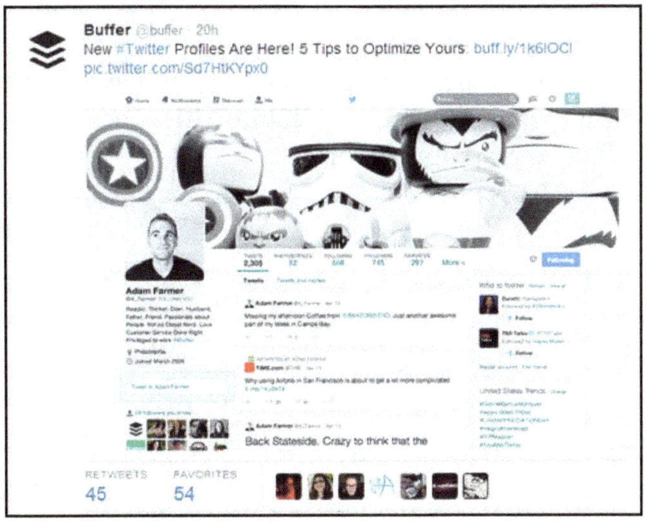

Buffer understands their audience will respond to content that keep them updated on changes in social media

Context fits with your company voice and platform trends. Should your content be funny, serious, highly detailed and educational or something else?

There are many studies that give you a specific time when you should post on social media. Use those studies as guidelines rather than hard rules. Remember, your audience is unique, so you need to test and figure out the best time for yourself.

Posting frequency is as important as the content you share. You don't want to annoy your fans or followers, do you?

Finding the perfect frequency is crucial because it could mean more engagement for your content or more unlikes and unfollows. Use Facebook Insights to see when your fans are online and engaging with your content.

7. Allocate Budget and Resources

To budget for social media marketing, look at the tactics you've chosen to achieve your business goals and objectives.

Make a comprehensive list of the tools you need (e.g., social media monitoring, email marketing and CRM), services you'll outsource (e.g., graphic design or video production) and any advertising you'll purchase. Next to each, include the annual projected cost so you can have a high-level view of what you're investing in and how it affects your marketing budget.

Many businesses establish their budget first, and then select which tactics fit that budget. I take the opposite approach. Establish a strategy first, and then determine the budget that fits that strategy.

If your strategy execution fees exceed your budget estimate, prioritize your tactics according to their ROI timeframe. The tactics with the fastest ROI (e.g., advertising and social referral) take priority because they generate instant profit you can later invest into long-term tactics (fan acquisition, quality content creation or long-term engagement).

8. Assign Roles

Knowing who's responsible for what increases productivity and avoids confusion and overlapping efforts. Things may be a bit messy in the beginning, but with time team members will know their roles and what daily tasks they're responsible for.

Role	Member
Visual content creation	John
Video content creation and editing	Kevin
Social media management	Sarah
Advertising (Facebook, Twitter, retargeting)	Deb
Social referral program	David
Customer service	Megan

An example of assigning roles

When everyone knows his or her role, it's time to start planning the execution process. You can either plan daily or weekly. It is not advised to put a monthly plan together because lots of things will come up and you may end up wasting time adapting to the new changes.

You can use tools like Basecamp or ActiveCollab to manage your team and assign tasks to each member. These tools save you tons of time and help you stay organized.

How AgoraPulse Helps in Social Media Management

AgoraPulse is no newcomer to the social media dashboard scene, but they have been traditionally known as a Facebook application platform. Most people don't know that AgoraPulse is a full-fledged social media dashboard which now includes support for Twitter and Instagram in addition to Facebook. While there's no shortage of great social media tools to help you manage these social networks, here are 4 ways in which AgoraPulse's unique functionality can help you save you time as well as make your social media marketing more effective.

1. Monitor and Respond to Engagement from One Dashboard

What social media dashboard do you currently use? If you use Tweetdeck, you can only monitor Twitter. If you use HootSuite, arguably the most popular social media dashboard, it might be difficult to manage conversations and engagement – in fact, once you become very active on social media and receive a lot of engagement, it might be fair to say it is impossible to manage the engagement without losing your sanity. SproutSocial has a social inbox concept built into their dashboard, but while they do Twitter nicely, their capabilities for Facebook, Google Plus, or LinkedIn might be lacking – and they do not have a solution for Instagram yet.

Enter AgoraPulse, which covers the main social networks for engagement – Facebook, Twitter, and Instagram – and allows you to easily monitor and respond to your social media mentions utilizing a social inbox. For users of HootSuite, you will find that AgoraPulse's approach is very different in that the streams of tweets and content do not form the main part of the dashboard but are merely one menu selection item among others including Users, Reports, etc. AgoraPulse also intelligently and automatically monitors each social network for mentions of you and will place these messages in a separate "Monitoring" tab (as opposed to your Inbox tab for direct mentions).

After using AgoraPulse, the Instagram monitor and response functionality is one thing that we found compelling and is a true timesaver. Beginning to utilize AgoraPulse for monitoring and managing your Instagram engagement might be the first step in having it eventually replace your other social media dashboards.

Here's what the dashboard for Instagram looks like as well as responding to a single comment:

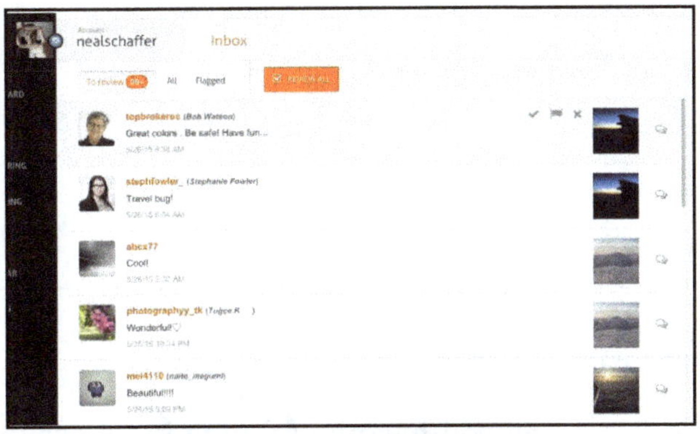

Of course, once you start using AgoraPulse you realize that you have the extra ability of tagging social media users to qualify them to do user outreach later on based on their profile.

There are other benefits to using AgoraPulse, but clearly the rest of what I will be explaining are mere icing on the cake in comparison.

2. Easily Find your Top Fans

It is surprising how few solutions exist to the basic problem that many businesses face: How can we find out who are biggest fans are on any given social network? AgoraPulse solves this by monitoring your engagement on those platforms you've authorized and provides you a list of top users in addition to further breaking them down into top Engaged, Ambassadors, Likers (Facebook & Instagram), and Influencers (Twitter). What you do from there is up to you, but this data is invaluable in leveraging your fans for greater things, including launching a brand advocacy program.

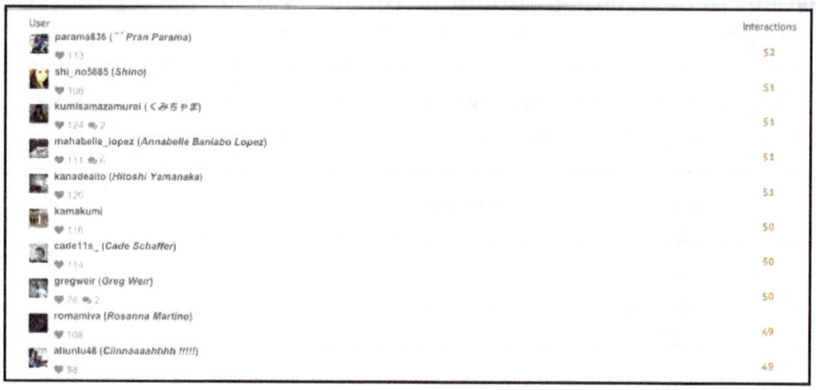

3. Get a Clear View of your Performance Metrics

AgoraPulse clearly excels at providing you meaningful data in an easy-to-understand format for your reporting needs. The reports provide unique data that are not seen on similar reports, such as the ROI report for Facebook Pages, which calculates the ROI of your Page based on the value of impressions and clicks. The Facebook report also includes functionality that is normally found in standalone analytics apps like EdgeRank Checker such as recommending the best (and second best) day of week, three hour time slot, and type of content to publish. The jewel here is clearly the Facebook Report, which is exportable in a beautiful 19-page Powerpoint that includes the following information:

- Key Metrics Summary
- Fan Growth
- Fan Source
- Fan Reach
- Page Tab Visits
- Fan Demographics
- Community Management & Moderation
- Page & Fan Activity
- Best Posts

- Worst Posts
- Best Time to Post
- Best Day to Post
- Best Type to Post
- Competitors.

While some of this data also appears in Facebook Insights, it simply isn't presented in the same clear-cut and actionable way as AgoraPulse displays the data. Here's a sample of popular posts data:

Best posts

POST	Organic reach	Fan reach	Engagement
How many of these did YOU know about?	21.45%	21.31%	5.65%
You know you need to "do" Instagram but don't know how? Start here!	20.35%	25.19%	2.37%
Definitive experts. Definitive social media tools.	16.71%	16.59%	4.91%
The ultimate list of social media tools!!! Which is your favorite?	13.39%	13.18%	5.19%
Here are the 11 ingrediens you need for a complete social media strategy plan.	11.9%	11.78%	4.5%
Are you Maximizing Your Facebook? If not, read on!	9.97%	9.95%	6.58%

4. Facebook Apps

Agora Pulse is the only social media dashboard that also has full support for a wide variety of robust Facebook applications as pictured below:

Facebook is still an essential social network and applications are a must-have for any business looking to engage with Facebook users. AgoraPulse brings Facebook apps into the dashboard so you don't need to use two different solutions.

As you know, no two social media dashboards are the same. AgoraPulse is representative of a new type of social dashboard which focuses above and beyond the usual "streams" to give you deep insight on your performance and your fans – and allows you to efficiently focus on the conversations and engagement.

How to Select a Social Media Monitoring Tool

Many businesses have accounts on Facebook and Foursquare, Twitter, LinkedIn and other social media channels as part of their marketing strategy. Social media marketing is a great way to brand yourself, get new customers to your website or store, and market your products. Although social media accounts are usually free, they are only as good as the results you get. You must be able to monitor your progress, sales, customer service and customer loyalty, in order to ensure it is a good investment of time. Not all businesses work well with every social media platform. According to your marketing plan and budget, you should choose a free tool or paid service to provide you with data on who is following you and how often they are using your services.

Method 1. Social Media Monitoring Preparation

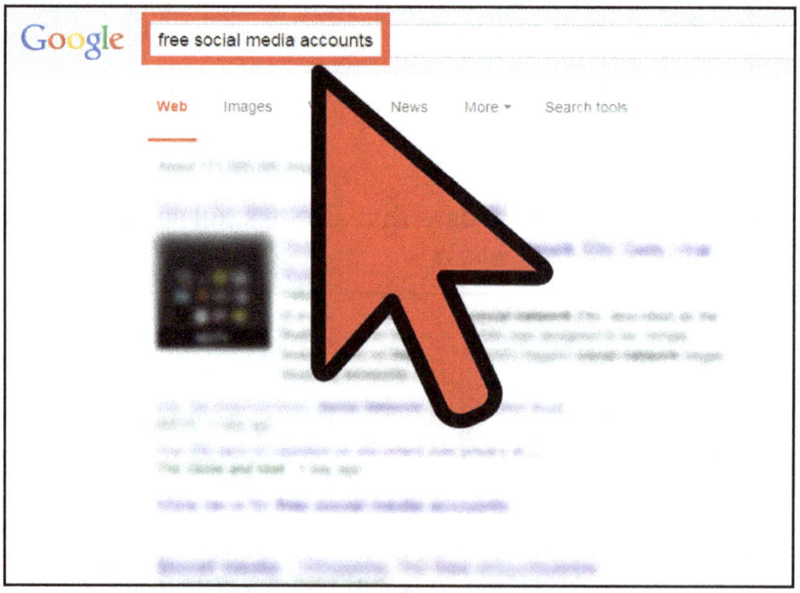

1. Establish your budget for monitoring social media. Whether you are a small or large business, you should create a plan for social media management and monitoring. It can be based on four basic factors which are reach, engagement, sentiment, activity. If you are able, you can use the money you save by using free social media accounts to invest in a more expensive social media monitoring tool.

2. Choose someone who is adept in handling social media accounts to research and choose your social media monitoring tools. If you want to make the decision as a group or board, ask the person to present the data from their research, give you the options and give their opinion on the best choice.

- Choose the keywords that you want to monitor. In the beginning, you should monitor the web appearances of your brand name, your products or services and the names of key executives. A company or paid service can help you expand your awareness by gathering the most common search terms that are used to find your site or social media accounts.

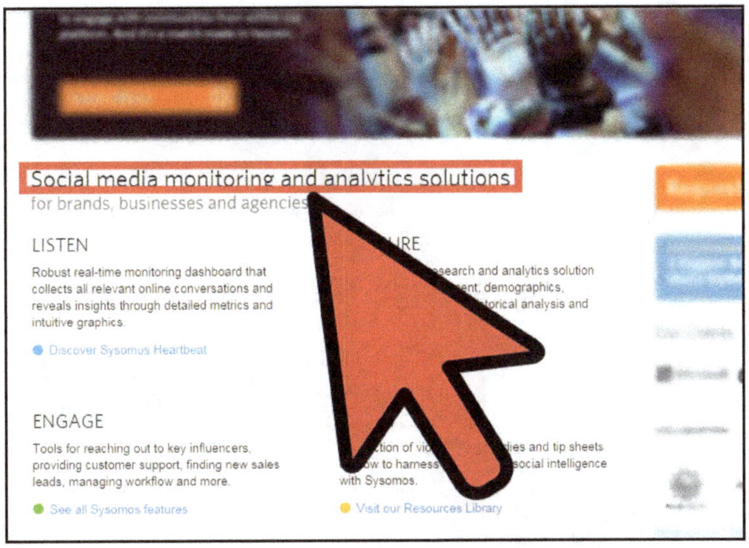

3. Define an objective before you start looking for services. Decide if you want to monitor social media to improve your customer service by finding complaints, or perhaps monitor the market better so you see what your competition is doing successfully. For many companies, social media monitoring can have more than 1 objective, but you should know what it is before you start getting quotes or spending company time on free monitoring channels.

Method 2. Low-budget Social Media Monitoring

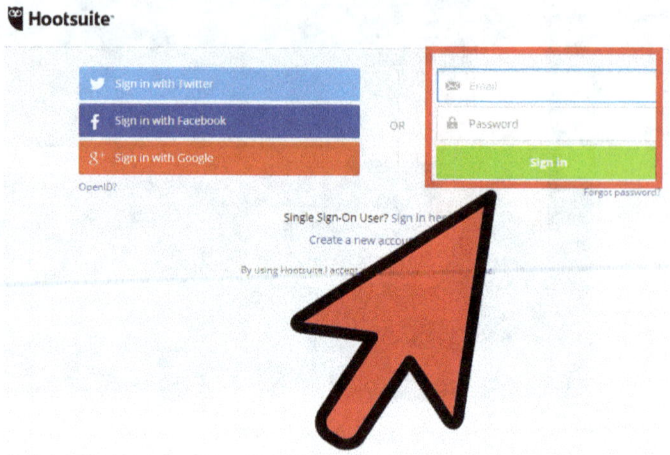

1. Choose free social media monitoring tools if you have a very low budget, or if you do not focus your marketing strongly on social media. The following are tools you can use to check how your social media is working.

- Google Alerts are the most basic social monitoring tool. By going to Google.com and clicking on the "More" drop down menu, and the "Even More" option, you will find Google Alerts amongst the list of free Google tools. Sign up for alerts by putting in keywords that apply to your business, entering an email and choosing to get the alerts either daily or weekly. You can also enter a specific site, such as "site:yourwebsite.com" followed by your keywords, and the results will be restricted to that site.
- Go to Social Mention. This free service allows you to create alerts as well. You can also download a widget that helps you to track analytic data on your website or blog.

Method 3. Medium-budget Social Media Monitoring

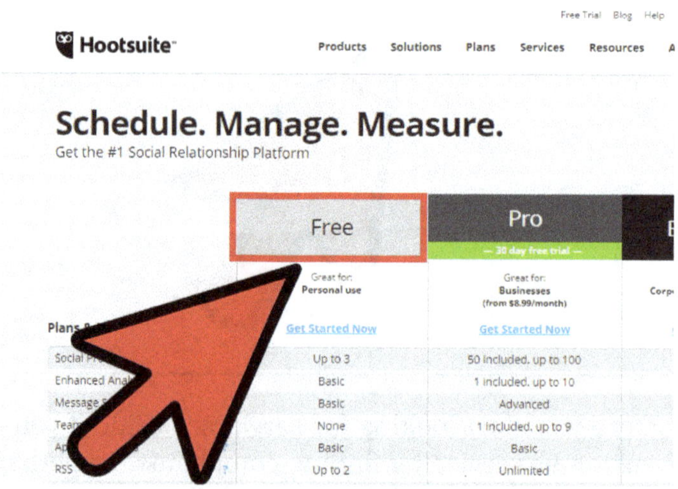

1. Search for an Internet-based option if you have a low to medium budget for social media tracking. There are a number of websites that pull your data based on your search terms and accounts.

They also give you reports based on your social media presence that you can bring to marketing meetings.

2. Do a free trial for all these services at the same time. Most online-only companies offer a 7-day to 1-month trial before you subscribe on a monthly or yearly basis. After a month, gather the data from each site and see which one did the best job at getting your information on your objectives.

- Try Trackur, Radian6, Ubervu, Viral Heat or other websites. The social media monitoring business is just taking off, so there are a high number of options on the market. Do an Internet search for "social media monitoring tool," and you should see even more options.
- Do an analysis of how each site gathers data, how it compares to the other sites and what fits your budget the best. Each site will differ in how they measure and track their data, so if they provide a customer service representative, quiz the person on how they gather data, what sites they focus on and why they would be the best choice for your company.

Method 4. High-budget Social Media Monitoring

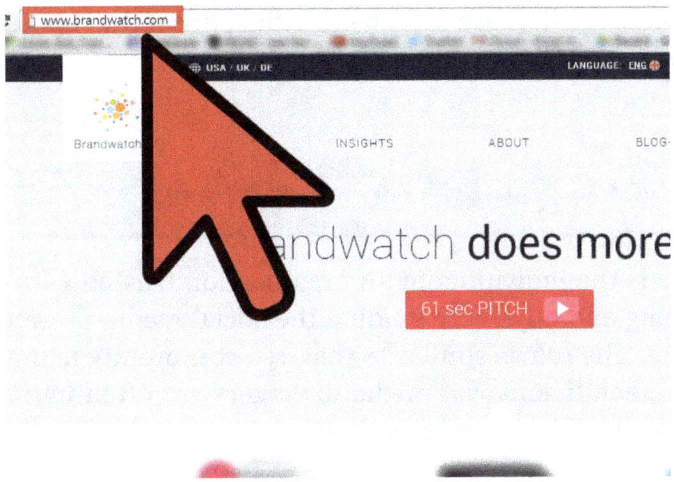

1. Get a personal quote from an online reputation management firm, if you are a big company or

you have a larger budget. For larger firms, it makes sense to have a personal approach and some careful customization according to your goals. Try NetBase, Lithium, Brandwatch, Sysomos or Alterian, or you can try a local company.

- Ask for a free demonstration and consultation of the monitoring tools and reports. Also ask the names of current customers they serve, if they monitor complaint sites, what social media sites they monitor, if they store an archive of all your keyword queries and posts, and why they are the best value over the competition. Interview 3 or more companies to ensure you are getting what you want at the best price.
- Don't be afraid to ask for a trial, discount or free premium services. If the reputation management firm is highly priced, they should also have some ability to work with their pricing. There are many options to choose from, so the advantage lies with the customer.

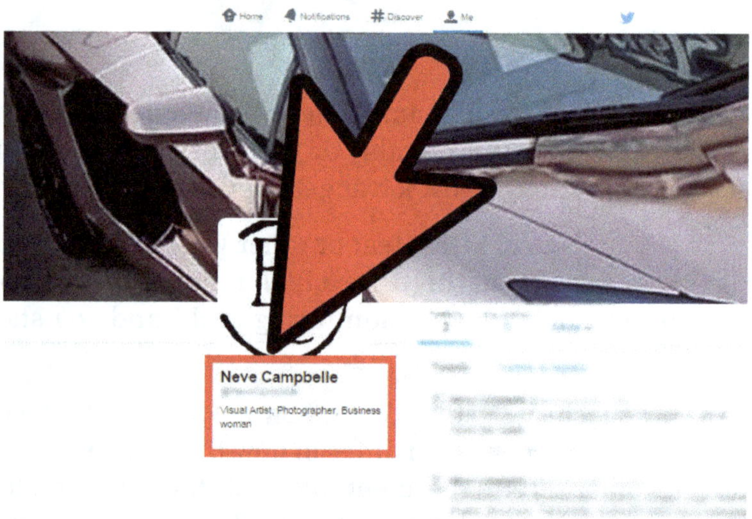

2. Make changes to your social media accounts, using what is successful and cutting out things that are not. A social media monitoring plan can help you decide where you should spend your money and time after 1 to 2 months. Make sure it is an essential part of the reports you develop for creating your marketing plan.

How to Become a Social Media Manager

A social media manager is the individual in an organization trusted with monitoring, contributing to, filtering, measuring and otherwise guiding the social media presence of a brand, product, individual or corporation. The role is similar to that of a community manager on a website forum or public relations representative. Social media managers are often found in the marketing and public relations departments of large organizations.

Social media managers create and maintain brand promotions, company information and marketing campaigns for their company across several different social media networks. They also monitor social media analytics using free or paid tools and respond to questions and comments according to the company's voice and guidelines. Social media managers work daily to produce new content for their companies, constantly innovating to push new ideas and formats and measuring how well those ideas perform.

Social media managers may report to a social media director (in larger organizations) or the head of content or brand. They work with other creative groups such as marketing and public relations, as well as the legal department, to coordinate campaigns with ongoing company initiatives and execute current marketing campaigns. A social media manager is expected to keep up with new trends and company and industry news.

Social media manager positions typically require a bachelor's degree in marketing, public relations or similar. social media managers earn an average salary of $47,000 in the U.S.

This infographic shows all of the tasks that a social media manager might do in one day.

Every day, a social media manager might be responsible for setting the strategy for an upcoming product launch, creating a video, designing gifs, coordinating messaging with internal communications teams, running paid advertisements and more.

Skills you Need to be a Great Social Media Manager

Now that you know what the role of social media manager involves, here are some of the skills you'll need to do your best in this role.

1. Copywriting

Social media managers do a lot of writing, sometimes more than a dozen posts each day. Each different social network requires a slightly different style of writing. Linkedin, for example, requires a more professional tone, while Facebook is more light and fun. SEO copywriting knowledge is also helpful. You must be able to create messages that are quickly understood by your brand's audience and promote a positive sentiment for the brand. As Forbes explains, your social media manager "will be communicating with customers on a daily basis – and 99 percent of this communication will be in writing." Some important types of writing include:

- Short and effective headline writing.
- Engaging introductions.
- Structuring text for easy only reading. (Because consumers will be skimming and scanning, subtitles, bullet points and numbering are absolutely necessary!).

2. Research

Social media managers must stay up-to-date with the ever-changing world of social and digital media, the new measurement tools others are using and what competitors are posting on a daily basis. Great social media managers set up Google Alerts on popular topics and use tools like Feedly and BuzzSumo to keep up with trending content. The Twitter Trends sidebar and Facebook Trending sidebar are also useful areas, and hashtag research can help, too. Here are some current trends that you'll want to track:

- The rise and role of mobile.
- The emergence of "pay to play" with Facebook how it reduces organic reach.
- The rise of visual marketing on platforms such as Instagram and Pinterest.

3. SEO Knowledge

Though SEO is often considered a separate department within organizations, it should have a large amount of influence on other areas of the organization, particularly content and social media. In fact, according to Hootsuite, SEO has great impact on your social media strategy. A great social media manager knows this and strives to always optimize content on social networks with SEO in mind. When you embrace SEO as part of your social media strategy, you attract a larger audience, leading to more potential customers. "Content is the cornerstone of your SEO strategy, and your social media manager is the gatekeeper and promoter of much of this content." When thinking about combining SEO and social media, task yourself the following questions:

- Do you understand the connection between exposure on social media and increased rankings in the SERPs?
- How will you promote your blog content on social media?

- Do you know how driving traffic to your company's website impacts revenue?

4. Social Media Expertise

It may seem obvious, but a social media manager needs to have social media skills. And though these can be learned over time through research and experimentation, if you're aiming for a job at a large company, you'll need a few years of experience under your belt. The type of knowledge you'll need includes:

- Knowing what type of content works best on what platform.
- Understanding how to optimize content based on platform.
- Ability to engage an audience through social posts.

The graphic below shows how consumer sentiment varies based on social media content types.

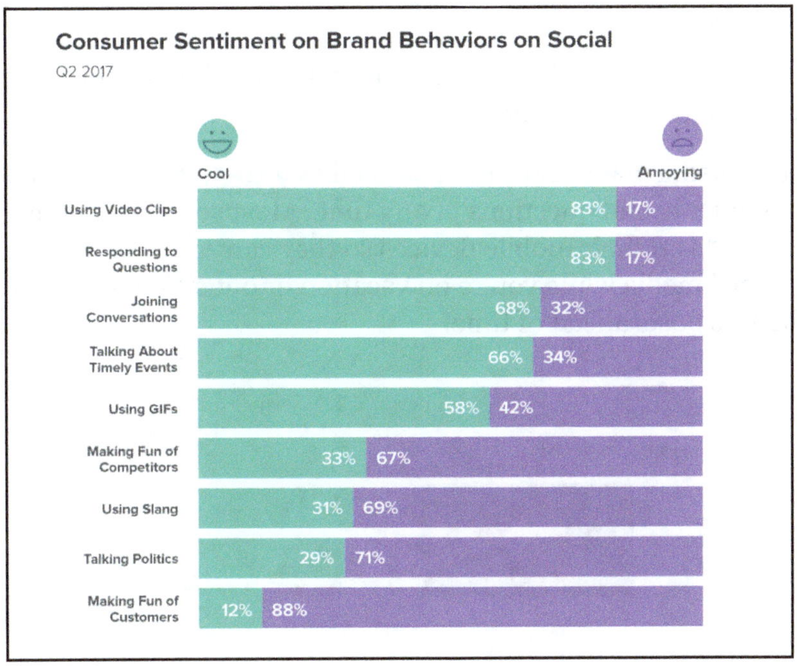

5. Customer Services Skills

When 34.5% of customers refer social media as their customer care option, social media managers need to make sure they have the skills to match. Customers often look to social media accounts for help answering questions about products and services, and if no one is there to answer those questions (even on nights and weekends!), their impressions of that brand will likely sour. "A successful social media manager knows that your social media presence is your brand's face online; that everything they say or do on social media is a representation of the brand – for good or for bad."

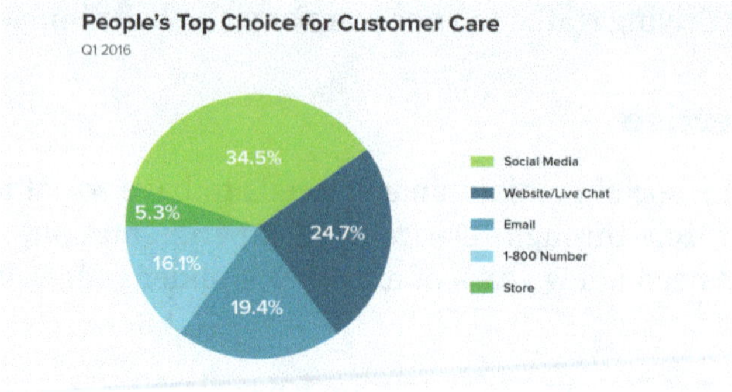

Here are some stats on the importance of customer service and social media:

- 86 percent of consumers quit doing business with a company because of a bad social media experience.
- 78 percent of online customers recommend a brand to friends and other contacts after a great customer experience.
- 80 percent of companies think they are delivering superior customer service, where only 8 percent of customers believe they are.

While the role of social media manager is often defined as 9-to-5, these individuals should be available to respond to comments and questions at any time. Most social media managers keep access to their company accounts on their mobile devices so they can respond when necessary. If there's no one to take over social media while you're on vacation or out sick, you may still be on the hook--even when you schedule posts ahead of time.

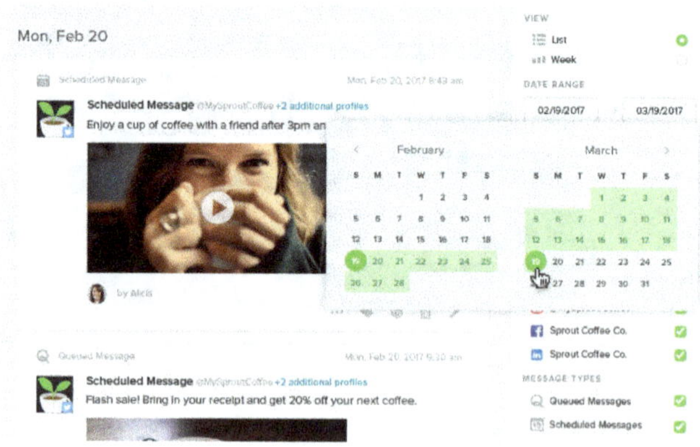

6. Visual Intelligence

While much of the content you'll put on social media will be written, visual content is also crucial.The right gif or photo can be shared hundreds, or even thousands of times, and you need to understand the types of images that work well on each social network. It's valuable for social media managers to have general knowledge of design so that you can create visually appealing graphics to complement your posts. Know Your Meme can be helpful in keeping up with daily development of new memes (if appropriate for your company).

Video is also an important component, so if you can gain skills in that area, it will be extremely helpful. As Hoostsuite explains, a great social media manager will "know great video when they see it, and most importantly have a firm grasp of social video trends and how they fit into each major network. Certain networks, like Vine and live-streaming tools Meerkat and Periscope, also have a far lower expectation of quality, so the average smartphone user can become a video content creator for your brand."

Struggling with creativity? Try taking some online classes from software companies like Adobe, or check out some local in-person art classes.

7. Adaptive

Flexibility is important in any marketing role, but even more so in social media management. The social media landscape moves so quickly that being adaptive is an absolute necessity. It's not enough to be able to schedule posts. You must be able to try out new features and change things up based on new trends and the continual testing and analytics that you should be running on your posts. Once you have the analytics in front of you, you also need the flexibility to try new things to make your social media work best for you. A/B testing (writing posts in multiple ways, with different images) can help you quickly determine which types of images and copy are working for your company - and which aren't.

How to Create a Social Media Strategy Map

Businesses have embraced social media as part of their Internet marketing plan. It is important to have an online presence that improves the reputation of your brand and drives new leads to your website. Social media thrives on consistent posting and communication with your fan base; however, it is often easy to forget the goals of a social media strategy as you attempt to keep track of this constantly changing forum. One way to ensure that your social media presence is working toward business goals is to build a strategy map. This is usually a tiered diagram that shows the goals of your work in specific steps.

Method 1. Developing a Social Media Strategy Map

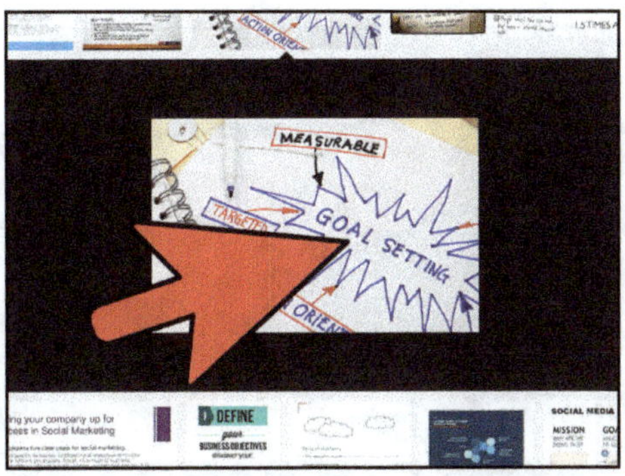

1. Identify your company-wide goals and objectives before beginning a social media presence. Research

and development of social media is the first tier of your social media strategy map. For start-ups and new businesses you will need to ask yourself some important questions to identify your strategy.

- Decide your place in your market. Decide if you are a leader, innovator, follower, customer service leader, educational leader, non-profit or community-centered organization. You can be more than 1 thing, but you should decide on 1 or 2 goals within your market, because you cannot cover all areas.
- Write down your value proposition to your customers. Ask what your customers achieve through buying your product. A business should look to increase the benefit to customers if they are not able to answer this important question.
- Develop a message for your customers, based on value and your business strategy. Break this down into 7 to 10 smaller messages that you can communicate to your customers via technology, such as your website, email blasts and social media. A website, database and, possibly, lead capture software should be active before signing up for social media accounts.

2. Identify your target demographic. Social media is only valuable if you are reaching your demographic of usual customers. For example, a demographic between the ages of 20 to 40 would mean you should develop a presence on Facebook, Twitter, LinkedIn, Pinterest and more.

- If you identify your target demographic as above 65, then you are likely to have less success with social media. Social media is not a good idea for every business. An older demographic may respond better to direct mail, newspaper ads or email blasts.

3. Start and begin using your social media accounts. Make sure you have an administrator on each

account that is given the company messages that should be delivered. Make sure to mix your content with educational, interesting and product/service messages.

- The first few weeks of a social media account are critical in setting up your tone. While you have fewer followers you should fill in all the information boxes, add company pictures and post at least 20 times before looking for followers. Internet users are less responsive to a "hard sell;" they prefer community oriented pages.

4. Integrate your social media accounts into your Internet marketing strategy. Cross-promote by posting links to your accounts on your website, e-mail blasts and printed materials.

Method 2. Creating your Social Media Strategy Map

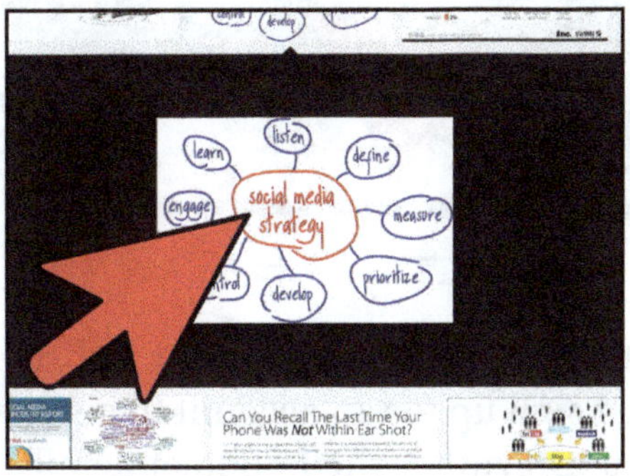

1. Begin using your social media accounts as a lead generation strategy. In visual terms, think of social media integration as the second tier of your marketing strategy. By posting interesting, funny, educational and valuable content with links to your website, you deliver targeted leads to your business.

2. Develop the third layer of your map, social media changes and growth. This involves training, gathering data and analyzing your lead generation process.

- Gather data from your lead capture software. Your website should be able to track where people are clicking on your links. If you do not have that capacity, sign up for a free Google Analytics account, and create links that will track who visits your website.
- Ask your social media fans and followers what they would like to see in your business. Use social media as a way to grow and change according to what your customers prefer. By studying the popularity of your posts, you can gauge the best way to communicate with your fans.
- Educate your employees on social media policies and social media strategy. By training the majority of employees on its use, you may also get helpful suggestions on ways to grow and improve your social media presence. Ask high-performance social media users in your company to contribute.
- Gather the lead generation data from your website, lead capture software or Google Analytics account. Bring it to upper management. Create "Social Media Champions" in upper management, who are willing to innovate the way your company adds value to its products through social media.

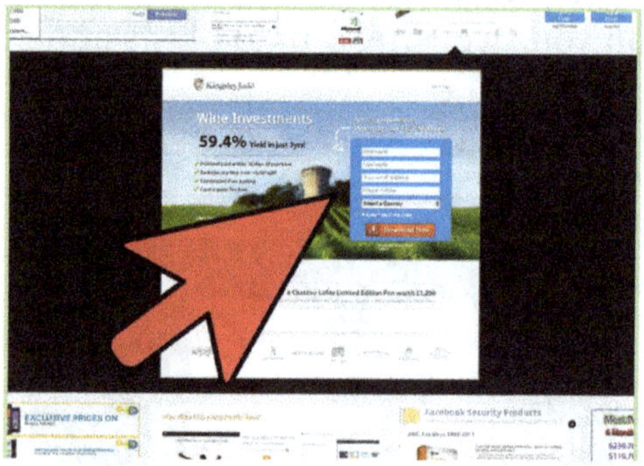

3. Establish added-value offers that are available via your website. This will help to convert leads into customers. If your leads must sign up for an account to get a free trial, free account, free song, free video or other offer, then you can gather their contact details.

- Make sure your fee value-added content somehow relates to your product or service. You want to attract people who would also be interested in what your website offers.

4. Communicate with your social media leads via email blast, mail or phone, depending upon your product or service. Offer products or services that are similar to what interested them in your website. This is the way you convert social media leads to sales.

- The process of converting a social media lead to a customer is often called a social media funnel. The goal of the funnel is to attract new leads and pull customers back into the funnel with new offers. Eventually, you should have a good base of repeat customers.

Method 3. Evaluating your Social Media Strategy Map

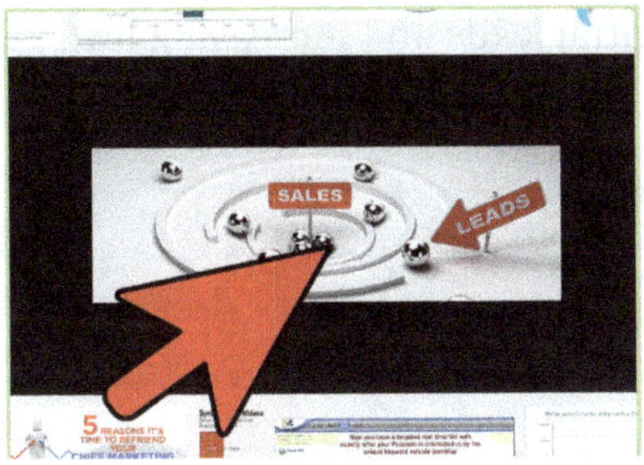

1. Gather the data of how many leads you acquired and how many leads turned into sales. If you have a high rate of conversion, then your map is leading you on the right path toward profitability. If you have a low rate of sales conversion, then you should adjust your map.

- Visualize the top tier of your map as business/shareholder profitability. The end goal of social media strategy is to deliver increased profitability to your business and shareholders.

2. Adjust your strategy map. Try to identify if you are hitting the wrong demographic, if you need to add value to your product or service or if you need to adjust your communication strategy. Try 1 thing at a time, so that you can isolate your problem area.

3. Study a rise in profitability over 3 months to a year. It takes at least a few months to gain a good online presence. Measure your increased profitability, which is the top tier of your social media strategy map.

- If you do not have increased profitability in 1 year, study your value proposition to your customers. Also, make sure you are targeting the proper demographic. You may want to keep social media as only a small portion of your marketing strategy.
- If you do have increased profitability, consider establishing a dedicated social media department. As soon as overall marketing messages are created, they can be tasked with communicating them to potential leads and increasing lead generation.

How to Develop a Strategic Social Media Program for Business

Method 1. Starting with a Strong Purpose

1. Know your purpose. Like any good corporate program or initiative, a strong purpose and a good set of objectives is important. This set of purposes and objectives has to be relevant and aligned to your other corporate objectives.

2. Know the limitations. It is important to know that not all objectives or purposes can be served by social media and it would be foolish to assume so just because 'everybody' is in social media. Social media is effective not only in PR, marketing and brand building but it is also effective when used for innovation, crowd-sourcing, building corporate culture and market engagements.

Method 2. Knowing your Social Media Landscape

1. Know the landscape. Before engaging social media for business purposes, it is important that the people involved in the social media initiative have a clear understanding of the attributes of the field they will be playing in. Know the landscape before you start constructing. The social media landscape generally consists of the following attributes that should always be in the mind of a social media strategist or planning team:

- Community-driven where people not only listen or view ads and news but they participate in this new media.
- Conversation is the new content king aside from videos and images. As David Armano said "It's the conversation economy".
- It's viral where people spread, shared and transmit content readily. That's what makes social media contagious.
- Personal spaces are even more pronounced, if you don't have permission, don't enter. Nobody wants to be spammed or get ad-bombed.
- Authenticity is what makes social media real and human. Don't bother with high cost production houses; real is soul here.

2. Build relationships. At the end of the day, these attributes are what builds relationships among friends. Get acquainted with people who were previously strangers to you. These attributes build a strong fan base for your brands and business. Small businesses and unknown musicians become famous because of them too.

Method 3. Build a Road - The 4Es of Social Media

1. Build a road. After you have understood what social media landscape attributes are, you will need to build a road before you can travel to your destination. The road here is acquainted to the 4 primary social media strategies that your company can deploy in your social media initiatives. These are the 4Es of social media:

- Education Strategy - Enriching your target community's knowledge with information and resources for them to better understand you.
- Entertainment Strategy - You create fun, sticky and memorable content that allows them to associate the image or message to your brand or business.
- Engagement Strategy - Your purpose is to engage the community by recognizing their presence, contributions and inputs.
- Empowerment Strategy - A space and role is created and provided to your target community to play an active role in what you are doing.

2. Tailor to your size. If your company is large enough, you can opt to deploy all at the same time but if your company is small choosing the most relevant and effective route will be your best investment and keeps your resources focus.

Method 4. Build, Hire but Don't Steal a Vehicle

1. Build slowly. You need a set of wheels to move forward. Once the road is ready, in order for you to move forward you will need a set of wheels. Depending on the size of your company, this means a bicycle, tricycle, motorcycle, car, F1 sports car, etc. The set of wheels that we refer to here are the social media tools and widgets that you will need to decide on what to use, how they can work together and when to use them. There are thousands of them around and there are few that are most popular like Hubpages here. In general the sets of social media tools can be divided into 4 major categories:

- Networking tools - blogs, micro blogs, social networks, etc.
- Collaboration tools - wikis, social news, social bookmarking, etc.
- Multimedia tools - videos, images, interactive contents, etc.
- Entertainment tools - virtual worlds, online gaming, etc.

2. Select according to need. Selecting the right combination of tools is important and helps you build expertise on these tools over time, because frankly you don't want to be managing 20 social networking sites at one go.

Method 5. Guide your Journey

1. Mark your map. Whenever you go on a long journey or to unfamiliar places, one of the most important things to have when you're traveling is a map. It tells you your destination, the dangers, and other necessary information to make sure you don't get lost or end up in a road that has no gas/petrol station. The same logic applies to social media. It is important that your social media initiative has a good set of metrics or measurements that will tell how you are doing at any one time. Nathan Gilliatt of Social Target LLC categorizes measurements into 4 distinct types:

- PR/media measurement - Viewing social media as media for their ability to reach an audience.
- Word of mouth measurement - Viewing social media as online interactions among people.
- Web analytics - Interested in people's usage patterns, as both audience and customers.
- Opinion research - Mining online opinions as the world's largest focus group.

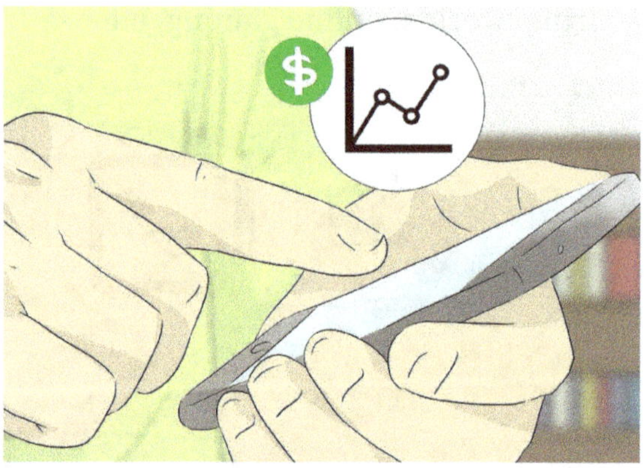

2. Translate into equity. All these are important to consider but even more important is to be able to translate the measurement information above into what we call "Social Media Equity" a set of fundamentals that are important for companies to make decisions about their social media investments.

- Strength of relationship (size, quality, relevance of type of activities etc)
- Degree of familiarity (with your business, brands etc, not just awareness)

- Degree of efficiency (where and how efficient are your viral logistics)
- Value creation (are there any?)

3. Be aware that measurement via loyalty is but one aspect. When you have loyalty without social media equity nailed down, it is hard to say whether your investment in social media has actually worked. This is because having 100,000 readers in your blog only says that you have 100,000 eyeballs of awareness but is this sufficient as a measure for performance?

Method 6. Don't Forget the Fuel

1. Get going. So you understand the terrain, you know which road to travel, bought your wheels, marked your map, so let's move it. Hold on a sec! Have you fueled? Fueling your social media initiative is no small task because when your company wants to take social media seriously, you have to seriously invest in:

- Time - yes, time to know how to use the widgets, set up your blog, create content, filter content, participate in conversations, spread your virus.
- Fresh Content - needs to be cooked up periodically whether it is from your company or from other sources. Social media is not a corporate website where you can stick up one article and let it stay there for time immemorial.
- Dedicated Team - yes, social media is no part time job for your HR manager, corp comm or PR or marketing team. If your guy has a business card that reads:

- Mr So and So - Sales, Marketing and Social Media Manager; your fuel is going to run low real soon.
- Creative Juices - to create value relevant content and conversations. Creative here does not necessary equate to fantastic designs but to content and conversations that delivered in ways that are of use. If you can put aesthetic make-up to that, this is even better.
- Good Design - because nobody wants to stick around a 1.0 design site and initiative.
- Widget Familiar - This is a given. Anybody who wants to be in social media has to get themselves familiar with at least 10 to 30 different widgets and how they work and inter-work with each other.

2. Get involved; be active in getting it moving. If your plan is to ask your IT department to hook it up for you via a memo or official request and then put that task to a queue of other stuff that the IT department has to attend to; that is really not going to work.

Method 7. The Take Back

1. Always be aware that there is nothing to lose when social media is done for the fun, but in business a lot is at stake and you certainly don't want your company, brand or initiative falling short.

How to Measure Social Media ROI

Marketers have always struggled hard when it comes to measuring social media ROI. (Return on Investment) Since social media is quite unpredictable and is still in transition when it comes to connecting social media to revenues, And thus traditional methods won't work. Marketers need to look for alternatives which are rapid and flexible.

Method 1. Using the ROI Formula

1. Calculate the new customer value using social media (*N*): This includes the sales, conversions, Business to business transactions (B2B), Contact value, etc. and placing a value on these things. Add them all to get new customer value.

- Use Google analytics or any other website tracking software to track these costs.

2. Calculate user lifetime value: Here you include the costs that you forgo to retain a customer plus the profit that you gain as a whole, while endorsing your brand to retain a customer.(It's like losing a little to gain more and adding the lost and the gained)

- Here is a formula on how to calculate user lifetime value:
    - User lifetime value (*U*) = (Gross distribution per customer) X Σ (yearly retention rate)^i / (1+ yearly discount rate)^i - (Retention cost per customer per year) X Σ (yearly retention rate)^p / (1+ yearly discount rate)^p+0.5
    - Where Σ runs from i= 0 to n in the first set while in the second set Σ runs from p= 0 to n-1. Here 'n' stands for the number of periods used in the calculation.

3. Calculate Impression value: This includes the easy costs that are used to impress customers via social media to ensure a quick viewership or membership.(In other words the internet advertising for which one has to pay for every time their advertisement is displayed) Here is on how to calculate it:

- Use this formula to calculate, Impression value (*I*) = (Add up all impressions from Twitter, Facebook, You tube (Cumulative views), website traffic and other online sources) X (Industry based cost per thousand impressions (CPM))/100

4. Calculate customer service Value: This includes the costs saved on customer service via social media.(Twitter, Facebook ,websites, etc.). Add all these values to get customer service value (*C*).

5. Add all the investment Returns: Investment Returns (*IR*) = {(Customer Value/ (Time Interval in years)) X Number of new customers + *I* + *N* +"C"}

6. Calculate social media expenditure: Here you need to calculate the amount that you spend on social media during the time of your campaign or just taking a specific campaign interval into consideration. Here are the steps on how to calculate the social media expenditure:

- Hard costs: Calculate the hard costs which denote the work or costs associated with the actual project during the campaign or during a specific interval.
- Soft costs: Calculate the soft costs which include the unseen work that composes the initial part of developing a project during the campaign.
- Cost/Time spent: Unlike other investments, social media has a greater value when it comes to time spent on it. Calculate the money spent per time spent on social media during the campaign.
- Sunk costs: Calculate the sunk costs involved during the campaign which include the costs that were required during a new addition or an internal fix during the campaign.
- Social media expenditure (*E*) = Hard costs + Soft costs + Cost/Time spent + Sunk costs

7. Calculate your Social Media ROI using the formula: *Social media ROI* = ("IR" - *E*) / *E*.

Method 2. Using ROMI and ROMO

1. Realize that the social media ROI has two subsets namely long term ROI and short term ROI which are famously called as Return on marketing investment (ROMI) and Return on marketing objective (ROMO). In this method we will calculate these two subsets and finally calculate the social media ROI.

2. Calculate the ROMI value. ROMI includes overall social marketing contribution over time usually year over year. Follow the below mentioned steps to calculate ROMI.

- Add all marketing expenditures: Marketing expenditures (*M*) = Social Marketing Budget + People and Resources + Technology Investments
- Calculate social marketing's contribution to business results (*S*) = Percentage of Sales influenced by social marketing (total number of leads, sales, cross and up sales) + Increase in revenue from existing customers
- Finally calculate social *ROMI* = Social return (*S*) / Social Investment (*M*).

3. Calculate the ROMO value. ROMO includes specific social marketing contributions to customer

engagement and sales usually campaign based and short termed. Here we will be basically calculating engagement. Follow the below mentioned steps to calculate ROMO.

- Calculate the lead generation effectiveness: Lead generation effectiveness (*G*) = Number of leads from social networks / Total number of leads
- Calculate marketing program effectiveness: Concentrate on specific metrics at the campaign level, the platform level and at specific levels (by post) for your customers. Example: Total number of followers on social platforms or the Growth.
- Calculating engagement = (number of like + number of shares + Number of retweets + Blog comments) / (Total number of published posts or pieces of content).

4. Calculate your Social Media ROI from there. Now for calculating Social media ROI just look for which plan do you follow. If you have a year to year based investments then your ROMI becomes your ROI and if you follow a campaign based or short termed based investments then your ROMO becomes your ROI. However if you follow the both then ROMI and ROMO combined become your ROI.

Social Media Optimization 3

Social media optimization (SMO) refers to the use of outlets and communities for generating publicity of a product, brand or event. RSS feeds, social networking sites, blogging sites and social news and bookmarking sites are involved in this process. Users are encouraged to use and share links to the website panning across all social media sites. The fundamentals of social media optimization and the techniques of improving and optimizing SMO have been extensively addressed in this chapter.

Social media optimization (SMO) is the process of increasing the awareness of a product, brand or event by using a number of social media outlets and communities to generate viral publicity.

Social media optimization includes using RSS feeds, social news and bookmarking sites, as well as social media sites and video and blogging sites. SMO is similar to SEO (search engine optimization) in that the goal is to drive traffic to your Web site.

How to Improve Social Media Optimization

There are a lot of lessons social media marketers can learn from SEOs to better optimize for social media. Here are six tips you can take from SEOs to improve your social media optimization.

1. Optimize your Strategy

A lack of social media strategy has been a roadblock for companies for a while now. Partly because it's still fairly new, and also because social media is always changing. Twenty-eight percent of brands feel that a lack of strategy is the top barrier keeping them from becoming a social business. In order to optimize your social media marketing campaigns, you have to have a strategy with clearly defined goals and objectives.

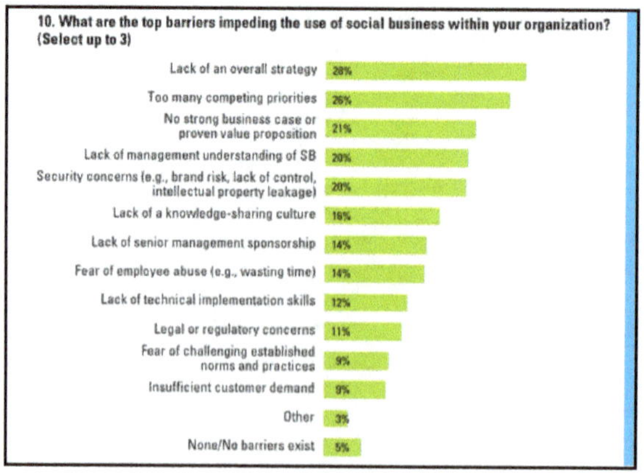

A social media optimization strategy should focus on growing your presence and achieving measurable results.

It outlines how to setup your strategy in seven steps:

1. Ensure your social goals solve challenges.
2. Extend efforts throughout your organization.
3. Focus on networks that add value.
4. Create engaging content.
5. Identify business opportunities through social.
6. Engage instead of ignore.
7. Track, improve and market your efforts.

When you have a documented strategy in place, youo measure where you stand and make improvements wherever necessary.

2. Do Keyword Research

One of the core competencies for SEOs is the ability to do keyword research. Keyword research is all about identifying the phrases and topics your target audience is searching for, so you can create relevant content for them. The same thing applies for social media optimization.

You need to know what topics, hashtags and keywords your target audience uses so you can share content that's relevant to their interests. Keyword research will also help you learn which hashtags and phrases to use in your social media posts so you have a higher chance of being found when people search for content relevant to your brand.

Here's an example. Let's say you're a vegan clothing brand in Chicago. People Tweeting about tasty vegan restaurants in Chicago or searching the hashtag #vegansofchicago on Instagram are more than likely a part of your target audience. So naturally, you want to make sure your social media posts show up for those types of searches. But how do you know which keywords are going to be the most important to your brand?

SEOs use a variety of tools to find out how often certain keywords and phrases are searched (search volume). But those numbers don't necessarily correlate to social media use. In order to get an idea of how often a keyword is used on social, you can use our Twitter keyword report.

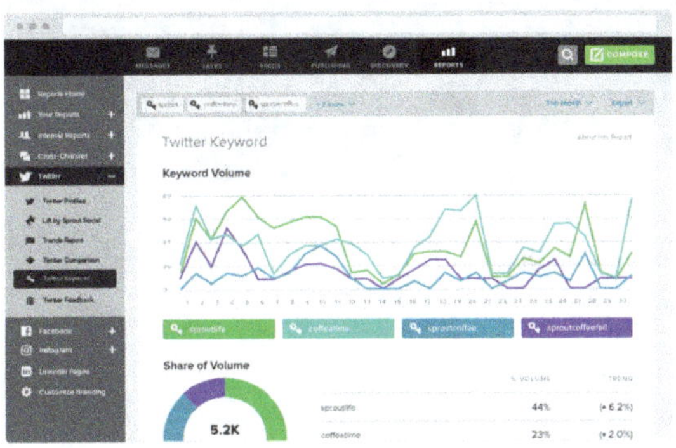

Most brands use this report to track trends in their branded keywords and hashtags. But you can also use it to do a little social media keyword research!

Start by coming up with a list of keywords your target audience might use. Then, go into the Twitter Keyword report and add your keywords.

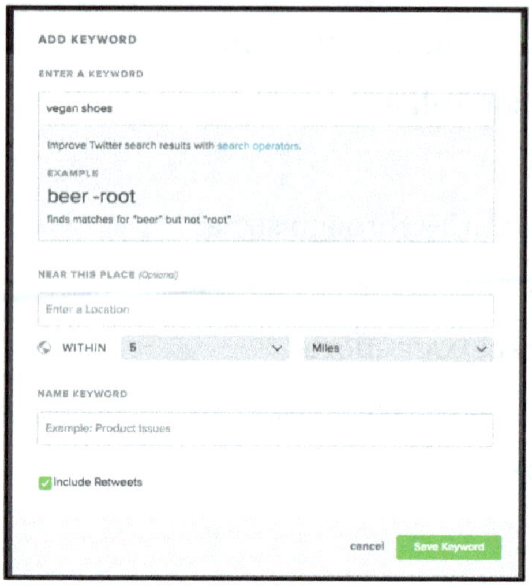

Now, you'll be able to see the keyword volume of all your target phrases over time. Pay attention to the phrases with the highest volume, then start adding them into your social media posts.

3. Optimize your Profiles

For SEO, optimizing your website is crucial. The content on every page helps search engines understand what your website is about. So when people are searching for topics relevant to your site, search engines know to recommend your content. Social media optimization is very similar. But instead of optimizing your website, you need to optimize your profile.

Creating your profile seems like a pretty simple task, yet it's one of the first areas of SMO where businesses fall short. Think of your company's profile page as your foundation. If it's weak, it's hard to build anything on top of it. Here's what it takes to build a strong foundation.

- Profile photo: Your profile photo should be your company logo. You can use a head shot of yourself if you're a freelancer, consultant or personality.

- Username: Use your company name. Social media username availability is starting to become a big factor for brands when they're choosing a business name. Using your brand name makes it easier for customers to find you when they're searching for your profiles on social. You can use a tool like Knowem to check if your company's name is available on different social media channels.
- Bio: Clearly state what your company does. If possible, place a trackable link back to your website within your bio to drive more traffic. Using relevant keywords in your bio will also give your page more visibility in search.

Most importantly, fill out your profile completely. Sites like Facebook and LinkedIn let you enter a lot of information about your company. Unfortunately many businesses leave these fields incomplete because they rush through the process. But the more complete your profile is, the more your page will stand out.

Pro Tip: Dedicate a block of time for completing your social media profiles 100% so you can give it the attention it deserves.

4. Optimize your Content

You've probably heard the saying, "Content is King" when it comes to SEO. Well the same thing is true when we're talking about SMO. Content drives social media. You can't succeed with social media marketing without sharing quality content.

There are two types of content that you can publish on social media:

1. Original content
2. Curated content

Ideally, your strategy should have a mix of both.

Original content is content that's specifically made for social media, and is usually part of a campaign. For instance, when Netflix launched its #NetflixCheating campaign, they created original graphics to share on Twitter.

Curated content is content that's shared from various sources around the web. Content curation is more than just tweeting out links. In order to optimize it for the best results, you should only share content that's valuable and relevant to your audience. Quality always beats out quantity. Determine what content your audience finds the most relevant by measuring the engagement for each post.

Guy Kawasaki is one of the top Twitter users/experts in the world, and his Tweets largely consist of curated content.

You can use Sprout Social's sent messages report to see exactly which content of yours gets the most engagement across all of your channels. Once you've identified them, you can start sharing similar content.

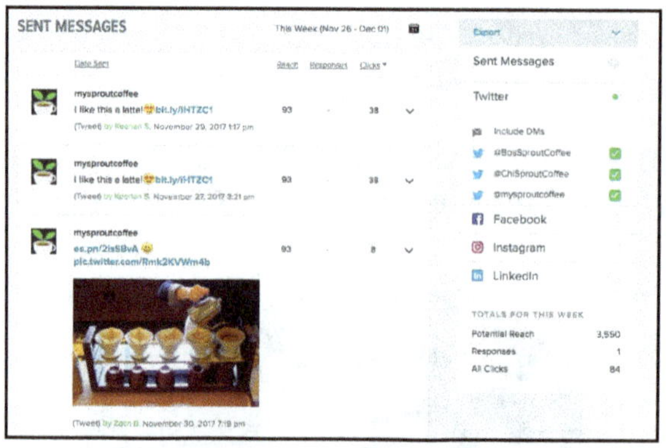

When you're publishing to social media, here are some tips to keep in mind:

Test Headlines

When you send out a Tweet or Facebook post, don't just use the same headline each time. Some headlines will work better than others. Plus, using a variety of headlines makes your feed fresh. Your followers probably don't want to see the same exact Tweet or Facebook post from you five times in a row.

Here's an example of two Tweets promoting the same article. Notice how they each have different copy.

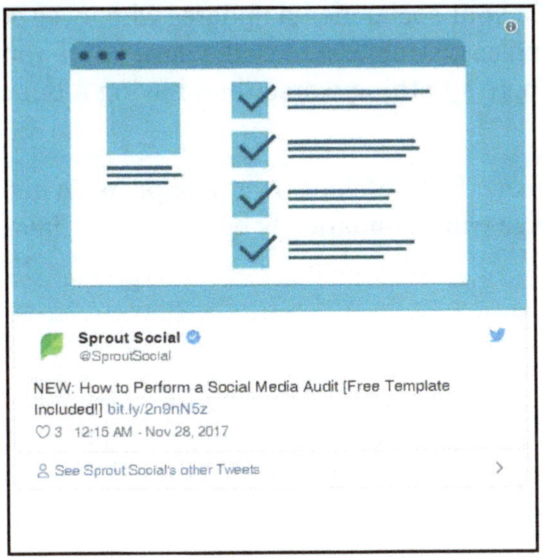

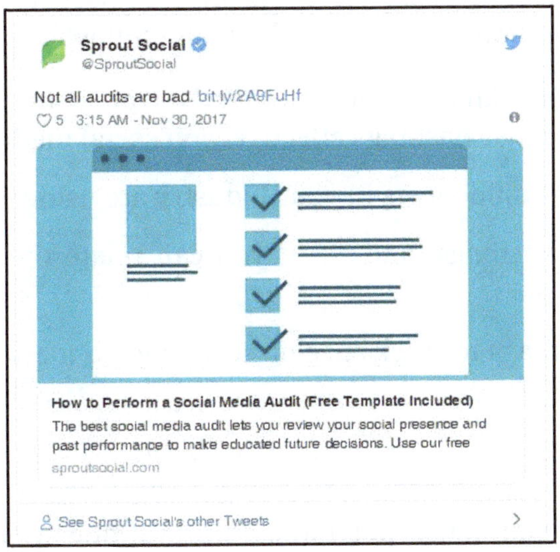

Use Images

A study from B2B Marketing Mentor found images were the most important tactic for optimizing content for social media.

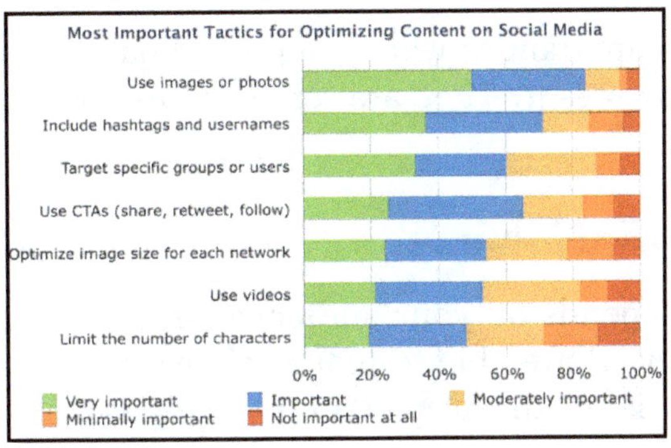

Include high quality images in your social media updates whenever possible. You can use our very own image resizing tool, Landscape, for free to make sure all of your images are sized correctly for each social media site. There's nothing worse than having a bunch of pixelated stretched out images in your Twitter feed.

Pro tip: Include a featured image in all of your own blog posts. Whenever people share your content on social media, the image will automatically be included. Check out this post on how to use Twitter cards for more info.

Hashtags

Hashtags have become synonymous with social media marketing. Instagram, Twitter, Facebook and pretty much all other top social media sites integrate hashtags in some fashion. They make it easy to track trending topics, categorize social media posts and they can be entertaining.

Hashtags help with social media optimization by giving your posts more reach, and making it easier for your content to be found even by people who aren't following you.

Even though hashtags can seem kind of random, there's strategy involved in getting the most out of them. Here are some tips to use hashtags effectively on social media:

- Look at what hashtags influencers in your industry are using. Use these tools to help.
- Search for trending hashtags, and see if you can relate them back to your industry or brand.
- Create your own hashtags to track specific social media marketing campaigns. Just avoid fails like these.

Post Length Matters

Twitter gives you up to 280 characters per Tweet, but that doesn't mean you have to use them all. Knowing the ideal status update length can increase the likelihood of people engaging with your content. We actually created an entire post with the ideal length of every social media post.

5. Optimize your Posting Schedule

The time you post is just as important as what you post. What's the point in sharing an amazing photo on Instagram if nobody sees it? Here are some tips to optimize your social media posting schedule.

Best Time to Post on Social Media

The optimal posting time depends on your audience and the social media site you're using. Luckily, tools like Sprout Social are able to make this process a lot easier by calculating the best time to post on your social media accounts for the highest engagement.

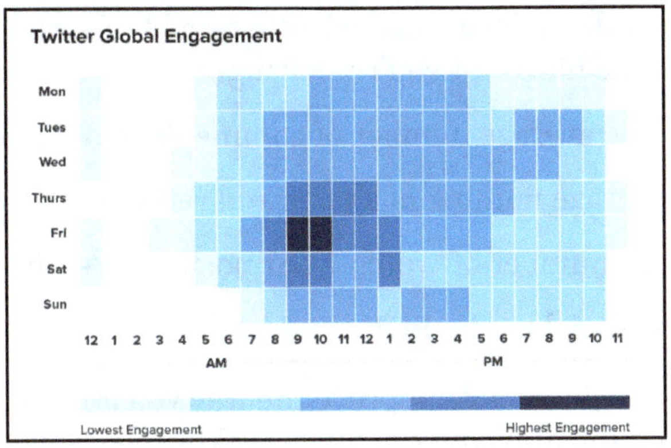

How Often to Post on Social Media

The second part of timing your social media posts is choosing the right frequency. You want as many people to see your posts as possible, but you don't want to completely bombard your followers' streams and timelines. Here's a breakdown of the optimal social media posting frequency for different social networks:

- Facebook: 3-10 times per week.
- Twitter: 5+ times per day.
- LinkedIn: 2-5 times per week.
- Pinterest: 5-10 times per day.
- Google+: 3-10 times per week.

Stay organized by making a social media editorial calendar for your business.

6. Track and Improve with Social Media Analytics

Just like with SEO, you should track your SMO efforts with social media analytics. Some of this can be done through Google Analytics using UTM codes. UTM codes and shortened URL's allow you to attribute the traffic your website gets from social media to a specific channel or campaign. In addition to that data, use the reports you get from your social media marketing tool to get a full picture of the impact of your campaigns.

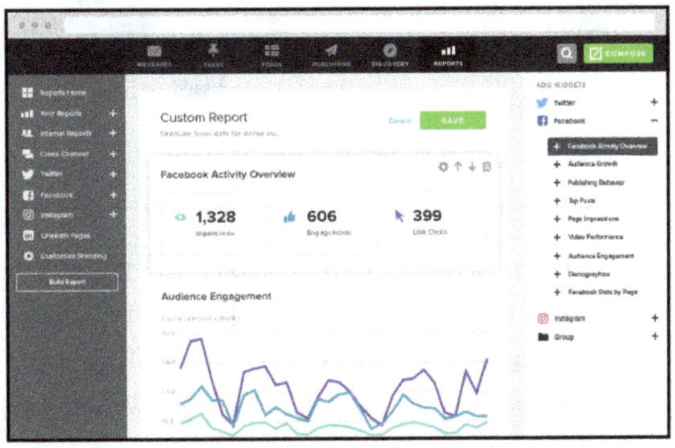

Aside from tracking traffic, tie in social media specific metrics too. Social media metrics are good because they're straightforward and focus on the key aspect of of social media—engagement. They answer the question: Do people like what you're sharing?

1. Conversation Rate: The average number of comments and replies your posts get.
2. Amplification: The average number of shares and retweets your posts get.
3. Applause: The average number of "votes" your posts get (+1, favorites, likes).
4. Economic Value: The social media ROI.

Social Media Optimization can drastically improve the way you approach marketing on Facebook, Twitter, Instagram and other social media sites. Start taking a strategic approach to social media marketing and amplify your results.

How to Optimize your Social Media Accounts

Social Media is where people go to connect with friends on the internet. For many, it is also a great place to find the latest updates on their favorite companies. With so many people using social media, having a company page on social media seems like a no-brainer. While there are many companies with accounts, there are few companies who have optimized their accounts to help customers find and engage with them. Get the most out of your social media sites with the following tips.

Steps

1. Have good content. The most important part of any social media marketing has to do with the content you post. Your content should engage and delight the reader and should not focus primarily on selling your products. Your content should help establish you as a leader in the industry. When consumers are ready to buy, they trust you have the most experience in the industry and the right products to match their need.

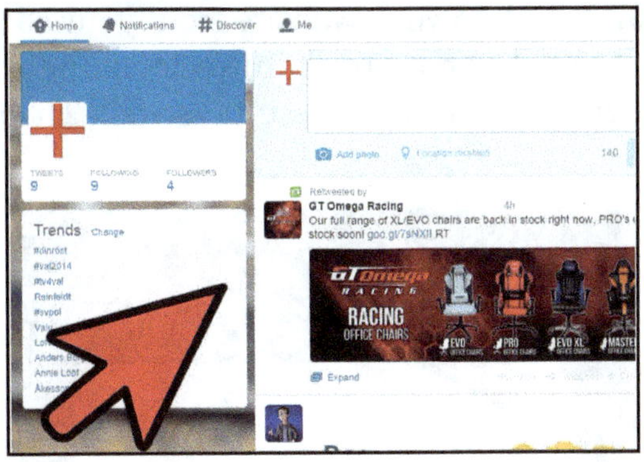

2. Consider your keywords. Do you want your profile to show up in at the top of search results? Then keyword optimization is the answer. For social media sites like Twitter and LinkedIn, the space below your name or Twitter handle is great for adding relevant keywords. If you are in the consumer electronics industry for example, you may want to add 'consumer electronics' and any other expertise you specialize in under your name. When people search for keywords you are related to, your profile will show up higher in the search results.

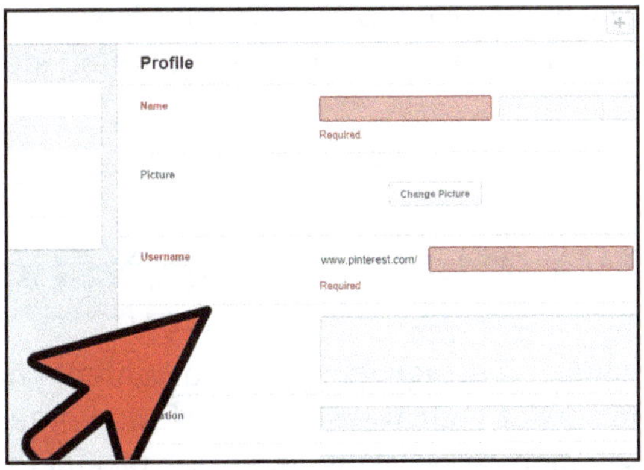

3. Complete your profile. With any social media site you are using, an incomplete profile will reflect poorly on your business. Start with a great profile and background photo. Since this is the first thing people will notice, it is important that it reflects your brand well. Information about who you are and what your company does is important too. If people are discovering you or your brand for the first time, make sure they can easily understand what you do with a complete profile.

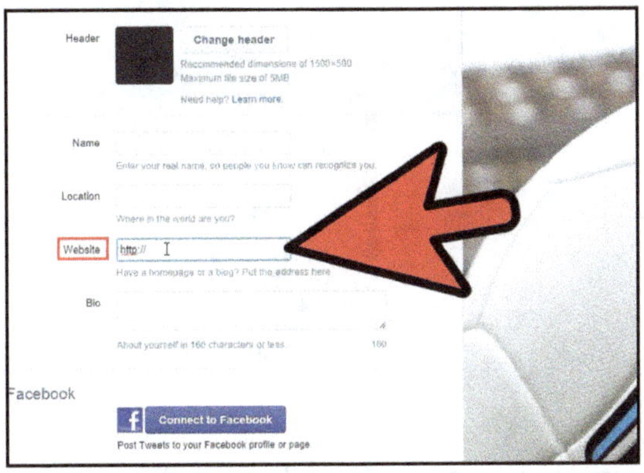

4. Use links. Many people visiting social media profiles want to visit the company's website after

checking out their page. Adding a link to your website from your social media page makes it easy for potential customers who want to learn more about your company. Adding links to your profile pages also help your search engine optimization results as well. The more links you have pointing to your website the better.

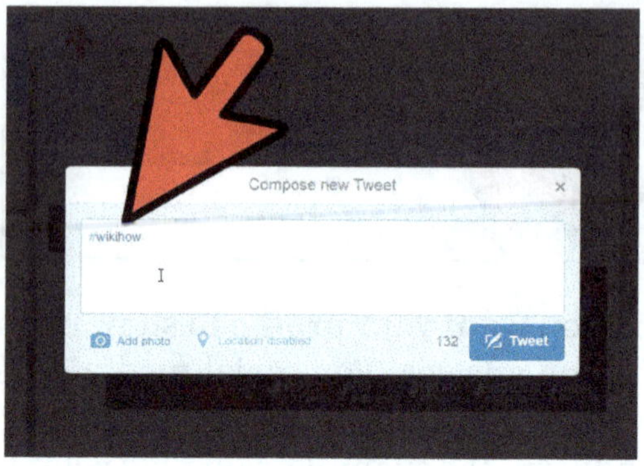

5. Use hashtags. Hashtags can be used in Facebook, Twitter, Google+, and Instagram. Hashtags allow you to emphasize important keywords in a sentence or summarize your post by adding a hashtagged word at the end. Hashtags group posts together based on the words people are using. People can also search hashtags based on subjects they are interested in. Stick to a max of three hashtags per post.

How to Check a Website for Optimization

Optimizing a website involves making design, coding, and content choices to attract more visitors to your website and help them stay at your website to perform some sort of action. This action is known as a conversion and may include ordering an online product from you or clicking a link to get more information. Online tools exist, such as Google's Website Optimizer, to test which design and content ideas are best for your site and lead to more visitors and conversions. Try these steps to check a website for optimization.

Steps

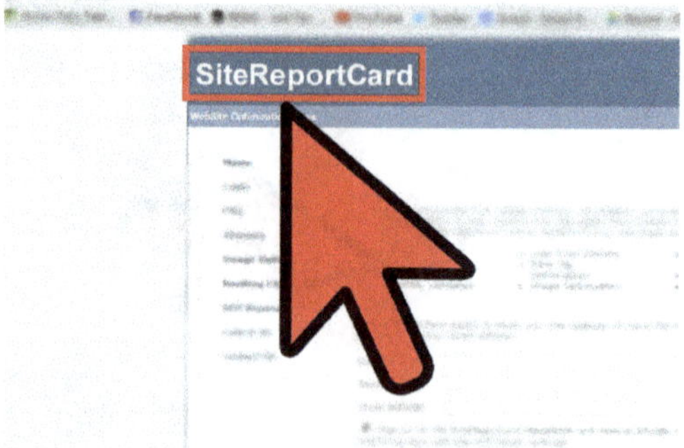

1. Search for a website optimization service. Google and SiteReportCard both offer free website optimizer tools.

- Sign up for an account to use the optimization service if needed.

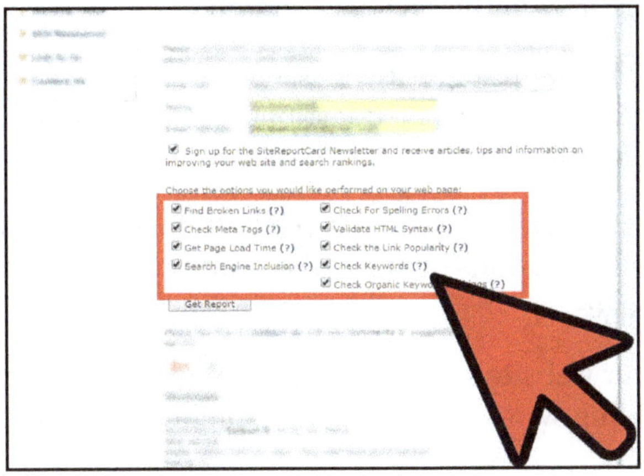

2. Choose what Type of Optimization Testing you want to do if Applicable.

- Before and After testing has you track visitor traffic and behavior on a web page. After making a change to the web page in some way, you continue tracking statistics to see if the web page's performance improved.
- A/B testing is a controlled form of testing that may not take long to prepare before being run. In this test, you divide visitor traffic between 2 or more web pages and see which page gets the highest number of conversions.
- Multivariate testing splits a web page into sections to test 1 section at a time. Different versions of each section's content are tested to see which performs the best. This type of testing may lead to high conversion rates but needs more technical work, time, and traffic than A/B testing requires.
- Segmented testing, also known as personalized or experiential testing, is the most sophisticated form of testing that uses the most time, technical effort and resources. It may be performed if you have improved your website as much as possible through A/B and multivariate testing and still wish to increase your conversions.

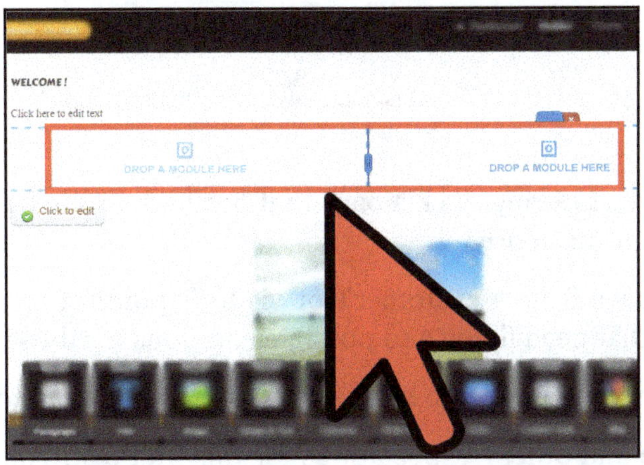

3. Decide which areas of a web page to test. Areas that you may want to focus on for optimization

purposes include web page titles, images, layout of content, your selling points, and the benefits or incentives to visitors for making your desired conversion.

- Consider changing the length of a title to see whether a shorter or longer title is more effective. Test rephrasing the title as a question or statement, making the tone more or less formal, or choosing a different point to emphasize.
- See how traffic and conversions change if your web page images are made bigger or smaller, if photos replace illustrations or vice versa, and the use of customer images is compared to using product images.
- Experiment with your website's layout, such as making it a single or multi-column layout. You can also try adding written content or reducing the amount of content your visitors need to read.
- Highlight different types of selling points. Compare quality to convenience, making money to saving it, and product features to customer service.
- Try pointing out different benefits or advantages to customers who make a conversion. Consider focusing on free shipping instead of a money back guarantee, for example. You can also measure whether taking orders by telephone does better or worse than receiving orders through an online form.

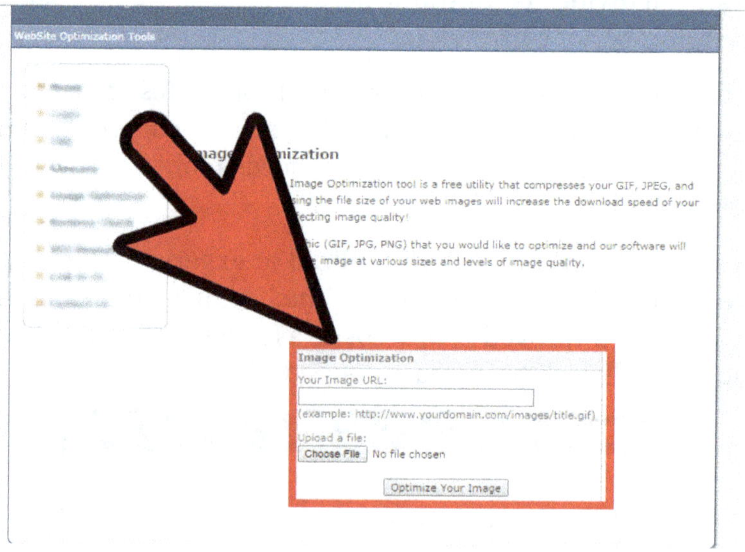

4. Choose a web page to start testing. Pick a page that has high traffic but does not get many conversions or otherwise performs poorly.

- Look at the web page from a customer's or visitor's point of view. Determine the 3 most important issues that need fixing and possible solutions for those issues.
- Consult with others, if possible, to brainstorm different content ideas to test.
- Manage your own and others' expectations for this first test. You may need to change the testing process or conduct more tests before seeing any results.

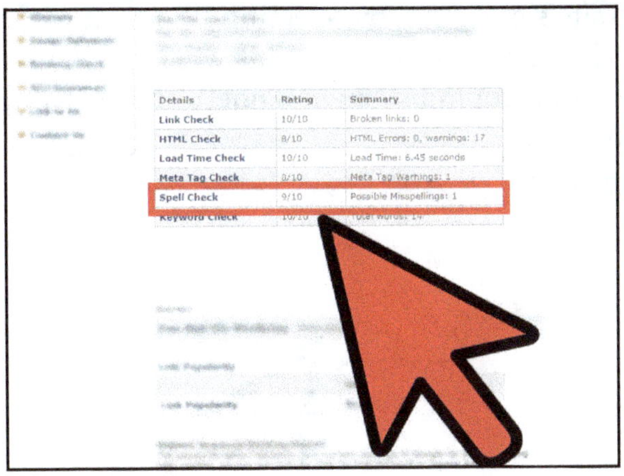

5. Check your website's code and text content for errors. Remove any bugs in the code or spelling errors you find.

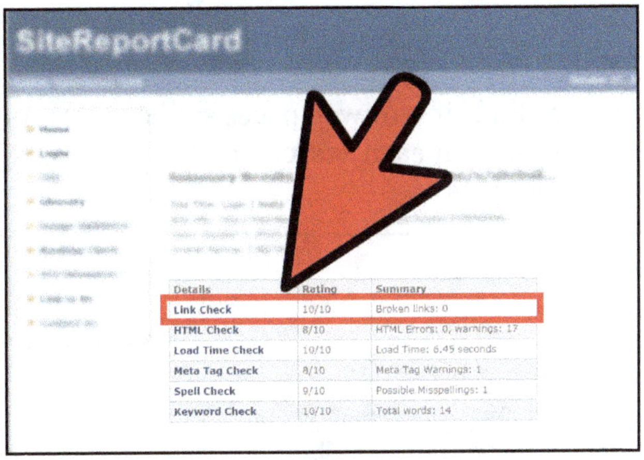

6. Test that your website's links all work correctly. Links that do not work, called broken links, may drive visitors to leave your site or prevent them from making a conversion.

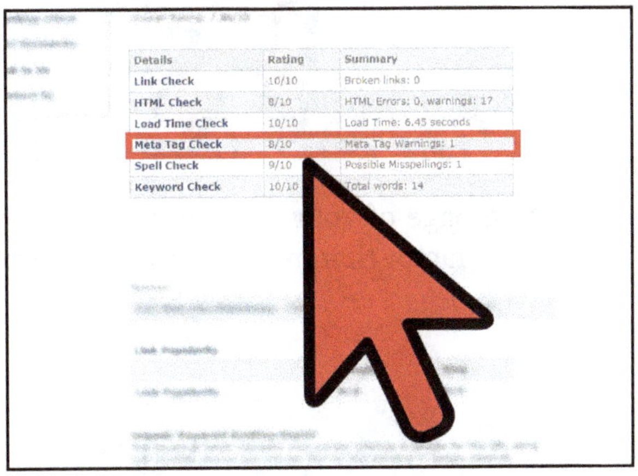

7. Compare your meta tag information to that of competitor websites. Meta tags are words or phrases embedded in HTML tags to describe that page and help search engines return the page address in its results.

- Inspect another web site's meta tags by selecting "View Source" from your browser's "View" menu or after right-clicking the web page. This will help you see the HTML code. Look for a section near the top that contains "meta name". The keywords are listed there as text to be used by search engines.

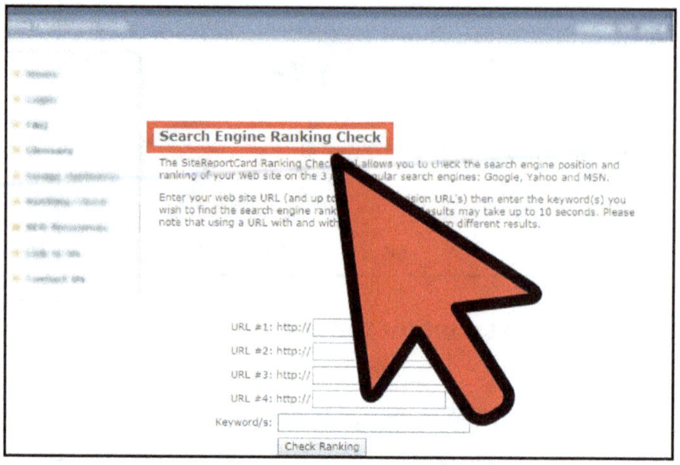

8. Use different search engines to find sites or web pages similar to yours. Check that your website or web pages appear in the results from each search engine. If don't, submit your site using the search engine's submission instructions.

9. Ask relevant web sites to link to a page of your site. Offer to link to their site in return. This should increase your link popularity, a factor that may be used in determining where your web site falls in search result rankings.

How to Optimize your Social Media Sites

Social media is where people go to connect with friends on the internet. For many, it is also a great place to find the latest updates on their favorite companies. With so many people using social media, having a company page on social media is good business sense. While there are many companies with accounts, there are few companies who have optimized their accounts to help customers find and engage with them. Get the most out of your social media sites with the following tips.

Steps

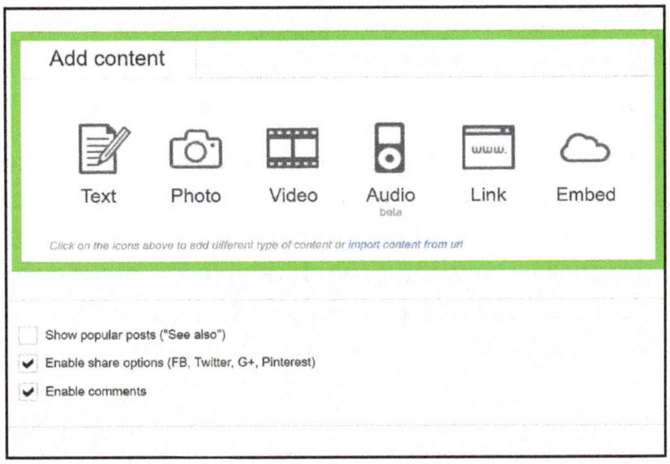

1. Provide quality content. The most important part of any social media marketing has to do with the content you post. Your content should engage and delight the reader and should not focus primarily on selling your products. Your content should help establish you as a leader in the industry. When consumers are ready to buy, they trust you have the most experience in the industry and the right products to match their need.

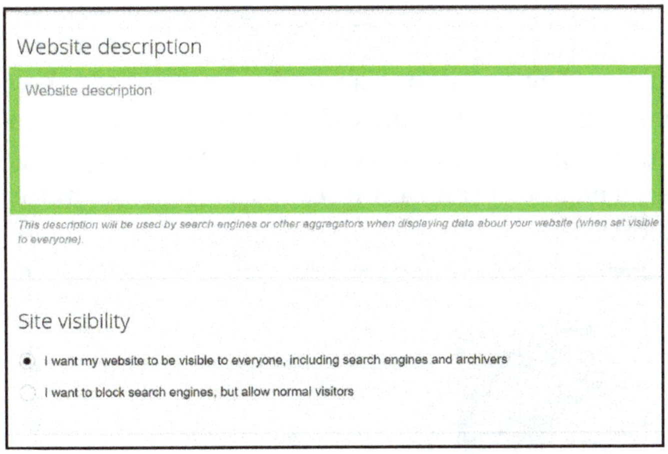

2. Use keywords. Do you want your profile to show up in at the top of search results? Keyword optimization can be somewhat helpful, depending on the platform used. For social media sites like Twitter and LinkedIn, the space below your name or Twitter handle is great for adding relevant keywords. If you are in the consumer electronics industry for example, you may want to add 'consumer electronics' and any other expertise you specialize in under your name. When people search for keywords you are related to, your profile will show up higher in the search results.

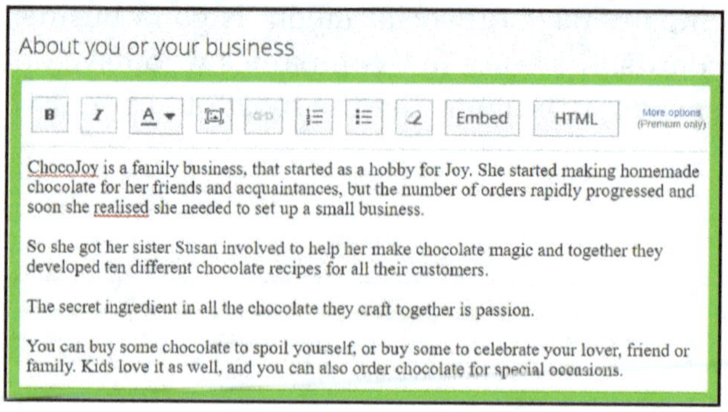

3. Complete your profile. With any social media site you are using, an incomplete profile will reflect poorly on your business. Start with a great profile and background photo. Since this is the first thing people will notice, it is important that it reflects your brand well. Information about who you are and what your company does is important too. If people are discovering you or your brand for the first time, make sure they can easily understand what you do with a complete profile.

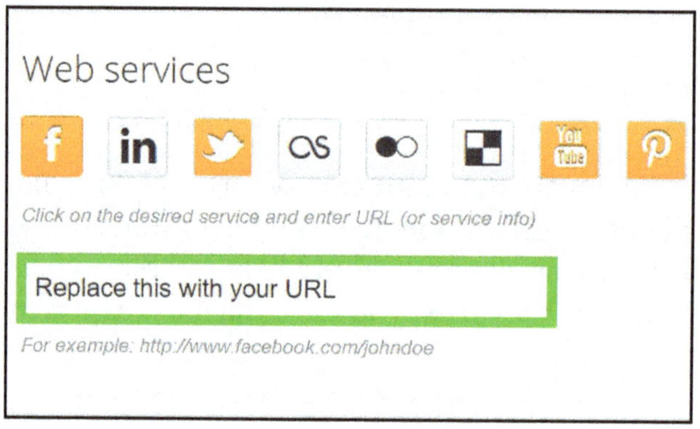

4. Add links. Many people visiting social media profiles want to visit the company's website after checking out their page. Adding a link to your website from your social media page makes it easy for potential customers who want to learn more about your company. Adding links to your profile pages also help your search engine optimization results as well. The more links you have pointing to your website the better.

5. Use hashtags. Hashtags can be used in Facebook, Twitter, Google+, and Instagram. Hashtags

allow you to emphasize important keywords in a sentence or summarize your post by adding a hashtagged word at the end. Hashtags group posts together based on the words people are using. People can also search hashtags based on subjects they are interested in. Stick to a maximum of three hashtags per post.

Brand Promotion using Social Media

4

Social media marketing is a modern tool for brand promotion. It uses social media platforms and websites for the promotion of a product or service. Such social media platforms have in-built analytic tools which allows brands or companies to track the success and progress of their ad campaigns. This chapter provides an insight into brand promotion using social media. It includes vital topics related to social media marketing, social media marketing campaign and promoting products in social media creatively.

Social Media Marketing

Social media marketing is a powerful way for businesses of all sizes to reach prospects and customers. Your customers are already interacting with brands through social media, and if you're not speaking directly to your audience through social platforms like Facebook, Twitter, Instagram, and Pinterest, you're missing out! Great marketing on social media can bring remarkable success to your business, creating devoted brand advocates and even driving leads and sales.

Social media marketing, or SMM, is a form of internet marketing that involves creating and sharing content on social media networks in order to achieve your marketing and branding goals. Social media marketing includes activities like posting text and image updates, videos, and and other content that drives audience engagement, as well as paid social media advertising.

Social media marketing can help with a number of goals, such as:

- Increasing website traffic.
- Building conversions.
- Raising brand awareness.
- Creating a brand identity and positive brand association.
- Improving communication and interaction with key audiences.

Here are a few social media marketing tips to kick off your social media campaigns:

- Social Media Content Planning – As discussed previously, building a social media marketing plan is essential. Consider keyword research and competitive research to help brainstorm content ideas that will interest your target audience. What are other businesses in your industry doing to drive engagement on social media?
- Great Social Content – Consistent with other areas of online marketing, content reigns supreme when it comes to social media marketing. Make sure you post regularly and offer truly valuable information that your ideal customers will find helpful and interesting. The content that you share on your social networks can include social media images, videos, infographics, how-to guides and more.
- A Consistent Brand Image – Using social media for marketing enables your business to

project your brand image across a variety of different social media platforms. While each platform has its own unique environment and voice, your business's core identity, whether it's friendly, fun, or trustworthy, should stay consistent.

- Social Media for Content Promotion — Social media marketing is a perfect channel for sharing your best site and blog content with readers. Once you build a loyal following on social media, you'll be able to post all your new content and make sure your readers can find new stuff right away. Plus, great blog content will help you build more followers. It's a surprising way that content marketing and social media marketing benefit each other.
- Sharing Curated Links — While using social media for marketing is a great way to leverage your own unique, original content to gain followers, fans, and devotees, it's also an opportunity to link to outside articles as well. If other sources provide great, valuable information you think your target audience will enjoy, don't be shy about linking to them. Curating and linking to outside sources improves trust and reliability, and you may even get some links in return.
- Tracking Competitors — It's always important to keep an eye on competitors—they can provide valuable data for keyword research and other social media marketing insight. If your competitors are using a certain social media marketing channel or technique that seems to be working for them, considering doing the same thing, but do it better!

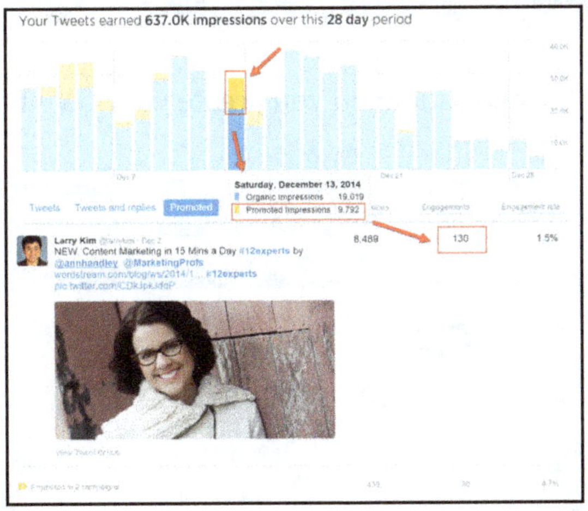

Measuring social media performance through Twitter Analytics

- Measuring Success with Analytics — You can't determine the success of your social media marketing strategies without tracking data. Google Analytics can be used as a great social media marketing tool that will help you measure your most triumphant social media marketing techniques, as well as determine which strategies are better off abandoned. Attach tracking tags to your social media marketing campaigns so that you can properly monitor them. And be sure to use the analytics within each social platform for even more insight into which of your social content is performing best with your audience.
- Social Media Crisis Management — Things don't always go swimmingly for brands on social media. It's best to have a playbook in place so your employees know how to handle a snafu.

How to do Social Media Marketing

Social network marketing can be lucrative provided you use the right tools. Here are some steps to follow if you want to try your hand at it. By implementing these steps, you will begin to create relationships with many people who trust you and will trust your business!

Method 1. Facebook

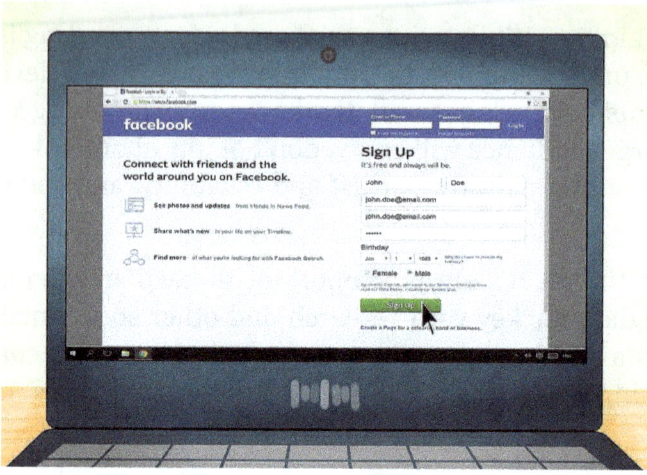

1. If you're just starting out, it's recommended you create your own personal profile.

2. Now you just need to add some friends. Facebook allows you to import your existing friends, add suggested friends and/or search for friends either by name or email address. This will allow you to build a large network of friends quickly. Once you have friends and have built a relationship with them, it's easier to let them know about your website and your business.

Use Facebook Events

As you start to grow, it's a good idea to host an event to promote your business. Many Facebook users enjoy attending events if it matches their interests. Once you've come up with the best event concept, let's see how to put it out there in Facebook land.

1. Go to the events page by clicking the calendar icon at the bottom of your Facebook page. Here you will see any events you have been invited to as well as an opportunity to create your own event by clicking "Create an Event" highlighted in green.

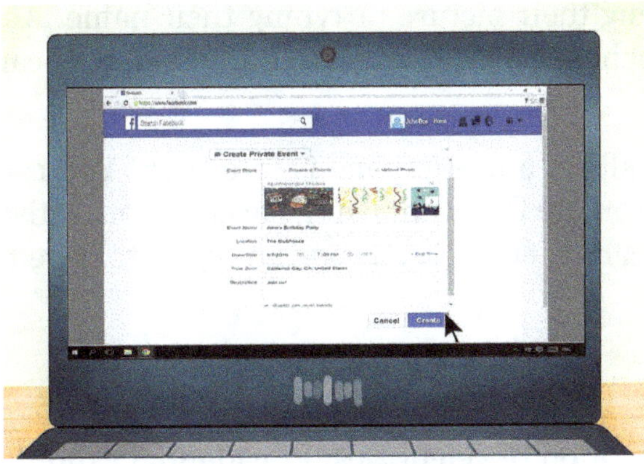

2. Now you can create the event with basic information. Be sure to add the street address! Then click "Create Event."

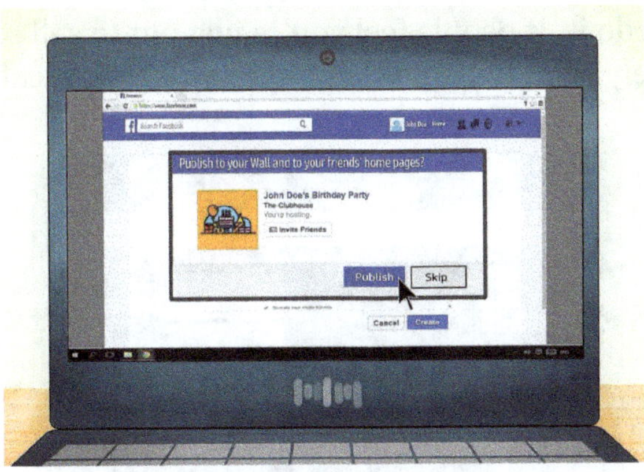

3. A pop-up page will appear allowing you to publish your event to your Facebook homepage. This also allows your friends to see your event without sending them emails. Very convenient! You can also add details of your event (highly recommended) to give your potential guests a chance to know more about your special event. Adding a picture is also recommended because people remember pictures more than words and it stands out amongst a sea of posts!

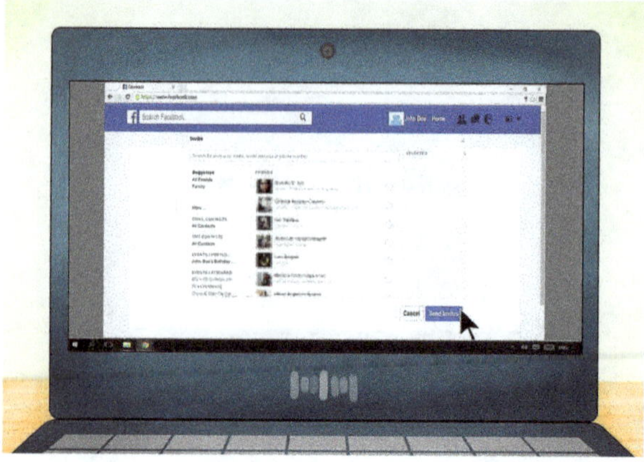

4. Send invitations. What's an event without friends! Although you already posted your event, not everyone checks their Facebook everyday. By sending an invitation, each friend will receive an email about your event. You can select All to invite all your friends to your event or choose a select number by either highlighting their picture or typing their name. Adding a personal message is optional, but adds a nice touch. When they receive your email, they can choose: "Attend" "Maybe" or "Not Attending."

- Voila! Your event is all set and everyone is informed! You can always go back and make changes if needed, promote the event using Facebook advertising, add pictures and videos to make it more appealing, etc. Most importantly, try to have fun with this. If you enjoy it, so will they!

Method 2. Twitter

Twitter has captured the attention of celebrities, Presidential candidates, businesses, street vendors and everyone in between! Twitter is a microblogging tool that allows you to send quick messages to anyone who is interested in what you have to say, "followers." You can also "follow" others and see what they have to say. This is also a great way to promote your website and your business. Again, be careful not to overdo it. If people feel you're just out to sell something to them, they will drop you. But if you genuinely want to help others, they will reciprocate! So let's get started.

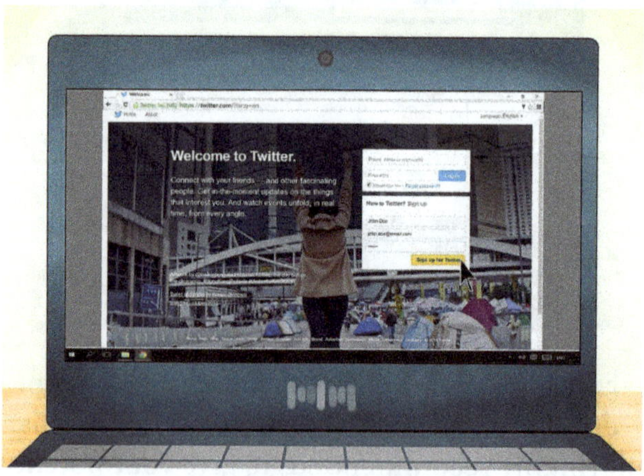

1. Learn how to use Twitter.

- If you have built solid a follower-base, then marketing via Twitter is as easy as posting a message up to 140 characters and hitting the 'Update' button.

Method 3. Digg

Digg is an extremely popular bookmarking site. If you've ever came across a webpage you really liked and wanted to bookmark it, perhaps you bookmarked it to your browser. The only problem is you can only access your bookmarks from that computer. However, social bookmarking sites such as Digg allows you to bookmark any page, access it from any computer and share with everyone! As a website owner, you also would like your pages bookmarked by others. Having your website on Digg, especially the front page, can open the gates to traffic!

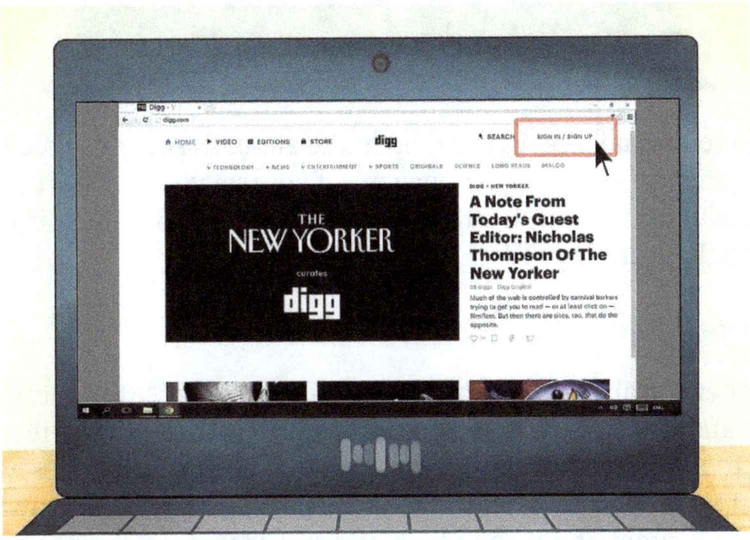

1. Start by joining Digg. Go to http://digg.com and click "Join Digg."

2. Fill out the necessary information, including Digg's verification form and click "I agree,. continue..."

3. That's it! Just go to your email account and open the email Digg sends you. Click the verification link and you're ready to start bookmarking pages. Of course, you can start by bookmarking your pages, but you definitely want to check out other sites and promote them if you feel they are that good. Trust me, they will return the favor!

Method 4. StumbleUpon

StumbleUpon is another social bookmarking site, similar to Digg. "Stumblers," those who actively participate in finding and bookmarking the latest news, can rate their favorite web pages. A toolbar can also be installed to make bookmarking even easier. If one of your pages get "Stumbled Upon" viewers can check out your site and vote to rank your page upward or downward. Make sure your website offers valuable content and a good look and feel that viewers crave and you will see your website fly up the ranks. This, of course, will add more traffic to your site. Try keeping your site fresh with new content and people will continue to stumble your pages. Be sure to return the favor! So let's get started!

1. Go to http://stumbleupon.com and click "Join StumbleUpon."

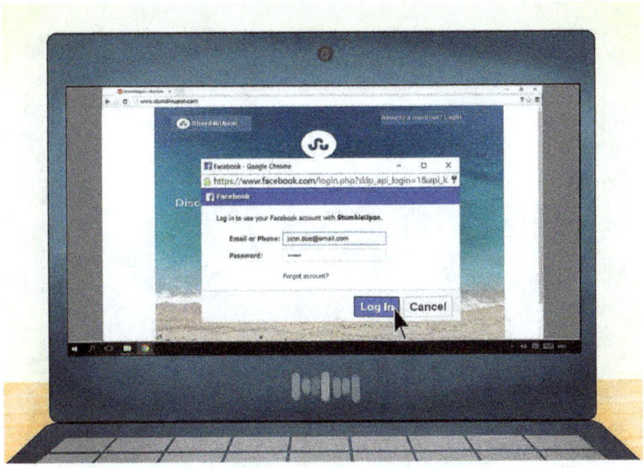

2. Fill in the necessary information and click "Join Now."

3. The greatest feature of StumbleUpon is the toolbar. After you join, SU automatically download the toolbar, which will allow you to vote and/or stories you StumbleUpon.

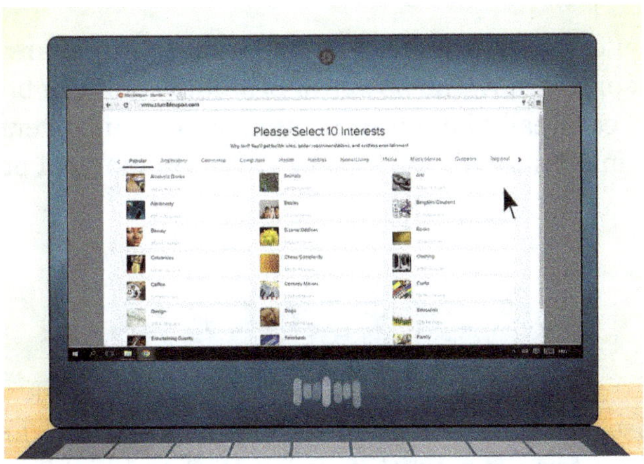

4. In order to give you stories that interest you, SU offer categories from which you can choose subjects that you would like to read about. Tick your favorite categories and click "Save now & Stumble."

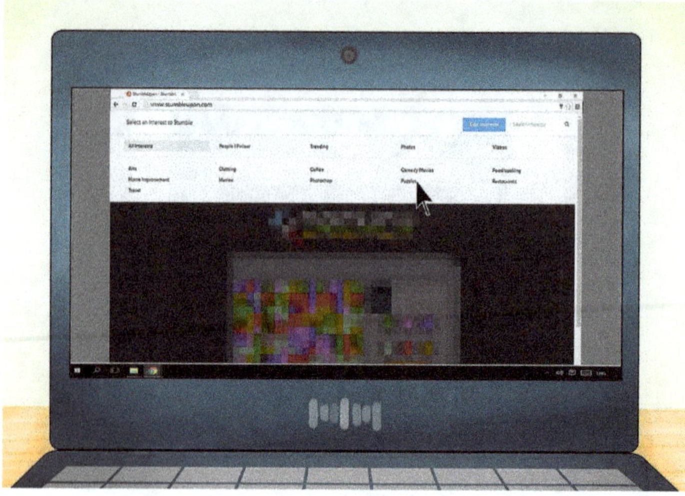

5. Browse through the list of stories until you find something that grabs your attention and click the headline link.

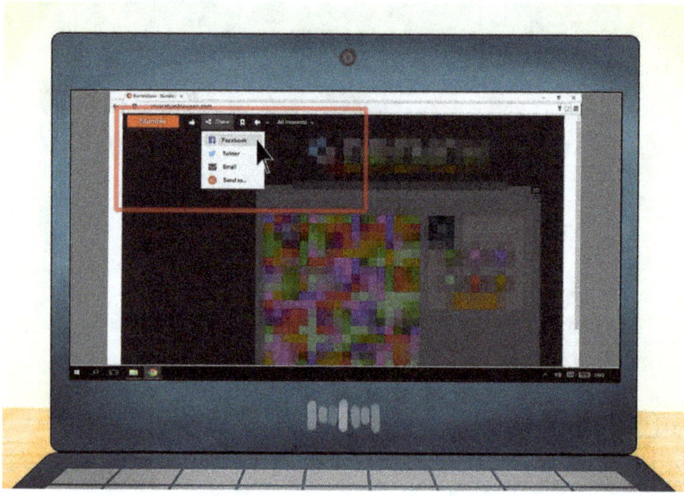

6. Here's the fun part. You can vote whether you like it or not, or share it with others from your email accounts, Facebook or Twitter. The power of StumbleUpon can be great! Create some content for your website that can really help others, unusual or controversial. The key is to attract attention to your site, but make sure it's the kind of attention that will positively affect your business.

How to Manage a Social Media Marketing Campaign

Social media marketing uses the power of sites like Facebook, Twitter, and Instagram to promote your brand or products. This form of marketing is low-cost and highly effective for reaching customers, but it requires a great deal of time and effort. By forming a social media strategy, maintaining a daily online presence, and optimizing your content, you can successfully manage a social media marketing campaign.

Part 1. Forming a Social Media Strategy

1. Outline your social media goals. When you first start your campaign, you'll likely just be posting content to grow your number of followers. However, you'll want to have goals other than just increasing your followers. This could be an increase in sales via posts, more positive reviews, or an increase in first-time customers.

- Increasing your number of followers is always a good goal to have in mind, but if your followers aren't interacting with your brand or buying your goods or services, you might need to focus on other aspects of your campaign.

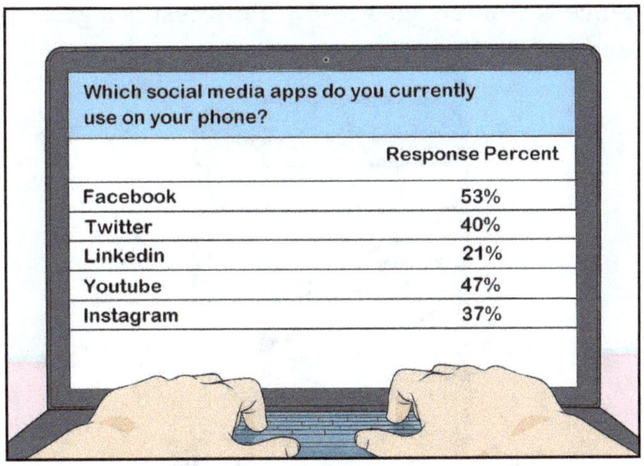

2. Conduct a survey of your brand aimed at current customers. Using a service such as Google Forms or SurveyMonkey, you can create an online survey to send to customers. To do this, you'll just input your questions into the survey generator and send the link to your customers via email. You can also post the link on your current social media accounts.

- Include a multitude of questions about their demographics such as age, gender, and location.
- Ask about social media use by saying "How often do you like or interact with posts by brands on Facebook, Instagram, or Twitter?" or "Which social media apps do you currently use on your phone?"

3. Identify the best platforms for your brand. Using the information that you gathered from your survey and your traditional marketing strategy, identify 2-3 platforms that will work well for you and focus on those. This will help your content reach people who are your targeted audience and are likely to become potential customers.

- Facebook is the most popular social media website overall, so if you're looking to reach a wide audience you should have a strong presence there.
- If your target audience is women ages 18-64, Pinterest is a great platform because women of all age groups tend to post there.

4. Invest in a mobile-friendly website. Because you'll be doing a lot of social media marketing, which is aimed at customers on mobile phones, you'll want your website to be mobile-friendly. It's a good idea to hire a graphic designer or HTML expert to create this for you.

- Most social media sites will have a "website URL" section where you can insert this link for users to click when they visit your brand's account.

5. Create a strong social media persona for your brand. In your posts, make sure you have a consistent tone and brand across all networks, even though you might share different content. Determine what kind of presence you'd like to have, whether it's witty, cute, savvy, hipster, or otherwise.

- An SEO professional does this on a large scale, and can help you manage your online business presence if you're struggling.

Part 2. Maintaining a Daily Presence

1. Make posts consistently. Make it a goal to share one picture, article, or funny story on social media per day. Make sure all of your content has something to do with your brand, whether it's product photos, user reviews, or seasonal sale announcements.

- Try to mix it up and not just post sales or reviews all the time. The occasional inspiring article or video will establish your brand as personable and keep your followers coming back.

2. Brainstorm a catchy hashtag to increase your exposure. Come up with a 2-3 word phrase that encompasses your desired brand image, your purpose, or is your brand name. Using a unique hashtag will encourage customers to repost your content, or post their own original image of your products or services that links back to your brand, growing your audience exponentially.

3. Contact influencers and ask them to be brand partners. Social media marketing is also done by regular social media users with a lot of followers. Most businesses send these influencers free packages of products or coupons for free services in exchange for them reviewing and tagging the company on their social media. This is a great way to reach new customers.

- In any case where you are providing free goods or services for review, make sure the influencer knows you want them to be honest about their experience.
- For example, you can ask by sending a private message that says "We really enjoy your feed and think you and your followers would like our product. Would you be interested in receiving a sample for free in exchange for an honest review posted on your Instagram page?"

4. Encourage followers to participate in the conversation on your page. In your posts and captions, ask questions and prompt your followers to respond. A post with comments in addition to likes will be more popular and will reach more audiences.

- You might also consider asking followers to post their own responses on their page and use your hashtag, or tag their friends to share the post.
- Ask questions or include prompts at the end of your captions, such as "Where's your favorite place to vacation?" or "Tag someone who inspires you in the comments!"

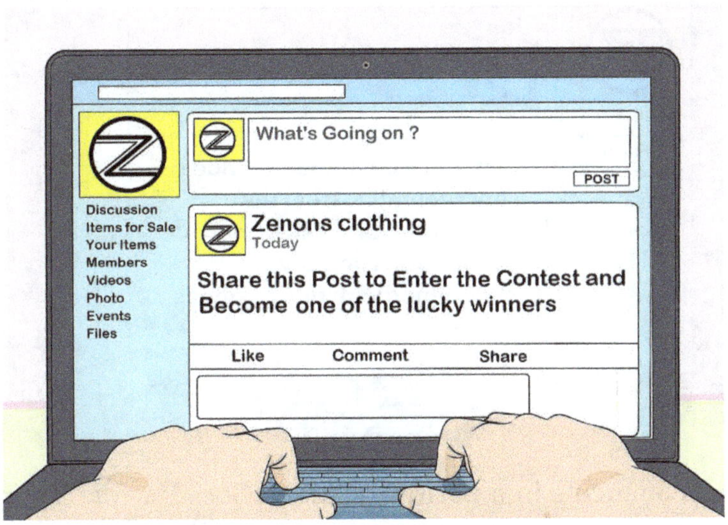

5. Use action-gating to reach a wider audience. Action-gating is when you prompt your followers to repost content or make their own content to participate in a contest with your brand. This method is highly effective at increasing brand loyalty and creating a network to reach new followers.

- There are many different ways to do this, whether it's by providing customers who give you their email with a coupon, or by having followers post pictures for a chance to win a prize.

6. Repurpose and share content. If you have an old picture from a few years ago, you can repost it by participating in #TBT or #FlashbackFriday. If you like a post by another brand and you have similar audiences, share it on your page and give them credit. Repurposing and sharing content will give you a break from creating original content while still keeping your brand engaged.

7. Respond to negative comments in a positive manner. Social media is a great place to exhibit exceptional customer service. It also gives your customers with bad experiences a public platform for their complaints. If you receive a negative comment, respond positively and try to turn the situation around.

- For example, you can send a private message saying "Hi Jen, I'm a customer service representative from the Thread Makers. I saw your post about a negative experience with our business, and I wanted to sincerely apologize for that. I'd like to offer you 20% off of your next purchase to make up for any frustration we may have caused. Could you reply with your email address so I can send that over to you?"

Part 3. Optimizing Your Content

1. Share the best content for each social media platform. It's no secret that Instagram is the best platform for sharing pictures and short videos, but there are some conventions for sharing posts on other platforms as well. Make sure you're sharing the best content for that specific platform.

- Facebook is great for sharing articles and links because the mobile user doesn't have to leave the app.
- Twitter is best for short updates or engaging with customers. The platform is also great for handling customer service issues.
- Visual content performs well on all varieties of social media, so it's important to have great pictures in your campaign!

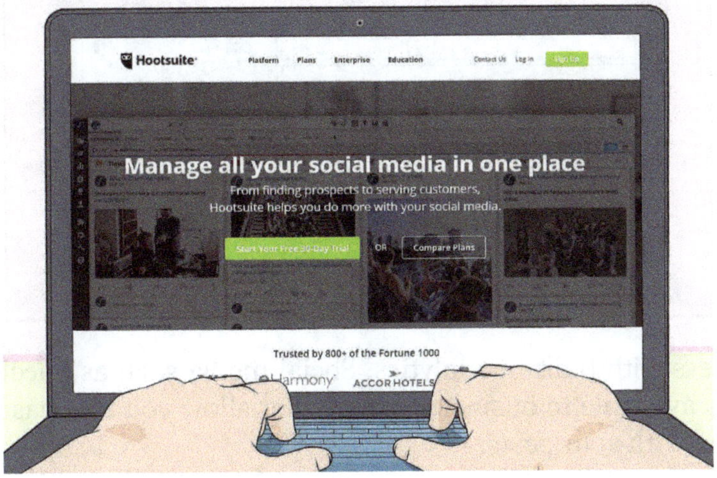

2. Utilize management tools to coordinate content across multiple platforms. Online tools such as Hootsuite, Buffer, and Sprout Social can help you to easily and quickly schedule and make posts on different accounts. If you want your brand to be active on Instagram, Facebook, Twitter, LinkedIn, and Pinterest, management tools can save you time and frustration.

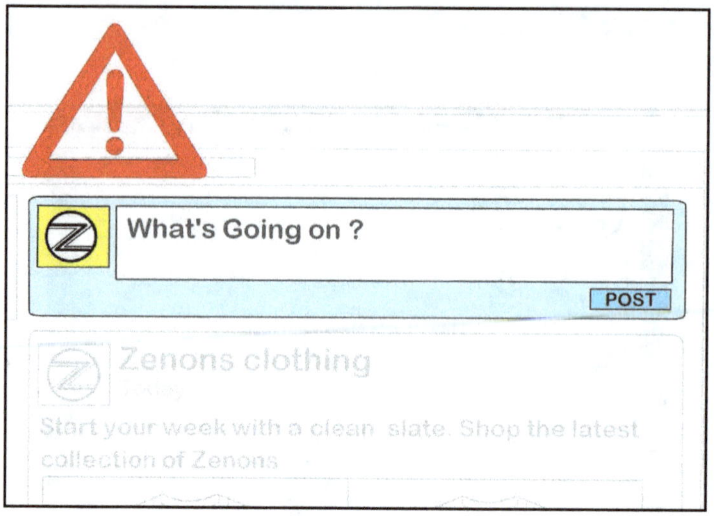

3. Proofread your posts carefully. Establishing a brand is exciting and you might be in a rush to get your content out in the world. However, you should always proofread your content entirely before hitting the "post" button.

- Many brands and companies have experienced major social media crises due to a typo, missed word, or accidentally published draft.
- Make sure all of your posts are on-brand and don't include language that doesn't fit in with the tone of your other posts.

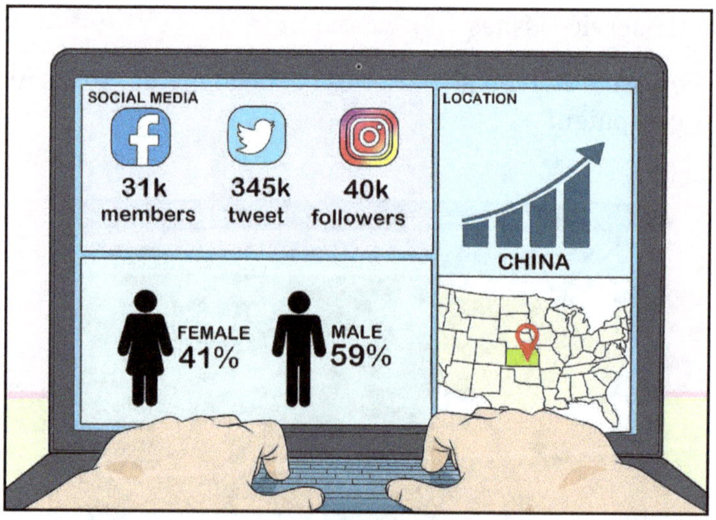

4. Measure your success with built-in analytics. Social media such as Facebook, Instagram, and Twitter have analytics available to business owners that allow you to measure how many people have seen or interacted with your posts.

- Make it a priority to check these analytics 2-3 times per week to make sure your content is effective and enjoyable for your followers.
- Pay attention to how many people see your posts, how many people like them, and how your brand is growing.

How to Market your Brand on Social Media

Companies are increasing their spending on social media marketing to market their brands for several reasons. Firstly, people tend to spend more extended hours every month on their social media accounts. They are not as inclined to visit company websites to acquaint themselves with the latest products and services. Secondly, social media allows users to share information faster. This enables companies to indirectly reach out to more potential customers for their brand awareness. Thirdly, the number of visitors and users for social media networks is multiplying, thanks to the widespread proliferation of smart-phones and cheaper computers now available readily in the market. Moreover, finally, social media allows you the flexibility of content.

Here are a few simple steps to market your brand.

1. Identify the Best-suited Network

Identify the social media network that best suits your needs. By far, Facebook remains the most popular social media platform worldwide and in the UK, as statistics we provide, prove. Facebook has users of all ages and genders. Additionally, Facebook offers the facility of opening a business page, free of cost. Further, Facebook also provides visitors to your company's page, to post comments about your brand. This is particularly useful for listening to client feedback, responding to complaints and building a brand. On the other hand, Twitter allows you to send instant updates about your new brands or improvements in a product or service.

Should you be looking at marketing your brand through images and videos, Instagram and YouTube are your best options. For most consumers, seeing is to believe, and you can use this old axiom to build your brand identity with pictures and videos. YouTube also offers a service through which your ads appear before or during a video. Pinterest is said to have a significant following among women. You may consider marketing your brand through this rapidly growing social media platform too. For building a brand for business-to-business purposes, you may consider LinkedIn. With high user base among professionals and the corporate community, LinkedIn is the right tool to reach out to B2B users for your products and services. Remember to include the Facebook, Twitter, YouTube, Instagram, Pinterest and LinkedIn links on your company's website. This improves your chances of getting more followers to market your brand on social media.

2. Excellent Content

Here is the tricky part of marketing your brand through social media. You will have to ensure, the content you provide is accessible to comprehend, concise and sharable. Consumers are not interested in content that is heavy on technical specifications. What they require is something they can identify with quickly. Furthermore, nobody likes to spend too much time reading content, because the attention span of modern-day consumers is relatively low. Hence, you will have to ensure your content is concise and yet contains all information relevant to your target consumers. Investing in high-quality images and beautiful videos will prove worthwhile.

Images, videos and other visual content by themselves are well remembered. Coupled with excellent user-friendly write-ups, they make a formidable combination. Great content tends to be shared on Facebook, Twitter, YouTube, Instagram and Pinterest users. It also draws attention from professionals and B2B users in your field on LinkedIn.

3. Influencer Marketing and Blogs

Getting bloggers to write about your brand on their websites is yet another great way to market your brand on social media. Bloggers provide links to other websites that speak highly about your product, as a reference. Additionally, Google AdWords sends videos and images of advertisements on such websites. All good bloggers have excellent Facebook pages with a huge fan following.

Roping in the services of a competent blogger who writes about products, services and developments in your particular industry is another great way to market your brand on social media. Getting a blogger to publish your content with links to your company's website also works wonders. In such cases, advertisements and videos of your products and services can appear alongside the blog, through Google AdSense. Your Facebook page can also be promoted by bloggers to get more 'likes' and followers.

4. Online Promotions and Campaigns

An integral part of marketing your brand on social media is by retaining the interest of followers on your Facebook, Twitter, Instagram, YouTube, LinkedIn and Pinterest pages. This can be efficiently done by launching frequent online promotions and campaigns on social media. Such online promotions and campaigns help develop your brand. It also encourages your followers to share your social media pages and web-links or blogs with other potential buyers. Admittedly, you will incur some expenses on such online promotions and campaigns. Offering attractive gifts, discounts and other incentives are known to help build and develop brands. Additionally, they also create a very positive and much desirable impact on your followers, clients and future customers.

5. Visual Branding on Social Media

This involves the use of your logo design and brand images that people can remember and identify with. A great example of visual branding remains British Airways and its former model Roz Hanby who would feature on the air carrier's advertisements worldwide. Of course, Internet did not exist in those days, and the concept of social media was never dreamed of. A flight stewardess for the airline, Roz Hanby was known as 'Face of British Airways' in the 1980s. Another excellent example is the Coca-Cola logo design, which has remained unchanged for decades since the soft drink was launched. Hence, visual branding is hugely vital to promote your brand on social media.

Creative Ways to Promote your Product on Social Media

Social media allows businesses to be in direct contact with target customer. Social media marketing is inexpensive and gives brands instant reach to billions of active users. For these reasons, social media has proven to be one of the most effective channels to promote products online.

However, with every business aware of it, competition on social media has become intense. To overcome competition, it is important that you leverage latest trends & techniques and promote your product on social media creatively and consistently.

Below are 6 such techniques that will help you in generating more leads for your product through social media in 2017.

1. Run Contests on Social Media to Attract Attention

A contest is a subtle way to promote your product without actually advertising it. Running contests on social media platforms will drive audience's attention towards your product. To reap maximize benefits from the contest, keep it fun, simple, and offer giveaways to all participants. Ultimately, this will create loyalty towards your product in customers; thus, will help you in generating leads in long-term.

Example: Dove, recently started a "Real beauty should be shared" contest on Facebook. It was a fill-in-the-blank contest wherein users had to tell why their friends represent real beauty by filling in their friend's name and things that make them a real beauty. As a prize for this contest, they gave entrants the chance of becoming the face of Dove (to be printed on Dove soap case). This was a brilliant branding campaign where Dove not only got a genuine face for marketing but also brought huge attention towards its product.

2. Provide Social Proofs to Build Trust in your Product

Customer review & testimonials act as an influencer that promotes your product to the consumer in a good light. It is always better that the consumer makes an informed decision by knowing other customers' experiences, rather than after being influenced by social media advertisements. That is why it is mindful to make customer testimonials or user-generated content the face of your brand on social media.

Example: The Facebook page of GoPro is filled with testimonials and user-generated content. Users submit their epic pictures clicked by GoPro camera, which GoPro share on social media to make a greater impact on the potential buyers of their products.

3. Run Deals and Promo Codes on Social Media

Newly introduced but proven to be a good way to promote products on social media is giving away deals and promo codes. Provide special deals to your customers on social media regularly so that they remain engaged at all times. You can also do a little brainstorming on how you can personalize the whole concept of offering discounts & promo codes to make your customers feel special. For example, providing discounts on birthdays, putting names of discount credit cards, etc. This will help them turn loyal towards your brand in long term.

Example: Lane Bryant took advantage of the end of summer to unload stock of clothes. The brand used social media to entice the audience for a 50% off on all summer wear. The discount was strategically planned by the e-commerce store as it engaged the audience by saying the summer clothing will be gone after this sale.

4. Advertise your Product to Reach Wider

People like your page on social media because they are interested in your product. However, for businesses, there is a fall in organic reach on social media, which is why they need to put extra efforts to make sure their products are being seen by target audience. Social media ads boost your reach and can help you achieve millions of views on your posts. This in turn, gives your product the promotion you want for it and ultimately brings you more lead.

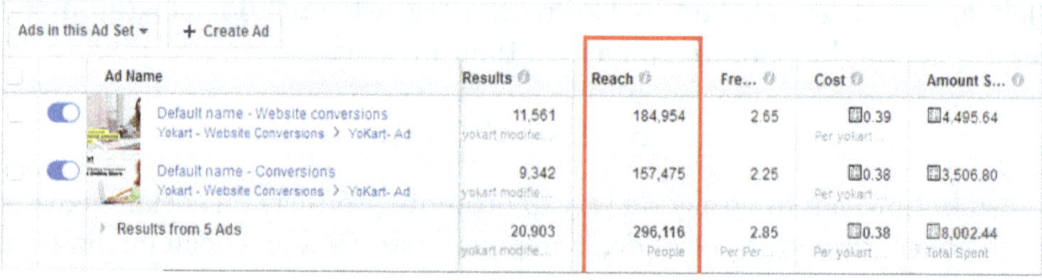

Example: Here are some stats from the recent Facebook ads for the product YoKart (a multivendor ecommerce platform). Despite having only a few hundred followers on Facebook, they were able to reach close to 300K people with Facebook ads; and that too by spending only $120 (INR 8000), as you can see in the image above.

5. Share Creative Visual Content for Better Engagement

Images, videos and other visual content have proven to be most effective for engaging users on social media. So, by posting creative pictures or product demo videos on different social networks, you can bring huge attention to your product.

Example: Slack is an efficient team communication tool that reduces the need of frequent team meetings. Most people hate to attend meetings. See how this creative social media visual by Slack would quickly make people interested in their product as it illustrates how it feels to sit in 25% fewer meetings.

6. Promote your Product in Social Media Communities

Joining social media groups/communities relevant to your niche can also serve as a good way to spread awareness about your product. Your product promotion efforts in social media groups will implicitly bring better results since members are already interested in a similar product. But it is really important that you connect with group members well, converse in their interests, and be transparent when providing details of your product.

If you pay attention to these points, social media communities will prove to be a good source for getting quality leads for your product.

How to Become a Social Media Marketer

As a social media marketer, you'll promote your company's products and services on various platforms. Sounds simple enough, right? But how do you get your start? That can be an intimidating question, but you might be more prepared than you think. After all, you've been marketing your personal brand while building your own social media following. With a few pointers, you'll be able to round out your media marketing skills.

Part 1. Developing Basic Skills

1. Focus on three main social media platforms. Though the opposite may seem true, specializing in one or two specific platforms is better than generalizing in many different ones. The three most important platforms for advertising are Facebook, Twitter, and LinkedIn.

- Social media platforms are frequently changed, causing once effective marketing techniques to be less useful. Staying updated on many platforms will be much more difficult than a focused one or two.
- Stay abreast of updates by subscribing to media marketing blogs or signing up for platform newsletters, like Facebook's Marketing Partner Weekly Update.
- Look up online resources to learn marketing techniques for your chosen platform(s). Many social media marketing gurus offer advice on their YouTube channels or Facebook pages.

2. Research your customer base. Different industries will require different marketing strategies, so

you'll need to choose the industry you'll become a marketer in, like technology, fashion, or automotive. Look at the forums on major company websites in your industry. What are people talking about? Use these conversations to learn about your customer base.

- Create a Reddit account and subscribe to subreddits in your industry to identify and monitor relevant topics to your customer base.
- Research doesn't have to be boring! Make color-coded spreadsheets with Google Spreadsheets or Excel to list topic areas in your industry. Use this list to improve variety in your posts.

3. Observe the marketing strategies of successful companies. Follow several companies you admire and follow them on your chosen media platform(s). Take notes on their marketing techniques. Ask yourself, "How could I duplicate this? What would I do differently? How would I use this to promote a product?" Ask yourself without hesitation – talking to yourself is completely normal.

- Bookmark or screenshot your favorite advertising campaigns from the companies you follow. Look to these for inspiration in your own advertising.
- Set up an RSS feed to follow advertising related news from websites like AdAge, PSFK, Creativity Magazine, and eMarketer.

4. Train yourself to post and update regularly. Even if it's only your Facebook status, get used to making frequent updates. When you're feeling tired, push through to victory and maintain a steady stream of posts. Hang in there! The more you practice, the easier it'll become.

- If readers feel like you're spamming them with useless promotion, they'll likely unfollow or block you. Keep posts relevant and useful. Avoid repetition to keep your writing fresh and interesting.

5. Intern or volunteer to build experience. As a volunteer or intern, much like a secret agent, you'll learn marketing techniques from experts by watching them in action. Take mental note, secret agent, of effective techniques and miserable failures. Save time in your own marketing efforts by avoiding techniques that look good on paper, but don't work in reality.

- Contact a local charity, politician, school, or business and express your interest in volunteering your services to their social media marketing department.
- Write a personal blog covering topics in your chosen industry to build your presence and reputation. Get some experience writing a weekly blog for a local business.

Part 2. Building a Professional Network

1. Join social groups in your industry. Some social networking sites, like Meetup or Sprout Social, can put you in touch with individuals interested in the industry in which you'll be marketing. Develop relationships with these people. Let them know how you might help them and vice versa. They may be invaluable in the future.

- Share some of your recent projects with people in your chosen industry along with future projects you hope to work on. This is a subtle way of indicating specific areas of expertise and interest to others.

- Search online for professional mixers, expos, and organizations, like the New York Social Media Club or the New Media Expo. Attend these events and exchange your contact information with other attendees.

2. Cultivate your online presence. Join conversations topical to your industry on Facebook, Twitter, and Instagram. Grow your own Twitter and Facebook following. If you have a large following, you'll be more desirable to potential employers.

- Drive up community engagement on your Facebook page by sharing relevant posts from other organizations in your industry or groundbreaking research.
- Reach out to notable users in your industry on Twitter by tweeting to them directly with an @ symbol followed by a user's name. The same can be done on Facebook by linking other users to posts.
- Grab the attention of online users by responding to posts. Don't be afraid to respectfully take a stance or voice your opinion on issues.

3. Develop meaningful relationships with other marketers. Your week is likely busy. It's hard to make time to keep valuable professional relationships alive. Why not set aside a single hour each week to go through your client list?

- Get in touch with contacts by phone. Keep the conversation short, but personal, by saying something like, "I'm a little busy today, but I wanted to call and see how you were doing."
- Similar to phone conversations, connect with contacts through email. Use a simple template and add a few personal comments to make the message more organic.

4. Collaborate with other social media marketers. Building your marketing life can be stressful, but as the saying goes, “Many hands make for light labor.” After making professional connections, reach out and suggest working on a personal project, like marketing for an event or professional organization you’re involved with, together with fellow media marketers.

- Make up for weak areas in your social media marketing skillset by bringing in a partner who’s good at what you’re not.
- To reach out to others, you might say, “I’ve got Twitter under control, but I think handling it and Facebook would be overwhelming. How about we work together and you manage Facebook?”
- As an added bonus (and who doesn’t love bonuses?), your project will have increased engagement from fellow collaborators’ online followings.

Part 3. Landing a Job

1. Collect data and testimonials to prove your skills. Use analytic tools, like Google Analytics, Datahero, or Yahoo Web Analytics, to track your media engagement. Make use of platform analytic tools, like the “Insights” tab on Facebook business pages.

- Pay specific attention to how you positively impacted growth, savings, and time. Keep track of analytics in a spreadsheet.
- Employers regard numerical proof of your skills highly. Instead of making broad statements, say things like, “I was able to increase unique views by 250% in three months.”

- Honesty is the best policy when applying with companies. You may be asked to back up your data. If you can't because you fudged the numbers, it could hurt your reputation.

2. Put together a portfolio. Collect samples of your best work. Write a table of contents for these samples and follow it with a short introduction that tells a little bit about yourself, your goals, and the included samples. Demonstrate your range of ability with samples from different projects.

- Some of the most useful portfolio samples include things like integrated marketing campaigns, new ideas, and particularly effective campaigns.
- A digital portfolio can be uploaded to your professional website or a platform page, like LinkedIn and Facebook.
- It'll show preparedness if you have a hardcopy of your portfolio at interviews. Print materials on quality paper and insert them into a professional binder.

3. Protect your online image. The phrase, "loose lips sink ships," is especially applicable to protecting your online image. Posting something inappropriate accidentally or in an emotional moment could lose you followers and hurt your prestige in your online community. Contemplate posts carefully before publishing them.

- To protect yourself from accidentally posting something inappropriate, run your content by a friend, coworker, or supervisor before publishing it online.
- When you're feeling emotional, give yourself some time to calm down. If you're ever on the fence about a post, give yourself a day or two to think it over.
- Consistency is an important key for locking down your image. Inconsistently posting or publishing dubious content could make you seem unreliable.

4. Write a unique resume. Applying for a job is basically marketing yourself, right? So you'll want to put your best foot forward with a unique, thoughtful resume. Display your design skills with a simple, pertinent graphic or two. Include links to your personal and professional social media pages. Showcase your knowledge of what clients want and how to promote it.

- Visual techniques, like the use of photos and memes, are an eye-catching way of promoting products and services. Employers will want to see evidence of your ability to include visual elements in your work.

5. Apply for jobs. Look for social media marketing position with major marketing agencies. Make use of job aggregating websites, like Indeed, LinkedUp, and Monster, to broaden your search. Peruse classified ads for marketing positions in print newspapers and on sites like Craigslist.

How to use Social Media for Advertisements

Social networking websites have become a tool for marketing and there has been a gain in their popularity in the last couple of years. The concept of social networks has become very effective in getting the adequate marketing leads for the company. It is one of the important tools for providing a platform, when you can make networking and gain new customers. The advertising has become a need for the businesses for marketing the products or services over Internet.

There are many companies, which use the marketing strategies for creation of the custom profiles on the social media websites and then the potential customers and business contacts are added into the list. Social network development tips are available on the blogs and forums for letting people express their thoughts on getting the best solutions for need of social interaction. The social networking websites are utilized for increasing the growth of the companies for producing effectual strategies.

The social network has the main motive of creation of the online communities for the people with similar interest and activities. There are many ways created for adding and sharing the information. It has become the right place to advertise the products and services at the lowest prices.

Steps

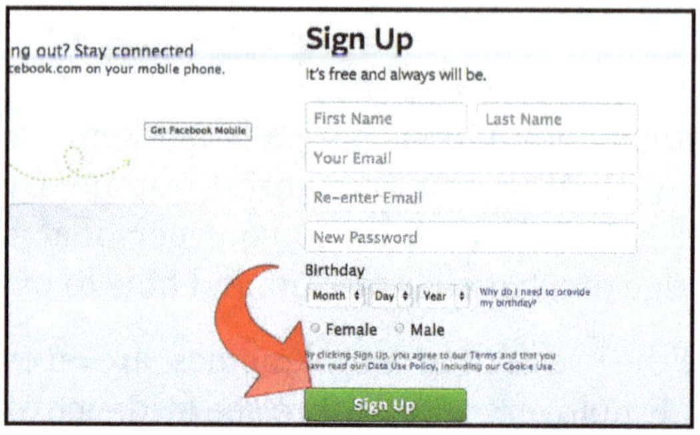

1. Create an account: It is important for the companies to create their profiles on the most relevant networks. The profiles have to be updated regularly. It is advisable to get online daily for responding to requests and getting adequate responses.

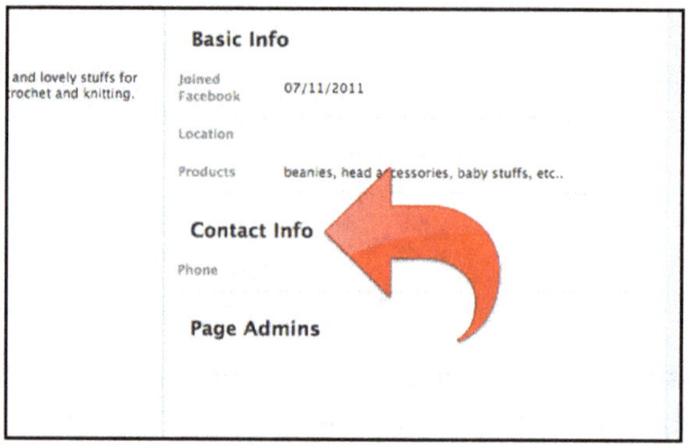

2. Expansion of network: Expand your network in such a way that you add the contacts, which share the similar interests or activities with you.

3. Socialize more effectively: It is important to take participation in the online forums and blogs,

which are related to your website. This practice can give positive results in making connection with your clients and getting good responses for your products or services.

4. Be consistent: The social marketing goes on best when you are persistent. Be in regular touch with your friends and give comments and messages. The more number of people are interested in your products, the more will be your profit rate by selling them. Try to judge the mentality of your fellow users and then only make efforts to throw sales pitches on them.

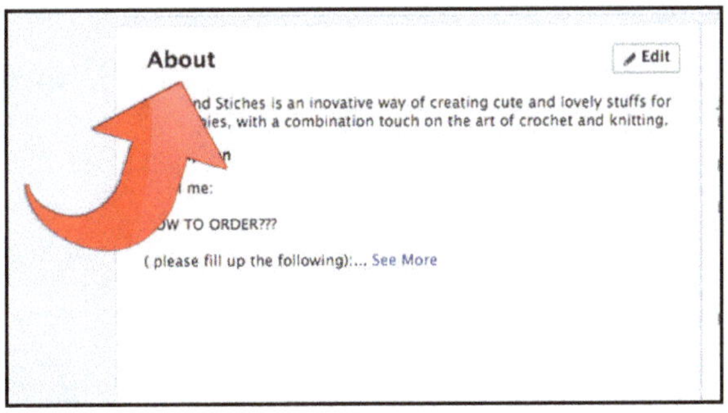

5. Reveal your expertise: Write informative articles or blogs about your products and make the postings to the best places, where members can read them. Address the needs of people and make them know why your product can be suitable for their needs.

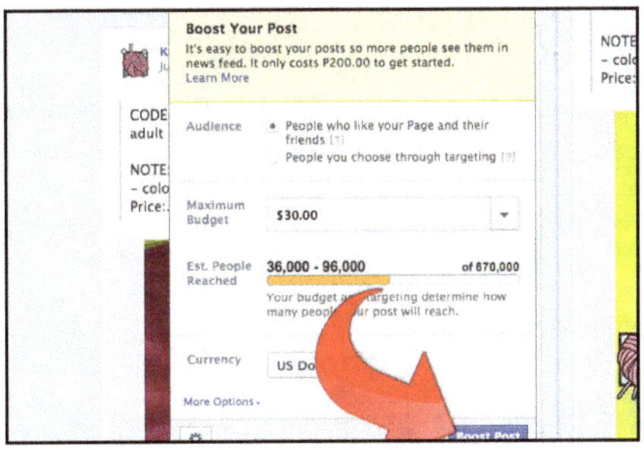

6. Paid ads: Paid advertisements can be a good way for rising popularity of a website. The advantages of social media websites maybe appreciated by choosing the appropriate ways to induce social network design information amongst the people.

7. Create service or product audio or video: This is the important way, which can raise the popularity by getting the interesting way to market. Videos are always appealing and interesting to watch.

Social Media Platforms and their uses

5

Social media platforms are used by organizations and businesses to advertise their products, services and brands, and inform about upcoming events, projects and new releases. Some popular social media platforms are Facebook, Twitter, Pinterest, LinkedIn and Tumblr, among others. The ways in which such platforms may be used by businesses as promotional tools for creating an online presence, promoting a crowdfunding campaign, etc. have been extensively discussed in this chapter.

How to use Social Media to Market your Business

If you own a small business, you can save money by transitioning more of your offline marketing efforts to an online presence. Starting a social media account is free, easy, and can help you effectively boost your company's online presence. Learning how to market your business via social media can help you reach your current customers while also targeting potential future customers.

Part 1. Setting Up your Social Media Platform

1. Identify your target audience. Generally speaking, your business has a split target audience: there are your business's existing customers (your current assets), and your potential customers (your target customers). A successful social media marketing campaign should make current customers feel heard and appreciated while also reaching out to potential customers in a way that promotes your business.

- Start by recognizing your current customer base. Are they generally young adults or middle-aged? Younger?
- Think about the kinds of social media your existing customer base might be using. You can conduct an informal survey by asking customers, while they make their usual purchases.
- You will need to make some predictions about your potential customer base, but a little online research might help. Try looking at the social media platforms of your biggest competitors, to see what demographics of their customers follow them online.

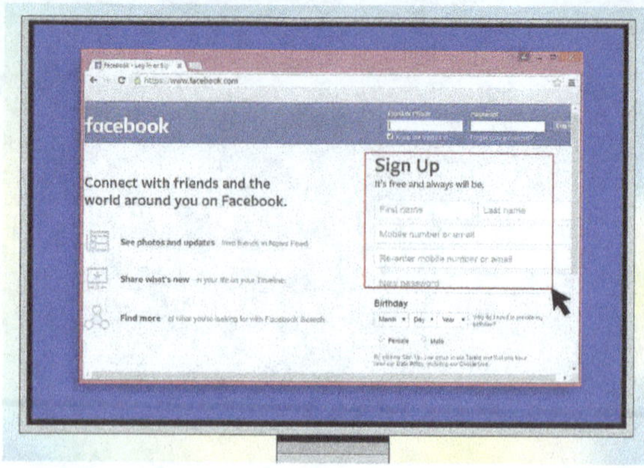

2. Sign up for your social media platform(s). Once you have identified your target audience, you are ready to sign up for a social media account. Social media accounts are free and are generally easy to manage, but you will want to check each platform's guidelines and user terms as the relate to business accounts; they may be different from those for personal accounts. Some of the most common social media platforms include:

- Facebook: This site is generally considered the most popular social media platform, and one of those most likely to attract all demographics (including adults over 65). This platform is best if you are trying to reach a broader audience across multiple demographics.
- Twitter: This is another popular social media platform, but predominantly popular with millennials and other younger generations. Though not as broad in its reach, Twitter does foster niche communities online, which could end up being helpful for your business.
- Google+: As it is linked to Google, Google+ is considered the best social media platform for increasing your business's search engine optimization (SEO) results. More people using Google to search for businesses will find your listing if you have a Google+ account, especially if you are a local business trying to reach local customers.
- Instagram: This image-based social media platform is very popular among adolescents and adults under the age of 35. It can be a great way to share images of your product, your business, or the visible results of your work.
- Tumblr: Though initially confusing for many users, Tumblr is an active and engaged way to reach potential customers between the ages of 13 and 25. Many Tumblr users are college educated and tend to be enthusiastically loyal to this social media platform.
- LinkedIn: This platform is often considered most effective for career networking. LinkedIn also lets you use its publishing platform to reach a wider audience. It can be very effective for reaching educated, wealthy customers, as well as for generating leads between businesses.
- Pinterest: This visually-themed platform works best if you have relevant images to share. It can be highly effective at targeting a female audience between 30 and 50 years old, especially those in a higher income bracket.
- Yelp: This website allows customers to post photographs, rank your business, and leave reviews based on their service and experience. It is also a great way to advertise, as many

people searching for a particular business (for example, a local bakery) will turn to Yelp for listings, hours of operation, and customer reviews.

3. Consider using a social media manager. Many people think a social media manager requires the hiring of additional staff to manage online accounts. You can manage your online presence, however, without having to hire any additional employees, and still maintain control of your business's online presence. Online social media managers are generally free and can help you improve your business's social media presence while also tracking your online outreach.

- Online social media managers like HootSuite and Ping.fm let you manage all of your social media accounts across all platforms on a single website.
- You will be able to schedule posts and messages, review how successful your posts are at reaching your audience, and view any and all online mentions of your business by social media users.
- These online social media managers are free, but there are also paid subscription managers.
- A paid service like SproutSocial will allow you to create contacts from your social media followers to track how successful you are at engaging them. You can also view and track how many customers use check-in apps like FourSquare at your business.

Part 2. Reaching your Customers

1. Let people know you are on social media. You might gain some traction with people searching blindly for your social media page, but the best way to promote your online presence is by letting

people know about it. Tell your customers that you are now online, or consider putting a little sign up next to your cash register or in your window. You can also provide the username or handle for your social media accounts on your business cards.

- Let customers know that you are increasing your online presence.
- Make sure you follow or send friend requests to your regular, loyal customers.

2. Find friends and followers online. Once you have established an online account, you will need to attract followers and friends who will view your posts. Start with current customers, and work towards reaching an increasingly broad audience of potential future customers.

- Try to reach out to current customers first. You want them to know that their loyalty is appreciated.
- You should also reach out to your local distributors, including any businesses that sell or promote your goods. For example, if you are a bakery and you sell baked goods wholesale to a coffee shop, network with that coffee shop online and tap into their audience.
- You can expand your audience online by searching for keywords and trending terms, then liking and sharing those posts or following the local people or businesses who posted them.

3. Start posting on social media. Your posts on social media should be more than just a self promotion. You can post information about your business, relevant information about the industry you

work in, and share (or post your own) photographs of customers frequenting and enjoying your business.

- Post photographs to showcase your product. If your business involves a service instead of a product, take pictures of your employees working, or of satisfied customers showing off the work that was done.
- You can offer some type of occasional deals that only your followers will know about. Hold a weekly or monthly raffle, where users have to share a post or photograph to be entered to win.
- Include specials of the day in your posts, and keep customers updated on your business. If you are running a bakery, for example, use social media to advertise the specials of the day, what types of baked goods you are offering that day, and your hours of operation.
- Keep your target audience in mind. If your customers tend to be retired, they may not know what hashtags are or what internet slang or abbreviations mean.
- Remember that your social media platform is a representation of your business. You can have fun, but keep your posts professional, and never post anything inflammatory about politics, religion, or your personal beliefs.

Part 3. Making Social Media Work For your Business

1. Listen to your customers. One of the best ways to foster a network of customer support online is by listening to what your customers say. Read the feedback that your customers give you and take it to heart. This can mean the difference between a returning customer and a former customer who will tell friends and family not to support you.

- Respond positively to all feedback, even negative comments. Reply gracefully to bad reviews by saying something like, "We're very sorry you had a negative experience. Please consider trying us again, and if you mention this post I will personally ensure that you have a better experience with us."
- Thank customers for their reviews and input. If multiple customers are saying the same things, you will need to consider implementing those changes, if possible and feasible.

- Make sure you like and comment on any customer posts to your social media page. You can also search for people who "checked in" at your business, and like or add to favorites any photographs or updates they shared about your business.

2. Specialize your social media presence. As much as you may want to appeal to every single person who views your social media page, that may simply not be possible. If that is the case, you may need to decide whether to keep a generalized social media presence, or one that specifically appeals to your target audience.

- Never willfully alienate anyone, whether they are a customer or not. However, do recognize that not every single person in your town will find your business appealing.
- Remember that if you run a specialized business (for example, a vegan bakery), you may simply be unable to tap into some potential customers (like those who do not like vegan food).
- If you tend to have a niche audience, you can share posts that will appeal to them. As with the previous example, you might share posts about the benefits and the personal appeal of living a vegan lifestyle.

3. Be consistent with your web presence. You may be hoping that a social media presence will instantly boost your business overnight, and that does occasionally happen. However, overnight

success is generally the exception to the rule. You will need to be patient and consistent with your online presence.

- Recognize that building an online presence and an online following takes time. How long it takes will vary, depending on your customers, your target audience, and how much time and effort you spend online.
- Be consistent. Try to post updates every day, and take some time each day to like, respond to, or share customer posts.
- Be patient. Having an online presence will not hurt your business. It will only help you, but you will only get out of it what you put into it.

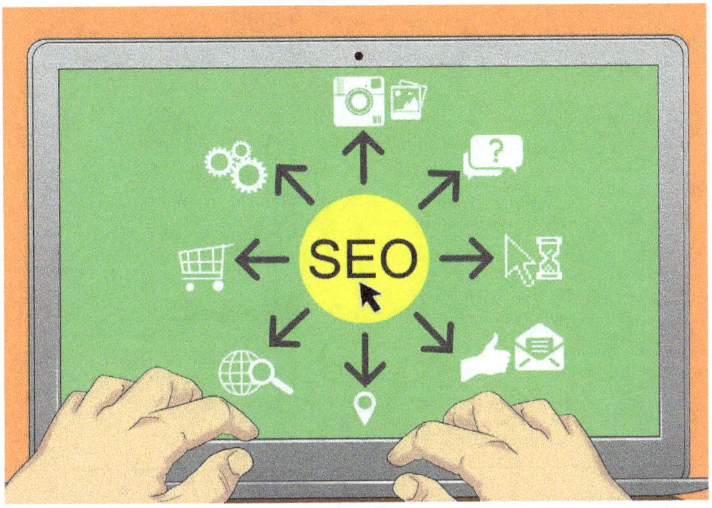

4. Use search engine optimization (SEO) methods. Search engine optimization, or SEO, involves altering your website and social media platform in order to better promote your business. When you use SEO, your business's website and social media pages will show up higher in the search results when a customer uses Google (or any other search engine) to search for relevant terms.

- Start by identifying keywords and terms that a customer might search for. You can use plural words, but try to avoid too much repetition (the fewer the keywords you use, the better, so keep it under 1,000 characters).
- Include any common misspellings of your business name in your keywords, so that someone looking for you will still be able to find you easily.
- Create meta tags on every single page of your website that incorporate those keywords. You will need to know how to use HTML code to do this, so learn how to code or find someone who knows how to help you.
- Audit your SEO effectiveness on a regular basis. You can use auditing tools, like DeepCrawl or Search Console, to assess how effective your SEO efforts have been at reaching customers.

How to Promote your Page on Facebook

A Facebook Page is one of the most popular way organisations, celebrities, political figures, and businesses showcase themselves on Facebook. Pages are visible to everybody on the Internet. There are different ways in which owners of Facebook Pages can market themselves to people to gain more viewers. All are pretty straightforward and easy to do.

Method 1. Updating your Cover Photo

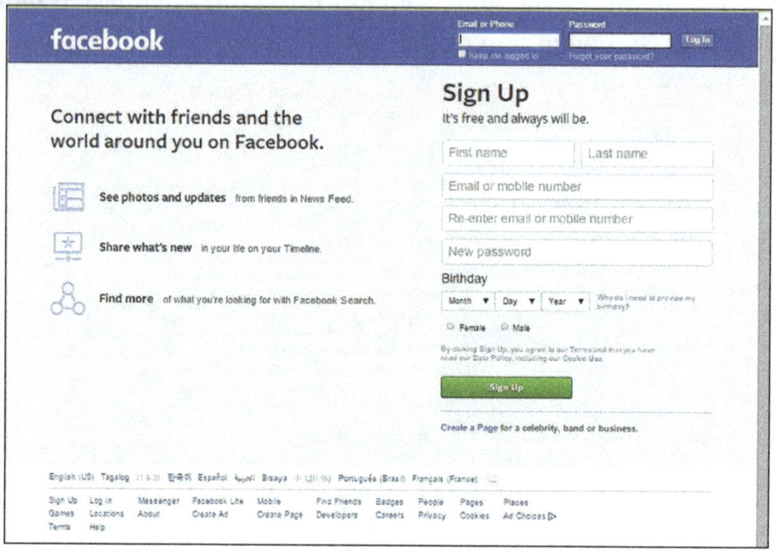

1. Log into your Facebook account. Visit the Facebook website on a new web browser tab or window. Enter your email address and password at the top right corner of the page to log into your Facebook account. You will be directed to your personal account's News Feed page.

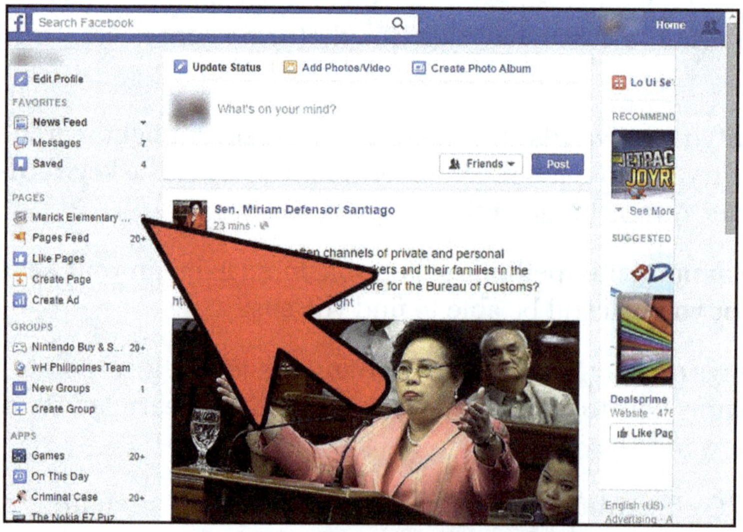

2. Go to your Facebook Page's Timeline. All the Pages you manage are listed on the left side of the News Feed. Take your mouse and click the Page name to go to its Timeline.

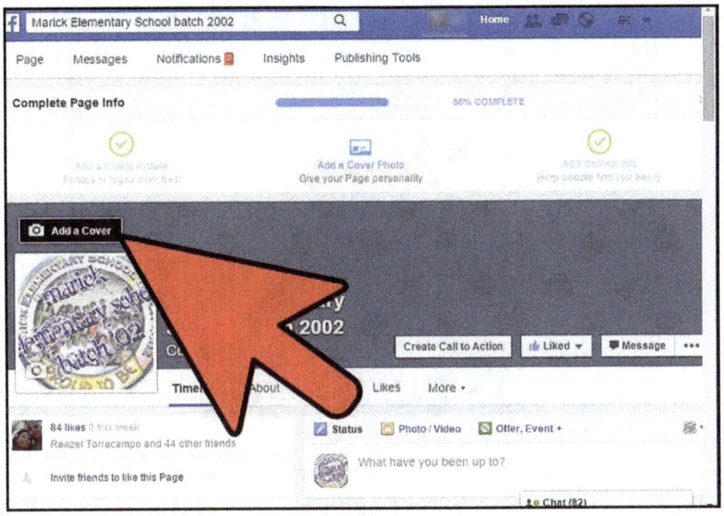

3. Upload cover photo. At the top left corner of your Facebook Page's Timeline is an "Upload cover" button. This button is represented by a camera icon. Click on it to browse for the appropriate photo from your computer.

- Try to select a photo that's interesting and in connection with your Page, like a picture from your latest event. Make sure that it's a clear shot, not blurry. The cover photo you upload should be 351 pixels by 815 pixels and should not exceed 2MB.
- Once it has been uploaded, the Timeline page will refresh, and you'll be able to see the new cover photo above the Timeline. Depending on your settings and the settings of your fans/ followers, they'll receive a notification of your changes so that they can check out your cover photo themselves.

Method 2. Engaging your Facebook Fans

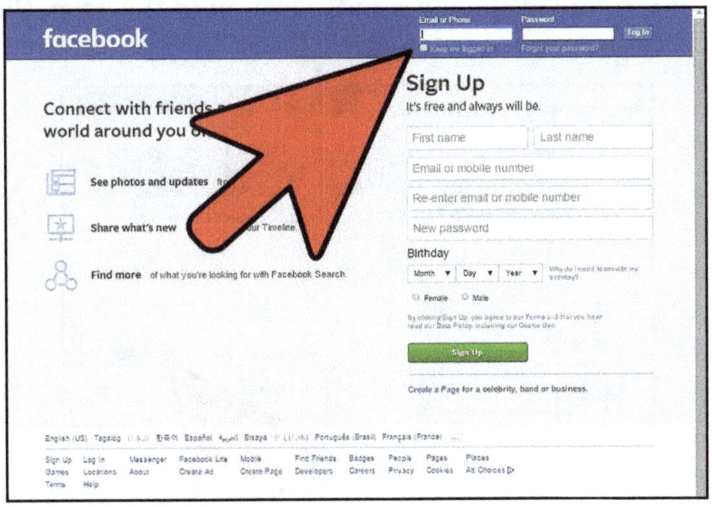

1. Log into your Facebook account. Visit the Facebook website on a new web browser tab or window. Enter your email address and password at the top right corner of the page to log into your Facebook account. You will be directed to your personal account's News Feed page.

2. Go to your Facebook Page's Timeline. All the Pages you manage are listed on the left side of the home page. Take your mouse and click on the Page name to go to its Timeline.

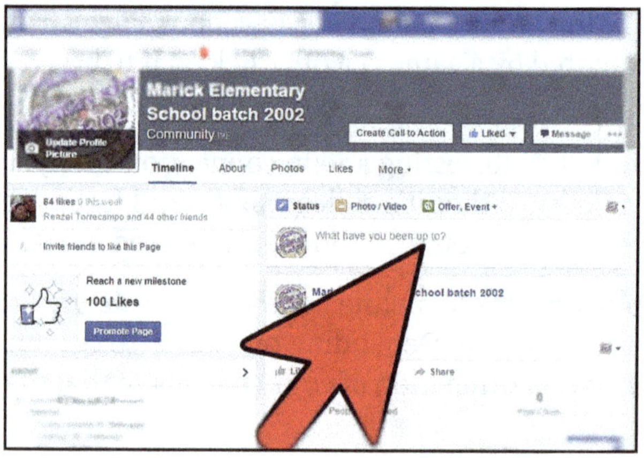

3. Find the status post box. On the Page's Timeline is a small text box with word hint "What have you been up to." It is found at the top middle section of the page. Click inside that box to activate it.

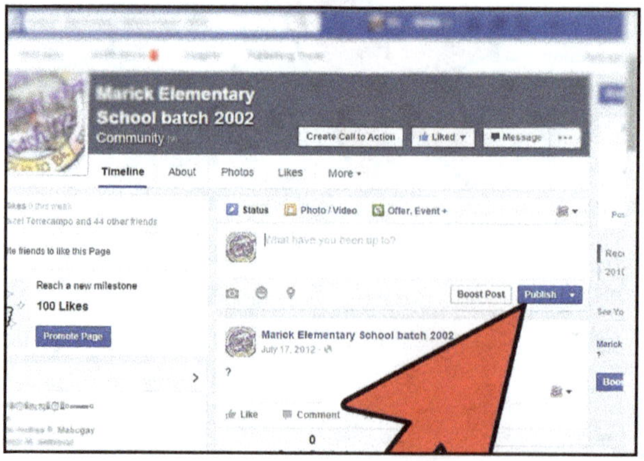

4. Write a status post. You can let them know of what you are up to, your achievements, or trending world news. Social media has taken most roles carried out by mainstream media. Hence, many people rely on status posts to get breaking news from around the globe.

5. Post regularly on your Facebook Page to keep your followers engaged. If you become the one always updating such information as breaking news or current events, many people who are on Facebook will be attracted to your Page.

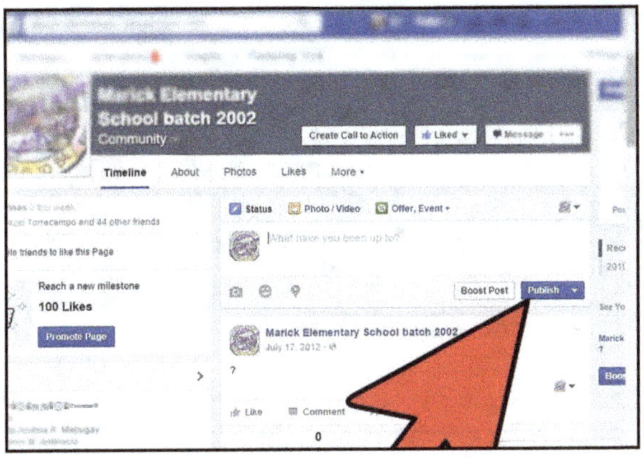

6. Publish the post. Underneath the box mentioned above is a bluish "Post" button. Click on that button to have your post published to your followers.

Method 3. Inviting People from your Email List

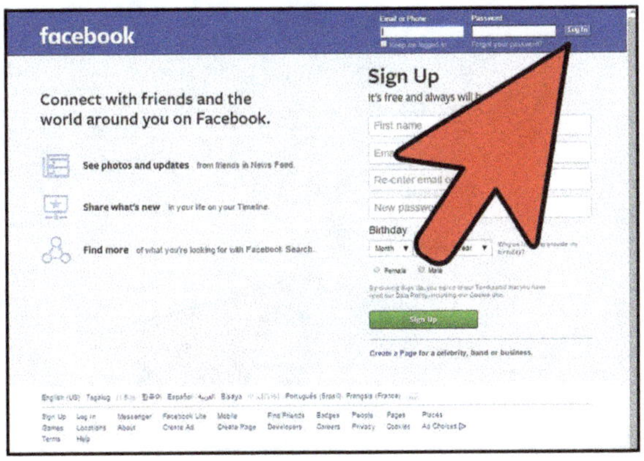

1. Log into your Facebook account. Visit the Facebook website on a new web browser tab or window. Enter your email address and password at the top right corner of the page to log into your Facebook account. You will be directed to your personal account's News Feed page.

2. Go to the Facebook Page. All the Pages you manage are listed on the left side of the home page. Take your mouse and click the Page name to go to its Timeline.

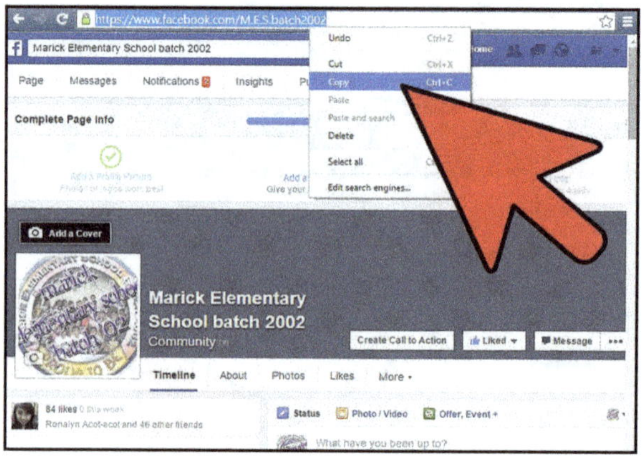

3. Get the Page URL. URL (Uniform Resource Locator) is the web address referencing the Page. Take your mouse to the address bar of your Page, highlight all the details on the bar, then copy it. You can copy by right-clicking on your mouse and choosing the "Copy" option from the list displayed.

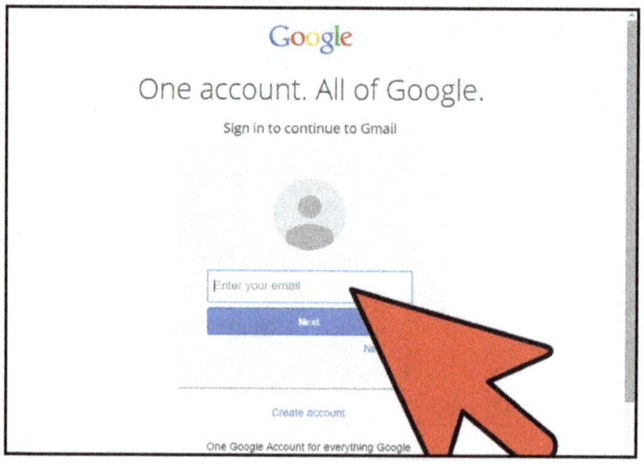

4. Log into your email account. This can be any email account, like Gmail or Yahoo. It doesn't necessarily have to be connected to your Facebook Page.

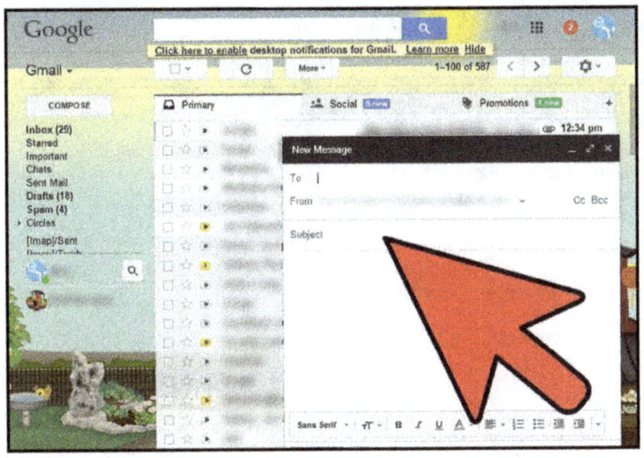

5. Compose a small email. Click the compose button to start the process of composing an email. On the first field enter the email addresses of people you want to send the email to. You can separate the email addresses with a comma.

- On the second field, enter the subject of the email, e.g., Invitation to my Facebook Page.
- On the body of the email, type the message you would like your recipients to receive.

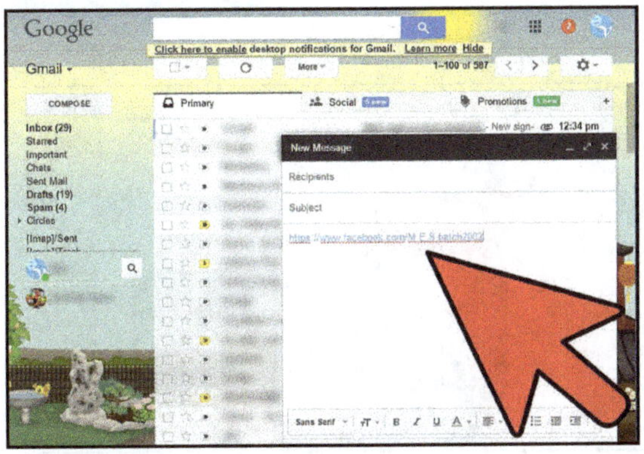

6. Paste the URL on your email body. It is important that you include the URL of the Page in the mail body by pasting it there. Right-click your mouse in the message box, and choose the "Paste" option from the list.

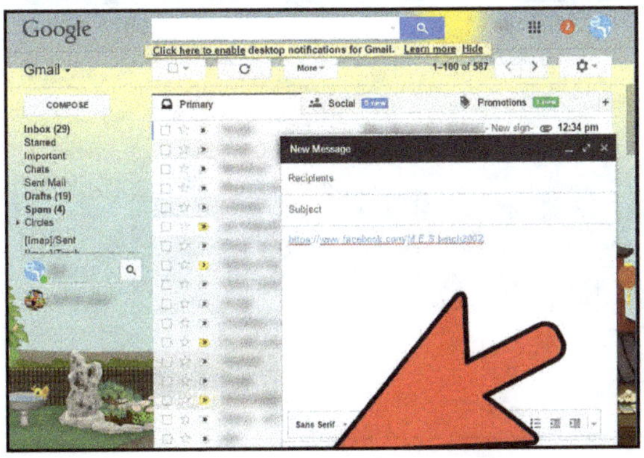

7. Send the email. Click the "Send" button to have the invitation delivered to your recipients. You'll be sure to get some viewers from your email list.

Method 4. Customize your Page URL

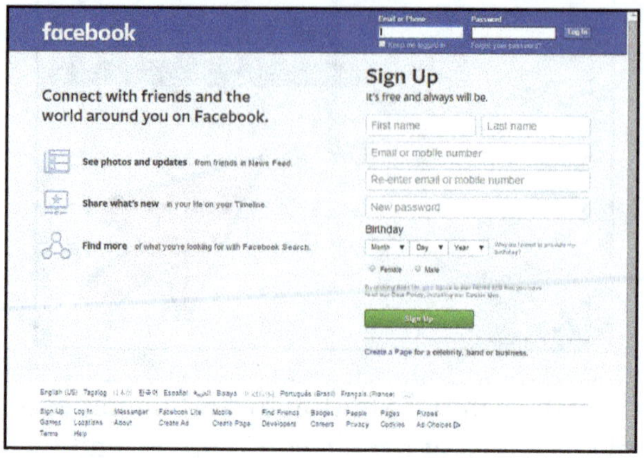

1. Log into your Facebook account. Visit the Facebook website on a new web browser tab or window. Enter your email address and password at the top right corner of the page to log into your Facebook account. You will be directed to your personal account's News Feed page.

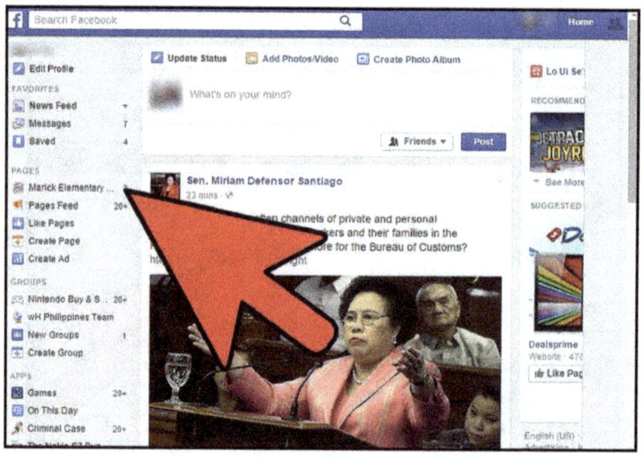

2. Go to the Facebook Page. All the Pages you manage are listed on the left side of the home page. Take your mouse and click the Page name to go to its Timeline.

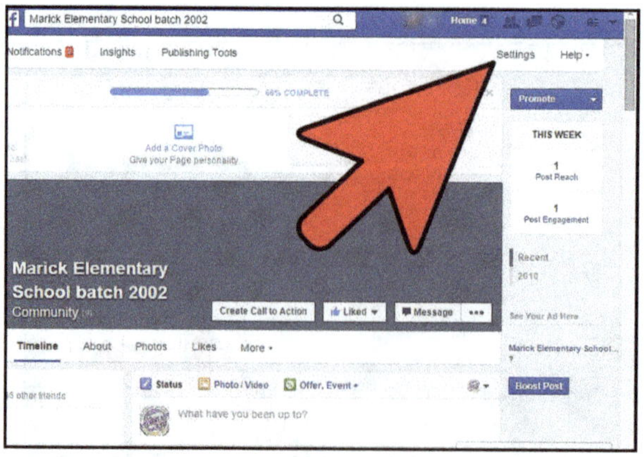

3. Go to the Page settings. On the top right of the Page is the "Settings" tab. Click on that tab to go to the settings menu of the Page.

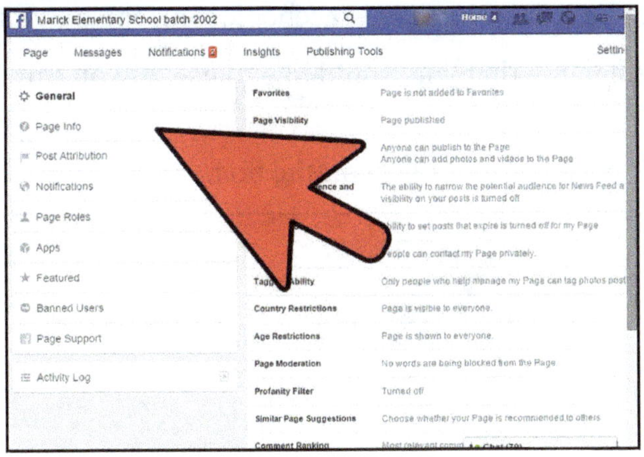

4. Select the "Page info" tab. On settings page, click "Page info" tab on the left side. This will return a list describing your Page.

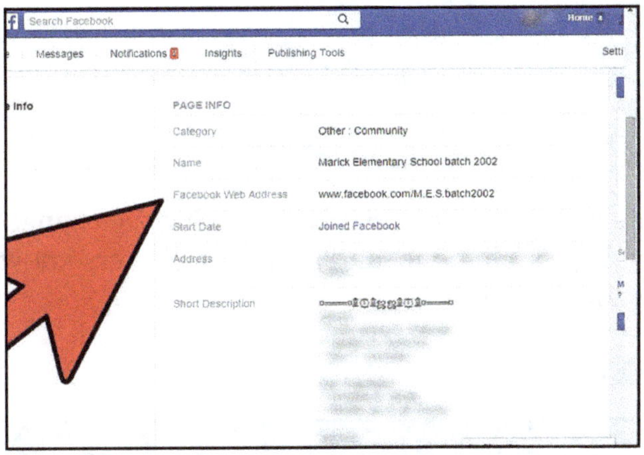

5. Go to the "Facebook Web Address" option. Scroll the list of options, and click Facebook web address to go to the screen to customize your address/URL. The customization screen has two boxes. The first one contains the Page name and the second one has the address of the Page.

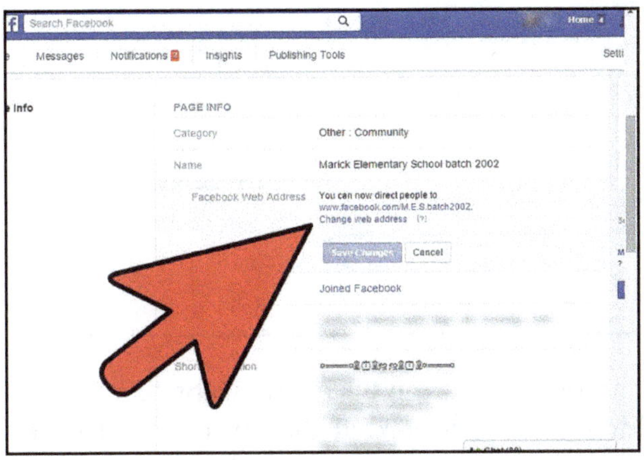

6. Edit the Facebook web address. Go to the second box that contains the Page address. Change the name to your preferred name. Make sure the name you type can be remembered easily by your

followers. The address can be something like "Facebook.com/companyname."

- Make sure that it's a name that you would like to use, as you can only change it once in the future.
- When you're done, click "Save" button on the box.

7. Let your fans or followers know. You can do this by posting the change as a status. Just go to the status box at the top of the Page's Timeline, and let your followers know that they can now easily find your page by entering the name you set.

Method 5. Promote through Competition

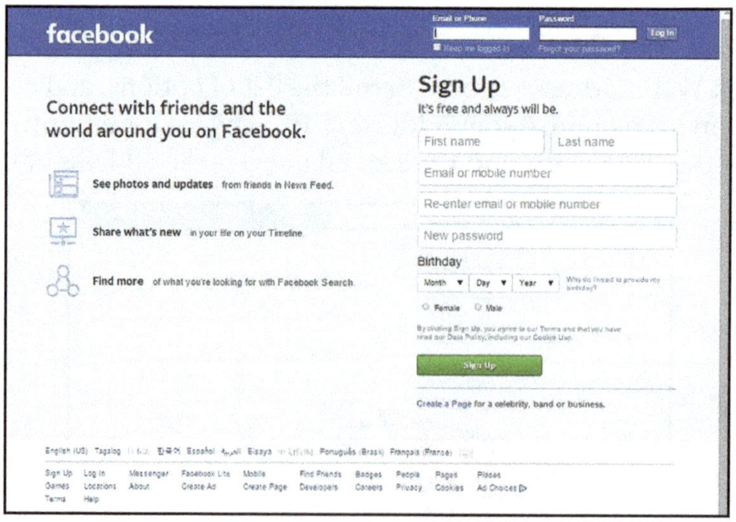

1. Log into your Facebook account. Visit the Facebook website on a new web browser tab or window. Enter your email address and password at the top right corner of the page to log into your Facebook account. You will be directed to your personal account's News Feed page.

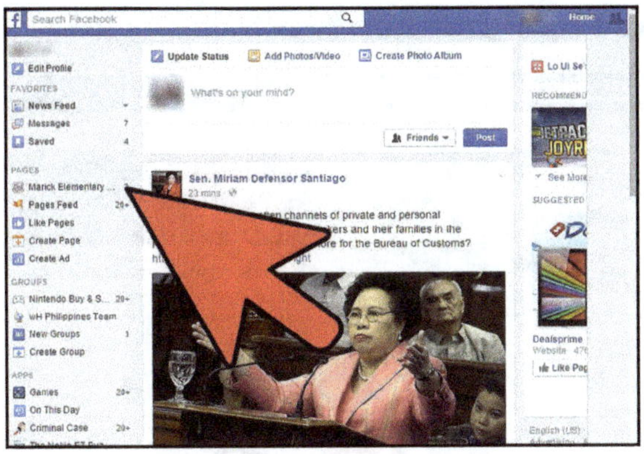

2. Go to the Facebook Page. All the Pages you manage are listed on the left side of the home page. Take your mouse and click the Page name to go to its Timeline.

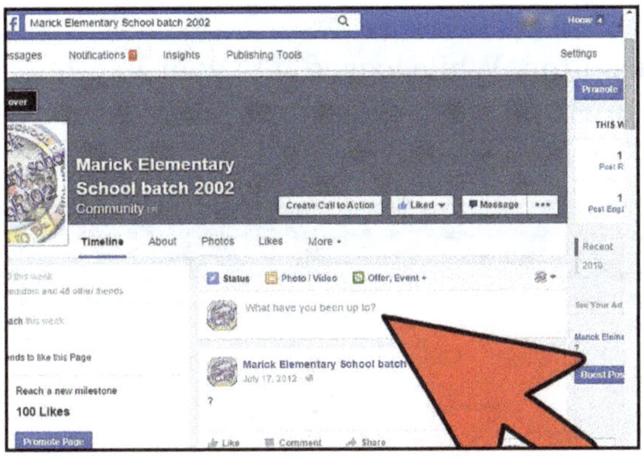

3. Describe the competition in the status post box. On the Page's Timeline is a small text box with word hint "What have you been up to." Click inside that box and write the details of the competition. For instance, let followers know the details of the competition (e.g., what it is for), the prize to be won, how to participate, and the period of the competition.

- An example of a competition would be asking your followers to tag photos on your Page and then share with friends. The photo that gets the most likes gets to win something.

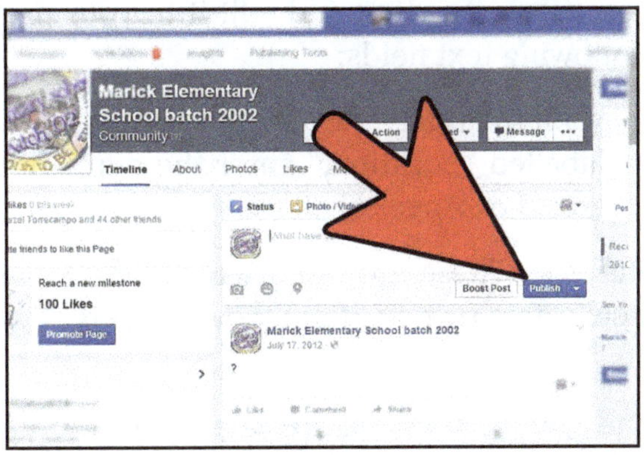

4. Post the competition. Underneath the box mentioned above is a bluish "Post" button. Click on that button to have your competition published to your followers.

Method 6. Promote the Page Using Ads

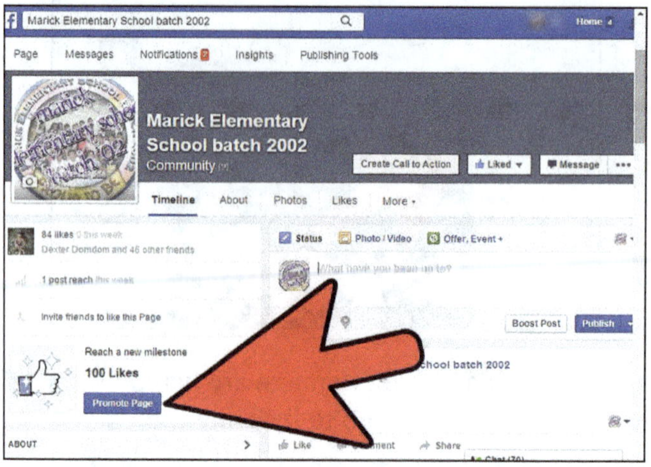

1. Click on the Promote Page button. While logged into your Facebook Page, click "Promote Page" button below the profile picture to go to the panel for setting the ads details. The ads panel has the Page description on the left. This is what will be displayed to users.

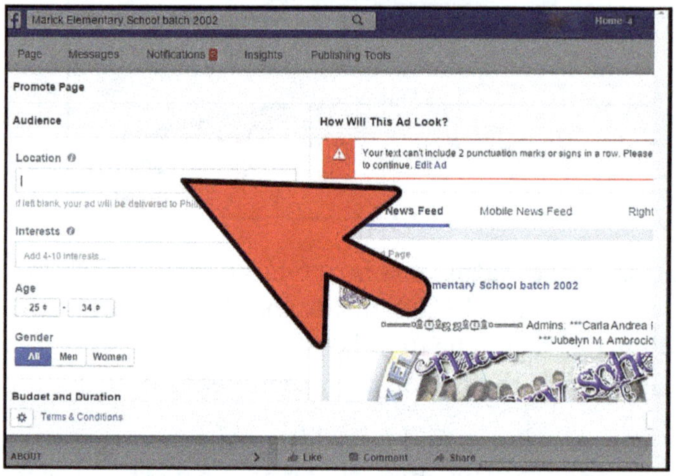

2. Edit the ad details. Click on the description and edit it to your preference. Then complete the panel details by answer the following text fields:

- Type the locations you want to target—Never run a promotion without specifying the target locations. On the box labelled "Location," enter the name of countries or places your ad targets e.g., Nairobi, Texas, Los Angeles, etc.
- Enter your target interests—These are the interests of people you are targeting, such as business managers, real estate owners, family owners, etc. Type your target interests on a box labelled "Interests."
- Specify age ranges and gender that you are targeting—For example, you can target men only, women only, or both of them. Specify the age ranges e.g., 21-40. You specify ages by just selecting the numbers listed on the start and end box.

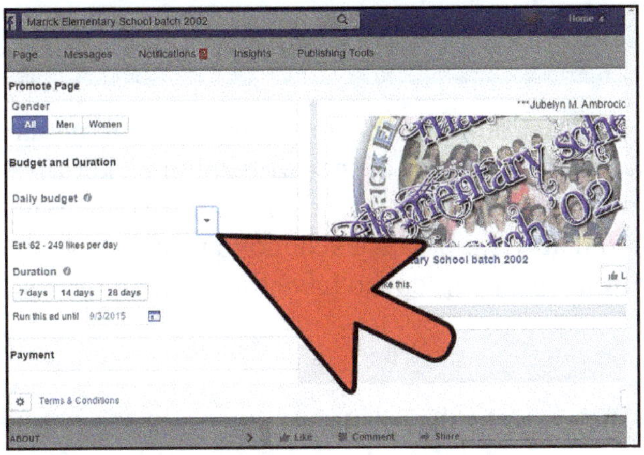

3. Determine your ad budget and duration days. On this section, specify your budget for the ad. You can choose 1 USD per day or even 10 USD per day. This depends on you and the number of people you want to reach out to. Duration days is the number of days you wish your ad to run.

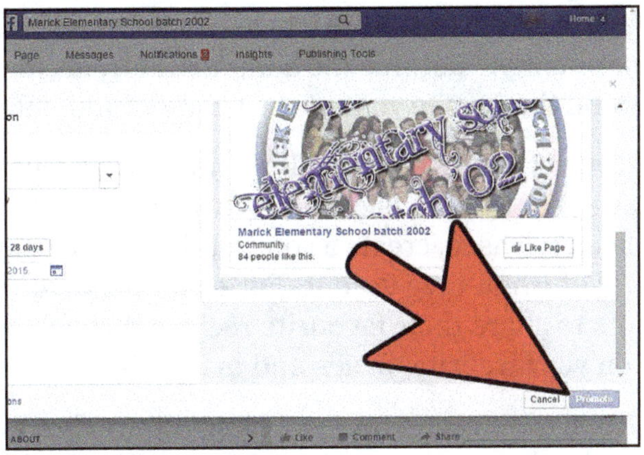

4. Promote your Page. Having filled the above information, click the "Promote" button to have your ad saved. A box will then pop up for adding your payment information.

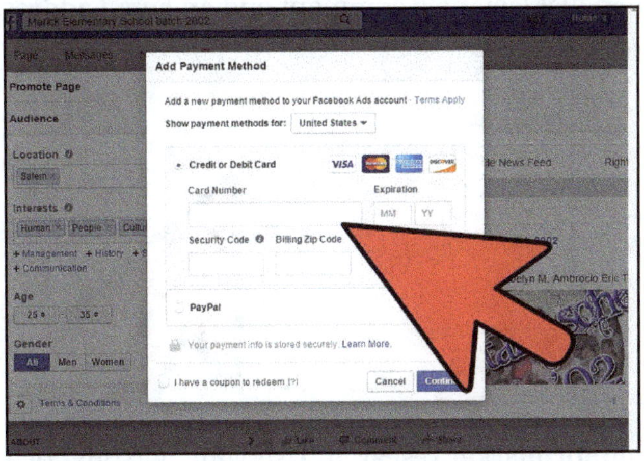

5. Add payment details. On the box that pops up, fill your payment method. You can choose to pay through a credit card or PayPal.

How to use a Facebook Group as a Promotional Tool

With over 800 million users, Facebook is at the forefront of social media websites. Many businesses now include Facebook as an integral part of their Internet marketing strategy. Facebook created ads, business Fan pages and has allowed thousands of applications to help businesses promote on their site. Along with personal and fan pages, Facebook groups are a way that people can connect and form a small organization with people who have the same interests.

Steps

1. Decide what community you would like to develop or promote. Unlike the Facebook business (Fan) pages, groups are designed to highlight the members, promote discussion and create opportunities for networking. Even if you are a business, you can create a community of people based on your business and services, and the following are some ideas for companies, bloggers and professionals:

- Create a Facebook group of referrals for your business. If someone is very excited about the service you have provided, ask them if they would be interested in being part of your "Company Name Review Community." Become the administrator, decide if you want it to be public or by invitation only and then invite your past customers and new customers to interact.
- Create a Facebook group around a product. Be careful not to announce the product through a Facebook group, as this is against Facebook's 2011 updated promotional rules. However, after a product has been released, create a community where people can talk about uses for the product or stories of when they used it. For example, if your company makes cooking utensils, invite people to share their favourite recipes through a Facebook group, and announce this option on your website, in ads and in emails.
- Create a Facebook discussion group for your blog, library, book store, club, magazine and more. Creating a Facebook group around 1 subject, such as a book, an important test, an article, a craft or a club will allow you to move past the "comments" section of a blog, website or Facebook wall. People who are interested will join the group and it can be a more intimate setting than just leaving a comment and an email address under a blog.

2. Create a Facebook group for market research. Use your personal or fan page to invite people who like your product or service to be part of a community, and you will ultimately network with your target audience. Communicate with your group daily, and ask them opinions on what changes they would like to see.

- Gather demographic information about the people who join your group. After seeing who is interested in interacting with your product or identifying themselves with it, you can create a Facebook Ad on through your Fan page that targets the same demographic.

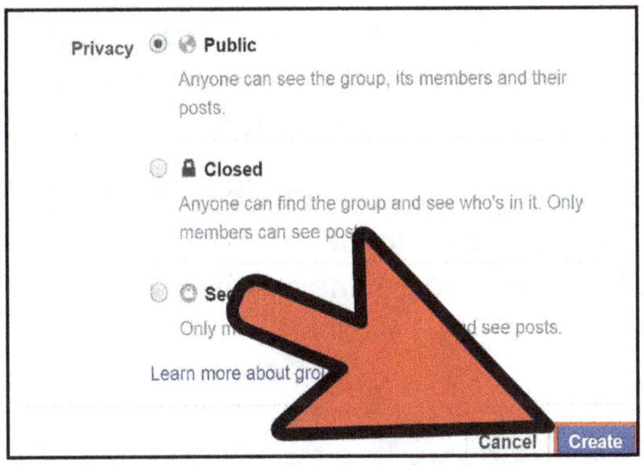

3. Sponsor your group on Facebook. Look at your group's home page options. Purchase a link with your credit card. This link will host ad content and message boards.

- Once you create a Facebook group, you become the "Admin" who can assign other administrators and approve content and members.

4. Build buzz for new products by hinting at them through a Facebook group. Although you are not allowed to hold contests on Facebook, you can promote some exclusive information for your members. Discuss sales, opinions and favourite products.

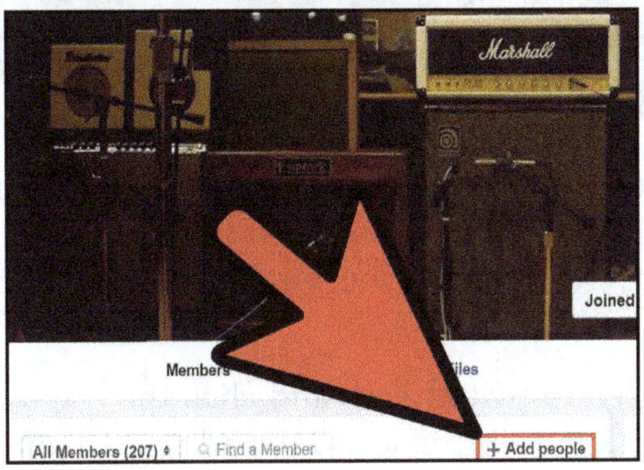

5. Create a Facebook group to promote a profession or region. This is a great way to create buzz

around yourself as a professional. Choose a catchy name and target friends who share the same interests.

- After a while, you may find friends of friends asking to join your group. Sometimes, creating a private group creates a buzz and a desire to join. For professional networking, you want to create a semi-exclusive club. For example, you can create a group of "Boise Marketing Professionals," that can discuss industry information and network.
- Use your Facebook group to go the extra step in marketing. Create regular in-person meetings, book clubs and meetings at large industry events. You cannot create a Facebook event using a group page, but you can create one by discussing it on your group discussion board.

How to use Twitter as a Promotional Tool

Twitter is a popular social media website that allows users to post "micro-blogs" of 280 characters or less. It began in 2006 and is now home to more than 300 million users. Many of these users are actually businesses that promote sales, customer loyalty and new products through their account. As with most social media outlets, consistency is the key to successful Twitter promotion. It is a good idea to create a personal account and become familiar with the way Twitter works, or appoint someone who will post to your account every day.

Steps

1. Create a Twitter account for your business. Make sure it is both the brand name of your company and includes the website name. For example, if your business is called Cooper City Promotions, and your website is coopercitypromo, you would want your account to be www.twitter.com/coopercitypromo.

- To set up an account, go to twitter.com and click the "Sign up for Twitter" button. Input your company description, website, location and upload your logo. Fill out your profile as completely as possible, including common search terms that people use to find your company in the bio section.

2. Use your Twitter link on all marketing materials, including business cards, letterhead, website, Facebook account, invoices and all other online or printed promotions. On your next email blast, include a section that asks people to find or follow you on Twitter.

3. Master the use of the hashtag. The hashtag is the "#" symbol followed by a keyword. This can be as specific as your business name, such as #coopercitypromo, or it can be keywords that people use to find your business, such as #marketing, #coopercity or #advertising.

- Include a hashtag with #deal, #coupon or #bargain, whenever you are having a sale or promotion. There are many aggregate websites that gather all of the day's tweets that include these keywords. Also regularly include any other popular search terms that people use to find your website along with a hashtag on your daily tweets. If you tweet a coupon code, you can track your sales by all the people who use the Twitter-specific code.

4. Find people to follow by using a Twitter directory like twellow or Justtweetit. Most Twitter users

receive an email when someone new is following them. Add a few people every day, and many people will choose to follow you in turn.

5. Avoid hard sales tactics. Twitter accounts that pressure or only post sales and business-related content rarely keep a large amount of followers for long. Post links and statements that show you are in touch, and on the cutting edge, of industry innovation and standards.

- If you have a strong relationship with your local community, post stories and links that support the community, other businesses and organizations. This will encourage people from your neighborhood or city to follow you for the latest updates, and they will receive your promotions at the same time.

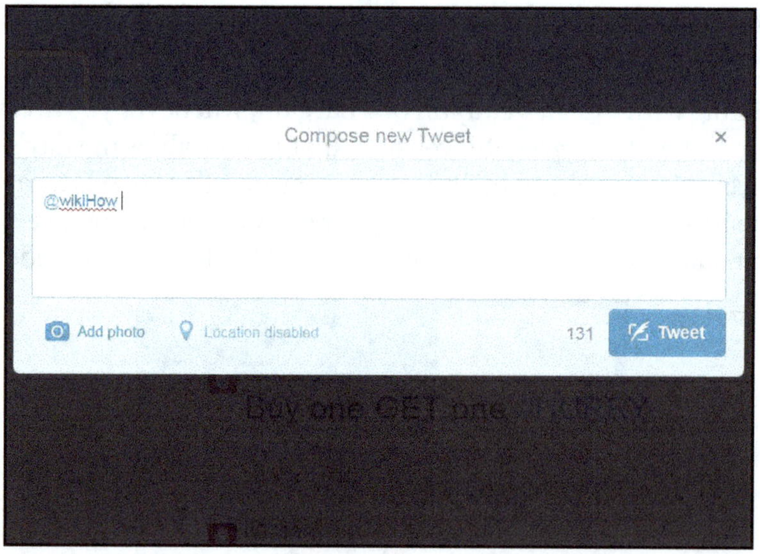

6. Encourage employees to communicate with the company Twitter account using their personal accounts or specially-made company Twitter accounts. Use the "@" symbol before the Twitter user name to direct message people or mention them in your tweets.

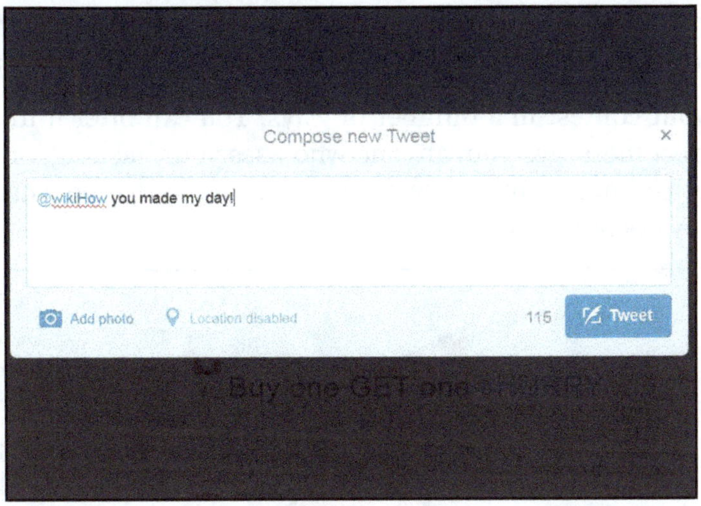

7. Announce all new events or products on Twitter, using product shots and details. Schedule your tweets so that they correspond with press releases for products or events. Make a hashtag for each event, such as "#coopershow."

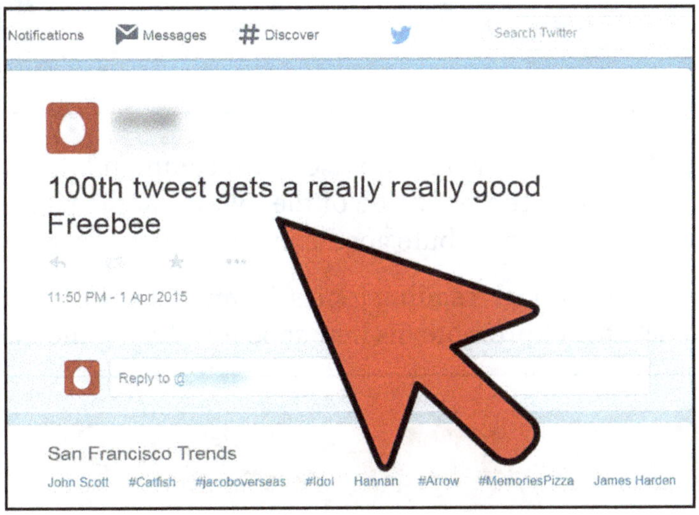

8. Use Twitter-based contests to promote your product. Many businesses have started to give away large items, like gift cards, phones or cameras to people who retweet or direct message their Twitter account during a day or week. The following are good general guidelines to follow when holding a Twitter contest:

- A contest will not have much impact if you have a boring Twitter account. You must first have a strong base of followers to create buzz about your company's contest. Follow new people every day, target people in your area or demographic and put time into creating a fun Twitter presence, and then hold a contest.
- Frequent contests of lower value are better than infrequent contests at a high value. Once users understand that you hold regular contests, they are more likely to follow your account on a daily basis, occasionally retweeting your content, and gaining you followers by referral.

- Be honest with your followers about what they will win. There were complaints recently when companies said they were giving away iPhones, but they were really sending gift cards.
- You can hold your contest in a number of ways. You can offer it to anyone who retweets, anyone who direct messages you, anyone who uses your hashtag, or anyone who responds in a short time. You may want to try different strategies to see what results in the largest increase in followers or response.

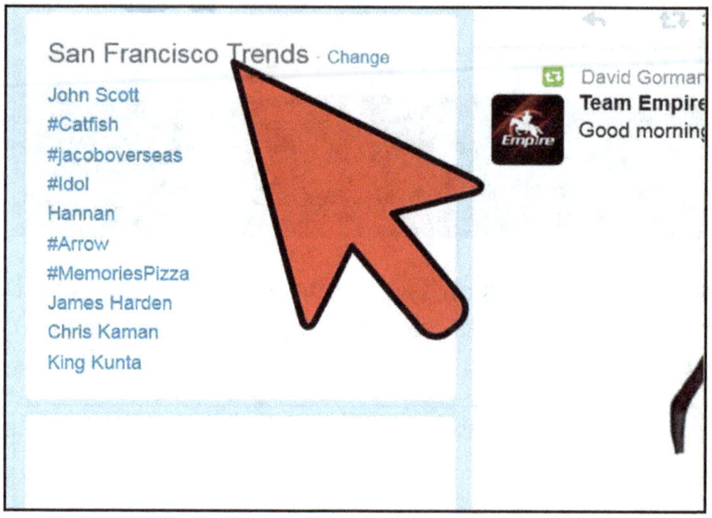

9. Follow the "Trending Topics" on Twitter and use these common hashtags when they apply to you. Trending Topics are listed on the right side of the Twitter home page. Don't be afraid to use the hashtag a few times, if you can contribute good content or conversation.

- Try to stay away from political trending topics. Kenneth Cole created controversy when he used the #Cairo hashtag to promote his new shoe line during the Cairo riots.

10. Employ a social media service, if you are unable to do all of this promotion within your company. Companies, such as Submitinme or coTweet, provide marketing services that focus on social media outlets like Twitter.

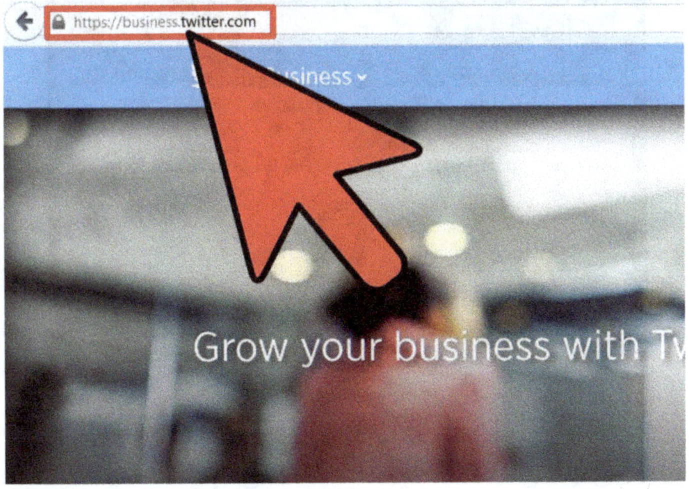

11. Buy a Twitter Promoted Tweet to try to target a new market. Promoted Tweets appear on top of the screen when a user searches for related topics. Go to www.business.twitter.com/advertise/promoted-tweets and use a special link, like 1 created through Google Analytics, to track website activity from Twitter.

How to Promote a Crowdfunding Campaign on Twitter

Consider the following 7 quick tips to market your crowdfunding campaign.

Steps

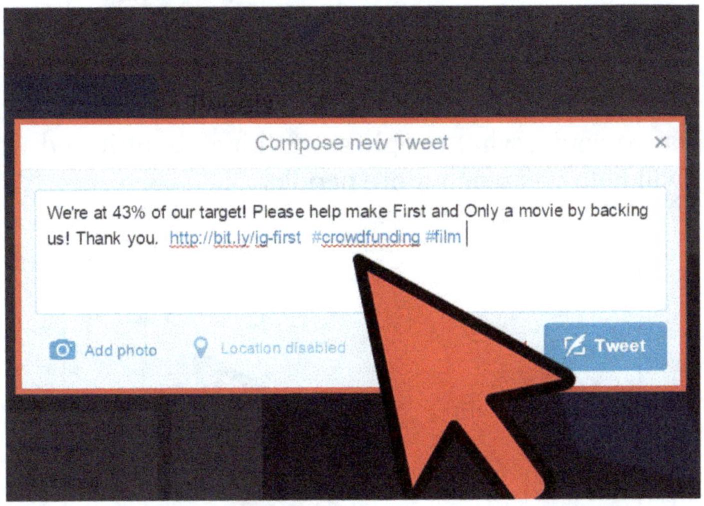

1. Share On Twitter 1x per day. Share your campaign on Twitter and increase your word count by adding a personal message. Tell your supporters about your cause, why you need their help and how their contributions will help you. A tweet is like a short Facebook status update. The difference is that every tweet arrives at every follower's feed, unlike the filter of Facebook's algorithm.

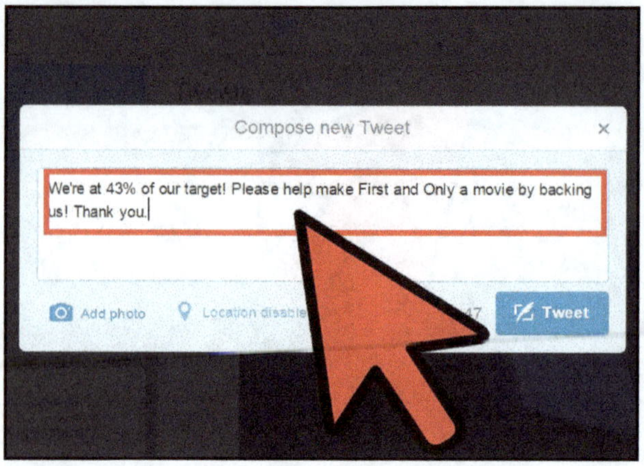

2. Make sure to create an engaging Twitter post! You should use words that you think will make an impact on your followers. Add some compelling details of your cause to this tweet to catch follower's attention. Keep is simple – tweets with less than 100 characters have a 17% higher rate of engagement than longer tweets do.

3. Search Keywords & Interact. Go to Twitter Search and find out if there is any conversation about a cause or project similar to yours, what people are talking about it and whether you can join or start a conversation. It will help you reach more people.

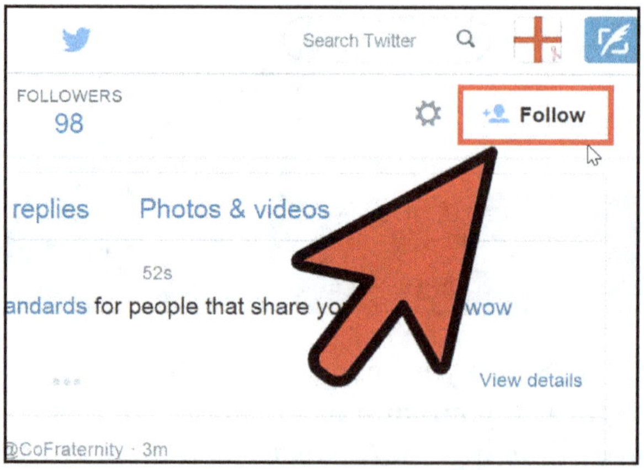

4. Follow Relevant People. Twitter is about connecting to people, building your own community.

To reach out to as many people as possible you should start following people you know, people in your neighborhood, non-profit organizations and communities related to your cause. Twitter can help you find people you know by scanning your email address book.

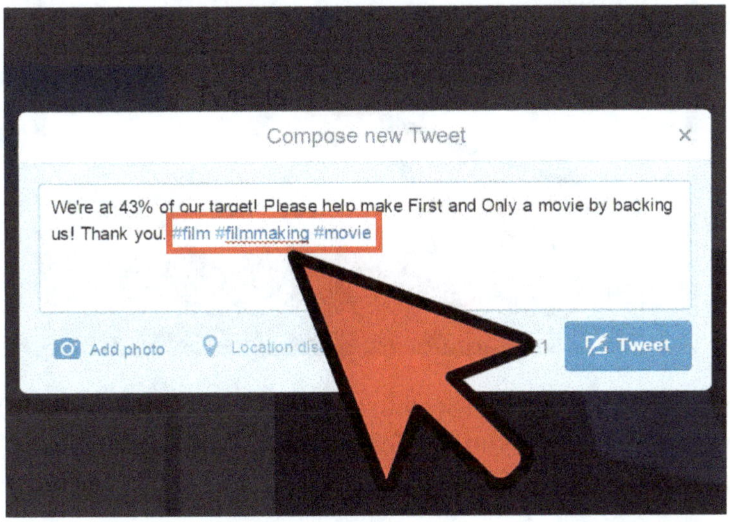

5. Increase visibility with hashtags (#). Make sure to include relevant and popular hashtags. You can have a hashtag that enables anyone to find your project easily. On the other hand, using relevant hashtags you get engaged in different Twitter community, which members can then tweet and Retweet your campaign several times a day. It allows you to maximize the promotion of your campaign to its fullest potential possible. You can reach out to as many people as you can without having to do it all by yourself. Remember, with hashtags other people can easily find and tweet or retweet your campaign.

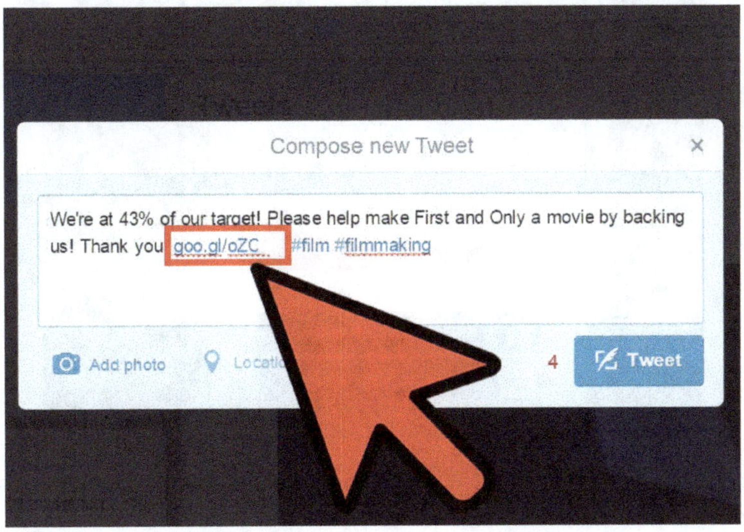

6. Include shortened links & images. People love to look at pictures, so include photographs in your tweets whenever possible. Twitter adds every photo you share to a photo gallery. The first six appear on your profile page. Take advantage of this feature to tell a visual story of your cause. Be sure to let people know when the link is a photo by adding [PIC] before the image.

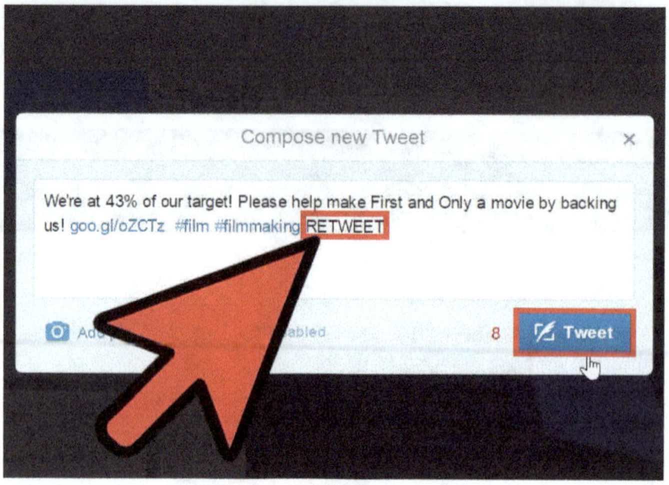

7. Request Retweets. Are you looking for more retweets? Just ask your followers. A tweet's retweet rate increases 12 times when you ask followers for a retweet. Asking followers to retweet using the whole word "Retweet" (instead of the short and casual "RT") increases retweet rates by 23 times.

How to use Pinterest

Part 1. Navigating Pinterest

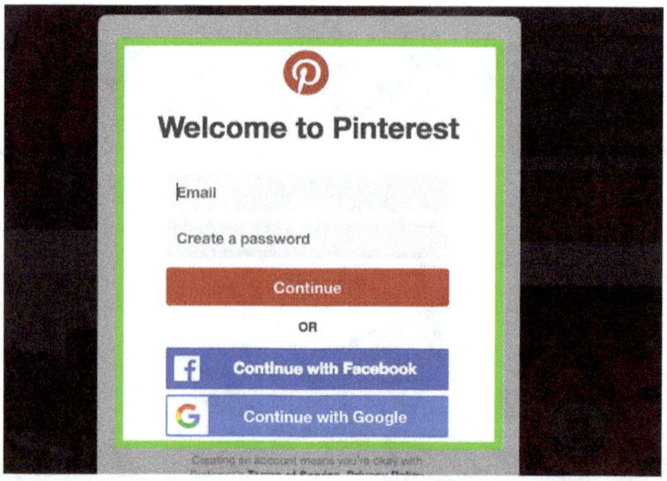

1. Open Pinterest. You can do so by tapping the Pinterest app (mobile), or by going to https://www.pinterest.com/.

- If you haven't created a Pinterest account yet, you'll need to create an account before continuing.
- You may need to sign into Pinterest by entering your email address and password when prompted (on desktop, click Sign In in the top-right corner of the page).

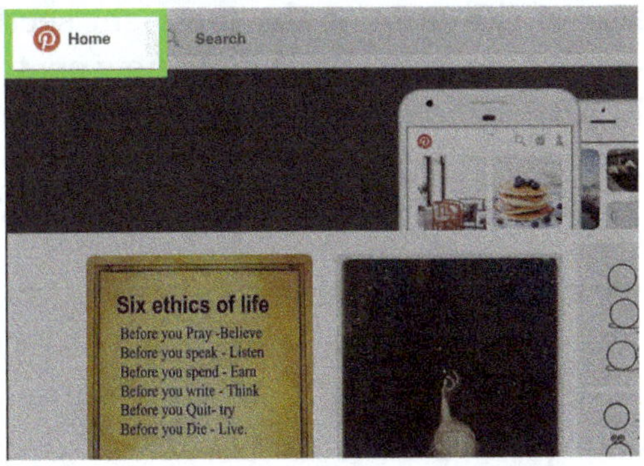

2. Review the Pinterest Home page. This is where all of your favorited topics will appear, as well as followed boards and users.

- You can get back to the Home page at any time by clicking or tapping the Pinterest logo. It's in the top-left corner of the screen for Android and desktop users, and the bottom-left corner for iPhone users.
- Android users won't see the Home page button when in another menu (e.g., the profile page); instead, you'll have to tap the "Back" button in the top-left corner of the screen to return to the Home page.

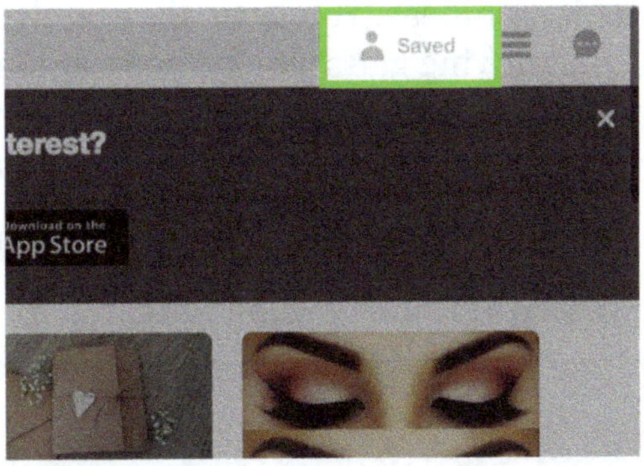

3. Open your profile page. You'll do so by clicking or tapping the person-shaped icon that's in either the bottom-right corner of the screen (iPhone) or the top-right side of the page (Android and desktop). You can view your personal boards--and their accompanying pins--here. You'll also be able to change your settings by tapping or clicking the hexagonal "Settings" icon near the top of the page.

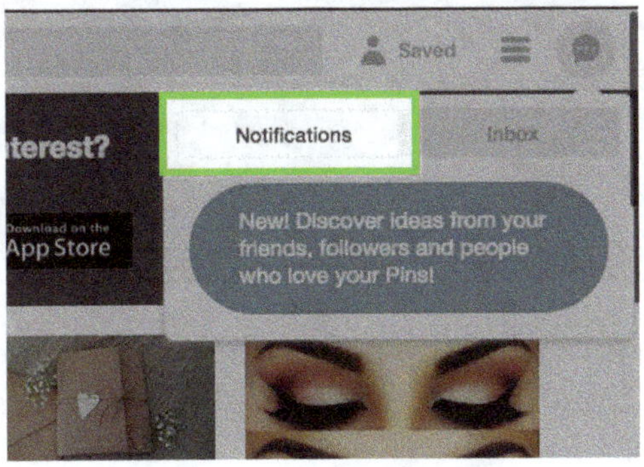

4. Check your Pinterest notifications. To do so, tap or click the speech bubble icon that's in either

the bottom-right area of the screen (iPhone) or the top-right section of the page (Android and desktop). This is where you'll see messages alerting you to new posts from people you're following, new followers, and your friends' activity.

- You can also select the Inbox tab at the top of the Notifications page to view private conversations and send your own.

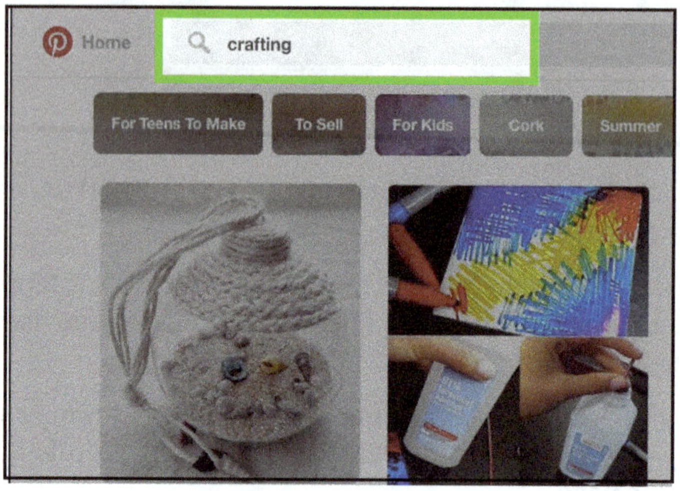

5. Search Pinterest for people, topics, or ideas. You'll use the search bar to do this; the search function is accessible by tapping the magnifying glass icon (iPhone and Android), or by simply clicking the bar with "Search" written in it at the top of the page on desktop. As you type, you should see search suggestions related to your typing appear below the search bar.

- You can select a search suggestion to search Pinterest for that suggestion exactly.
- You can also press your device's "Enter" button to search for your search term verbatim.

6. Use Pinterest's "Explore" feature (desktop only). Clicking Explore to the right of the search bar will open a page with currently trending topics, rising and new topics, content suggestions tailored for your preferences, and more.

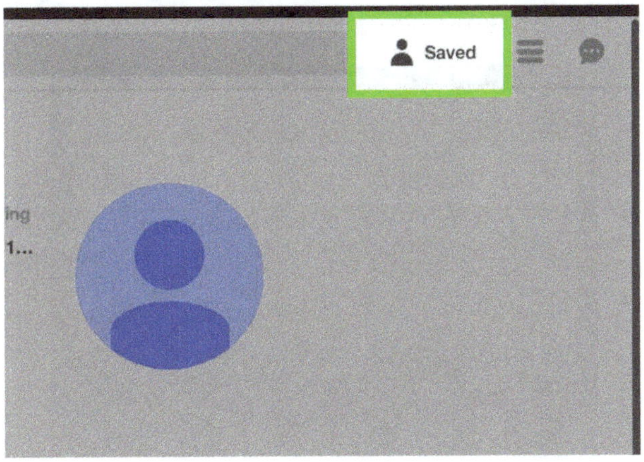

7. Select the profile tab. This will take you to your profile page, where you can get started by creating your first board.

Part 2. Creating a Board

1. Select the + button. It's in the top-right corner of the screen on mobile. Desktop users will instead click Create board on the left side of the page.

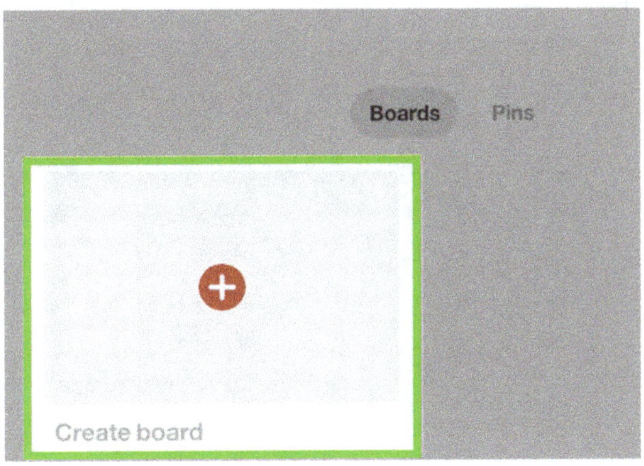

2. Select Create board. It's toward the bottom of the screen on mobile. If you're on desktop, skip

this step.

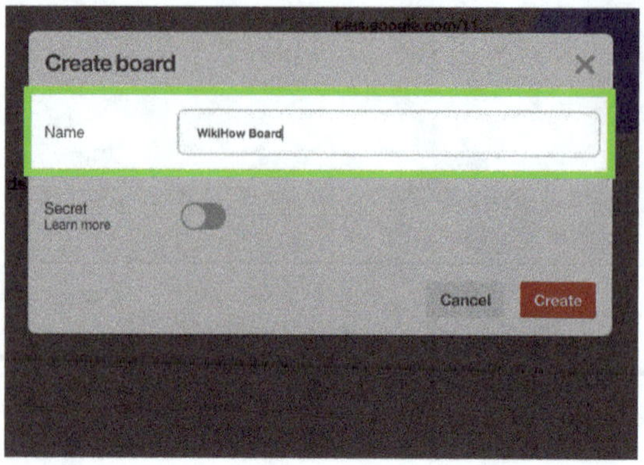

3. Type in your board's name. This title should reflect the kind of content you plan on posting to this board.

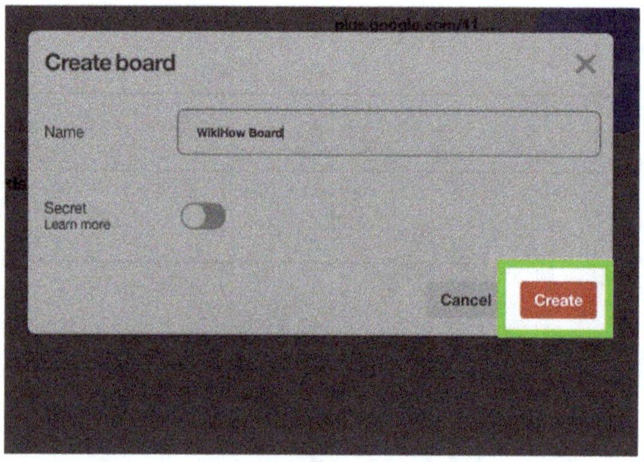

4. Select Create. Doing so will create your Pinterest board. Now that you have a place to store content, you're ready to upload and save some pins.

- You can also hide your board from other Pinterest users by selecting the Keep board secret switch (called Secret on desktop).

Part 3. Uploading Pins

1. Select the + icon again. This applies to desktop as well (you'll find it in the bottom-right corner of the page). You should see a couple of options appear:

- Photo (mobile)/Upload a Pin (desktop) - Allows you to select a photo from your device's default "Pictures" album.
- Website (mobile)/Save from a website (desktop) - Lets you search for a website (or enter a link to one), then search the resulting site for pin-compatible items.
- On mobile, you also have the option of tapping Copied Link to navigate to the last link you copied. This option is functionally the same as tapping Website.

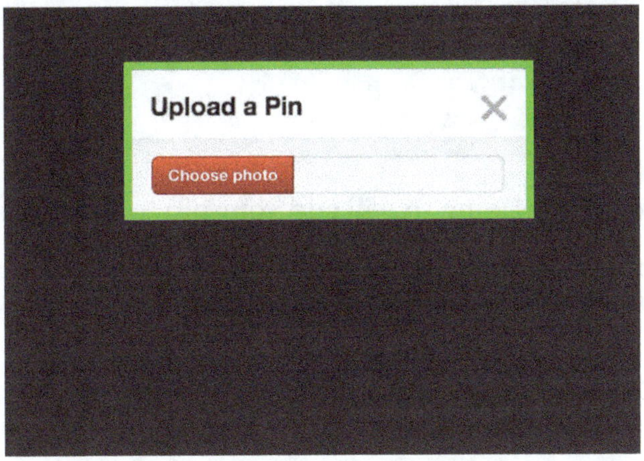

2. Select your preferred option. From here, uploading a pin will vary based on your choice:
   - If you chose to upload a photo, you'll have to allow Pinterest access to your device (mobile) or click Choose photos (desktop). You can then browse through your device's pictures to select the one you wish to upload.
   - If you chose to use a website, you'll enter the website's URL into the provided text field. Once the site finishes loading, you should see a list of all media that you can pin--though, on iPhone, you must first tap Save in the top-right corner before you see this list.

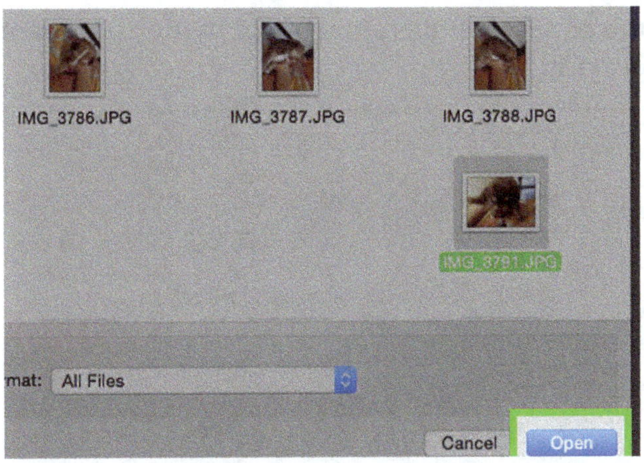

3. Select an item to pin. Again, this process will vary slightly depending on your chosen upload path, but you'll tap or click the photo you wish to save.

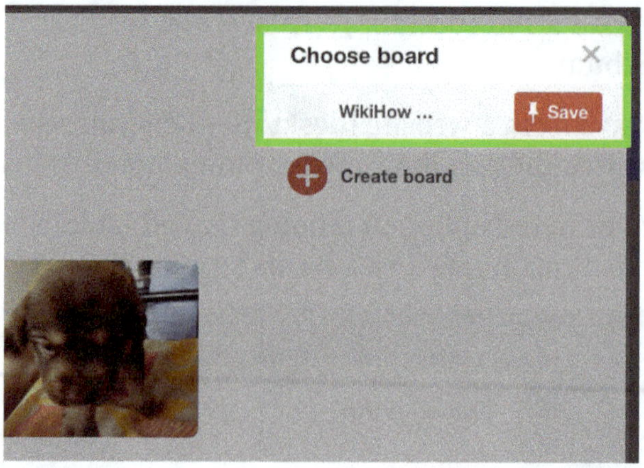

4. Select a board when prompted. Doing so will add your pin to the board in question.

- You can also add a description to your item in the field to the right of the item's icon.

Part 4. Saving Pins

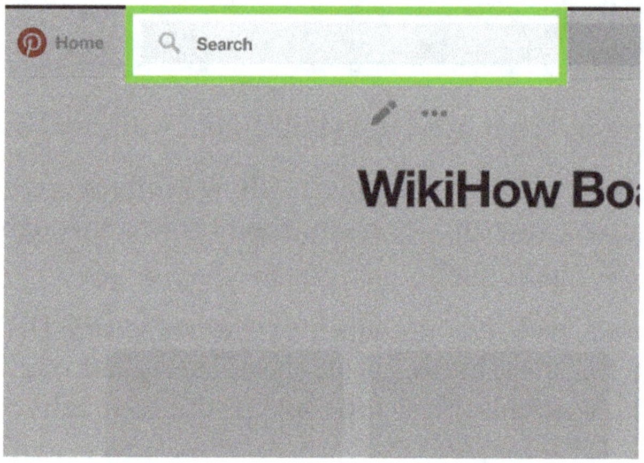

1. Open the Pinterest search bar. Remember, it's a magnifying glass on mobile, and a "Search" bar at the top of the page on desktop.

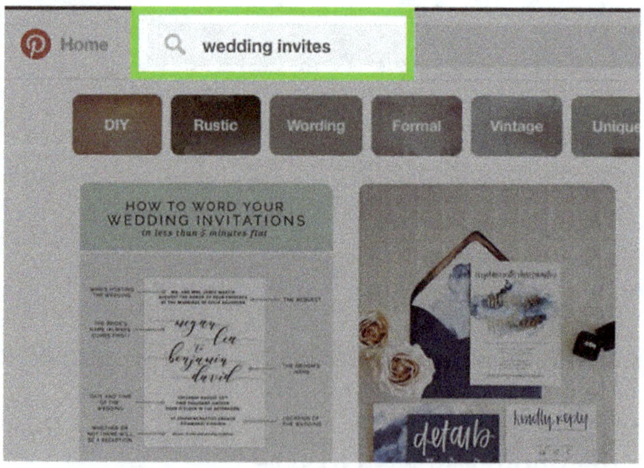

2. Search for a pin you wish to save. You can do this by typing a search query into the search bar,

or you can simply return to the Home page to view Pinterest's suggestions.

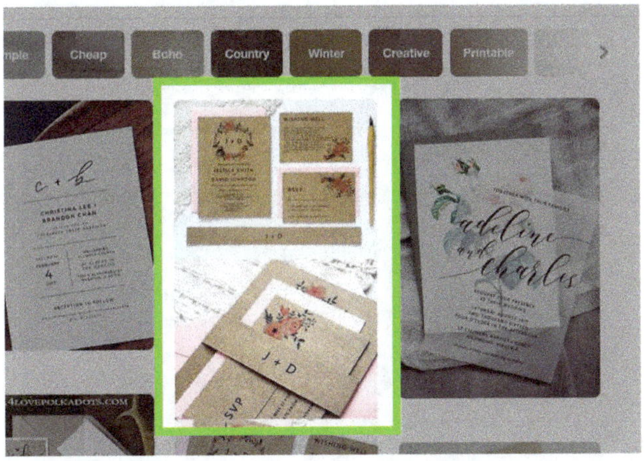

3. Tap or click a pinned item. Doing so will open it.

4. Tap or click Save. This option is in the top-right corner of pinned items on iPhone and desktop, and in the bottom-right corner of items on Android.

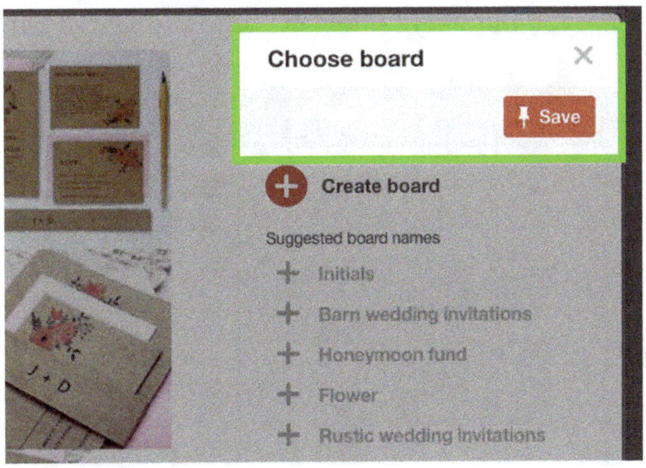

5. Select a board when prompted. Doing so will add your pin to the board in question.

- As with uploaded pins, you can also add a description to your item in the field to the right of the item's icon.

Part 5. Following Boards and People

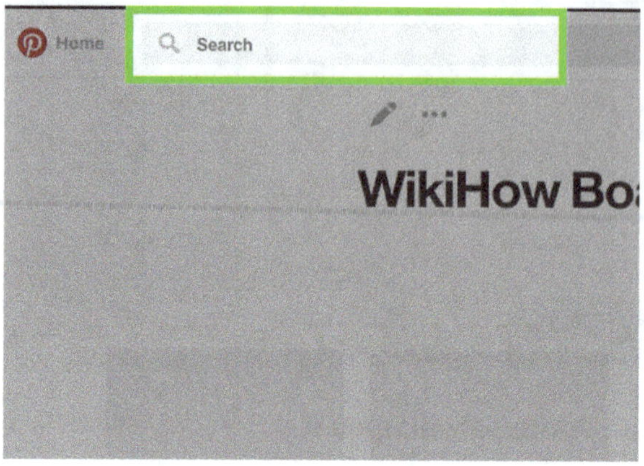

1. Open the Pinterest search bar. You can use keywords or more specific search terms to find boards and people to follow.

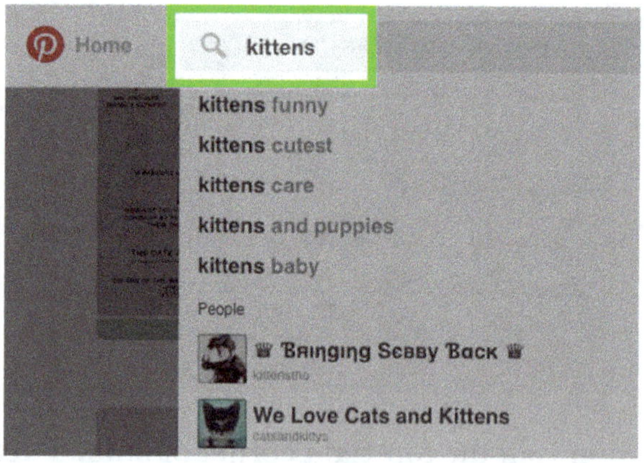

2. Search for a term related to your preferred content. For example, if you want to follow a board that posts pictures of kittens, you might type "kittens" into the search bar.

3. Tap the filter icon right of the search bar. You don't need to do this on desktop, since the "Filter"

options are in the second row of tabs below the search bar.

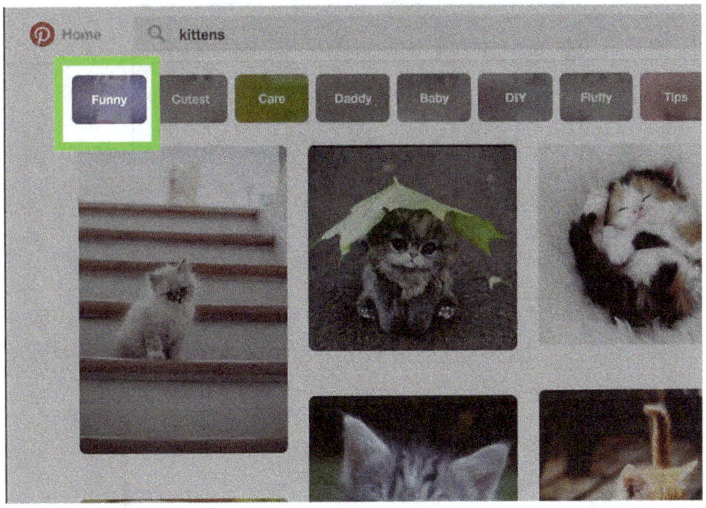

4. Select a filter. You'll select Boards to show only boards displaying your search term, or People to find Pinterest users to follow.

- On Android, tap Pinners to filter based on people.

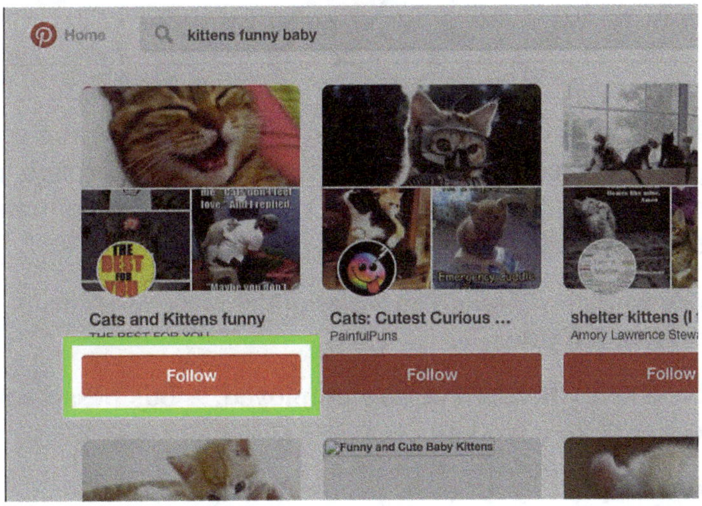

5. Tap or click Follow. This option is below a board or person. Doing so will cause you to follow the board or person in question.

How to use LinkedIn

LinkedIn is the largest and most dominant social network in the professional arena. Totally different from the likes of Facebook, it is used for maintaining a professional persona and brand. Other uses for LinkedIn include finding a job, networking, recruiting new employees, getting sales leads and even getting your business news.

Method 1. Signing Up

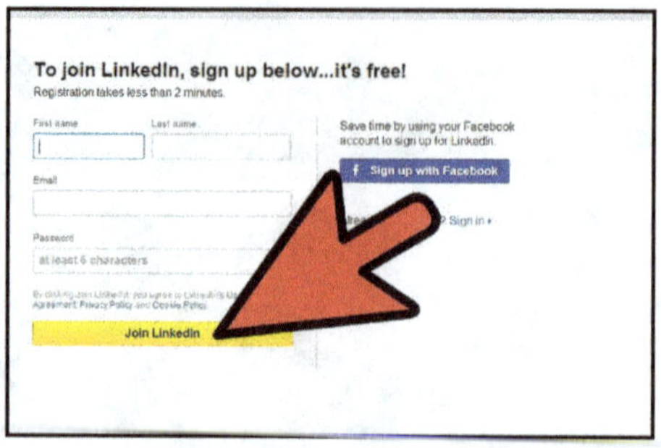

1.Join LinkedIn at their website. Click on the link, add your relevant personal information, and click "join LinkedIn."

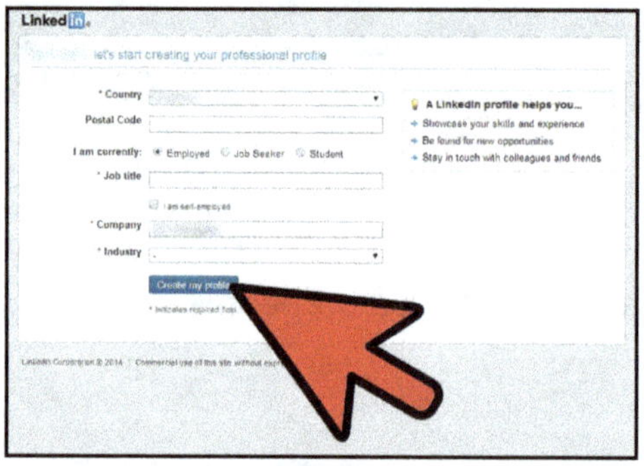

2. Create your profile. Your profile is the condensed picture of how the professional world sees you. A great, detailed profile projects someone who is successful, thorough, and connected. A thin or outdated profile projects someone who doesn't care or who can't be bothered. Make sure your profile says the thing(s) you want to project.

- LinkedIn's profile wizard will take you through the steps of entering your region, industry, company and current job title.
- You will also be asked whether you are employed, a business owner, looking for work, working independently or a student.
- This information completes your basic profile.

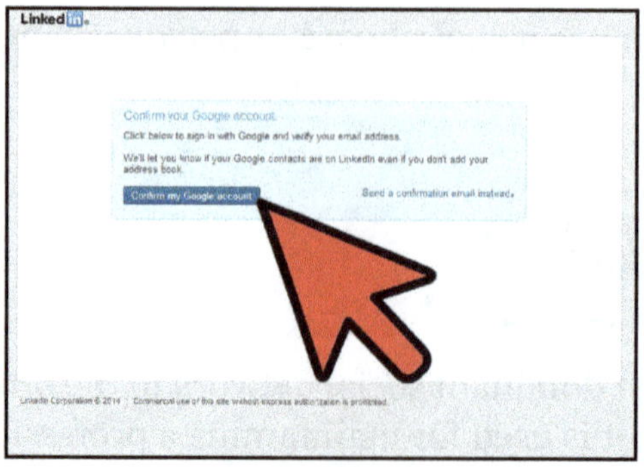

3. Confirm the email account you used to create your profile via the link provided. This will help you efficiently complete the next step, which is finding connections.

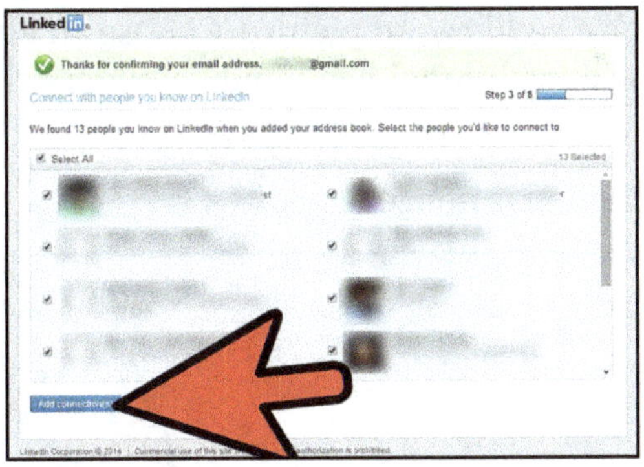

4. Add your connections. Connections are professional contacts whom you know or wish to know. The connections you add on LinkedIn become part of your social network.

- LinkedIn will prompt you to search for connections by crawling your email, which you give LinkedIn access to. You can use this to see who among your email connections already has a LinkedIn account and invite them to become part of your professional network.
- You may opt to skip this step if you prefer to add connections individually.

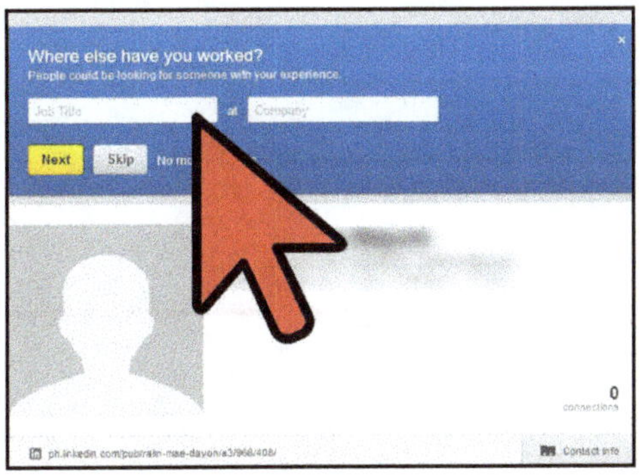

5. Continue to build your profile. Enter your previous employment details and your education information. Then enter a brief summary and/or headline. A brief summary or headline stating who you are professionally in a few sentences. This headline should give a sense of your most outstanding professional attributes.

6. Upload a profile photograph. Unlike other social networks, this picture should reflect you at your most professional. No pictures of binge drinking, girls around the arm, or smoke wafting

from the background, even if it's a *really* good picture. Choose an illustration that represents your professional image. This can be a traditional head and shoulders shot, a shot of you at work or a copy of your logo.

- Use a clear, vertical rectangular image.

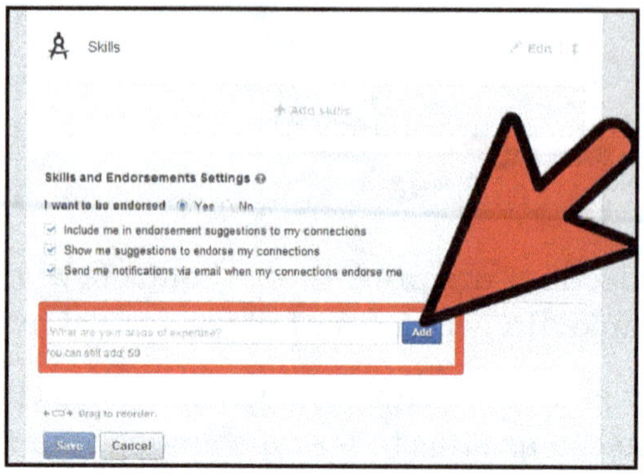

7. Add specialties to your profile. Including specific skills or specialties, such as veterinary dentistry or congressional campaign communications, allows other users can find you more easily.

8. Add your website or your company's website and your Twitter or blog information. The more ways there are for people to find you, and access information about you, the more valuable your LinkedIn profile will be.

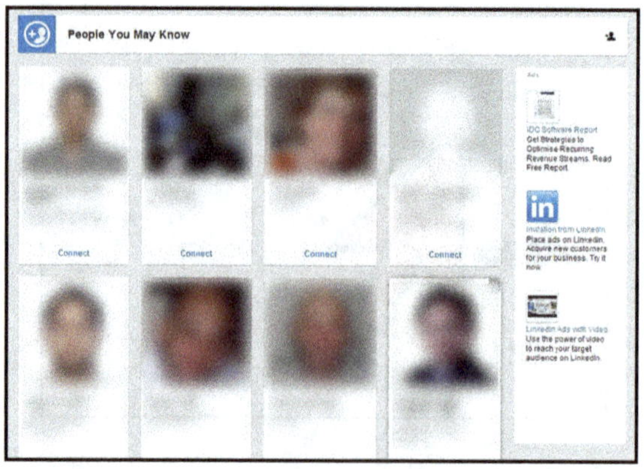

9. Invite connections suggested by LinkedIn based on your employment and education listings.

Method 2. Starting Out

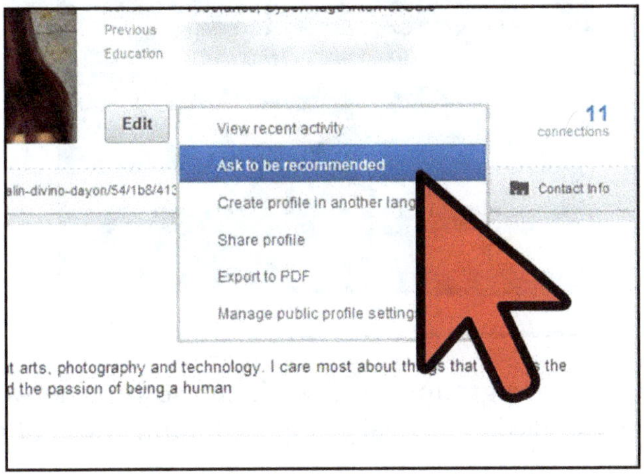

1. Ask for recommendations. LinkedIn allows you to ask connections for recommendations and post them to your profile. You will see the recommendations and approve the postings. This feature reinforces the information in your headline summary and specialties sections. Prospective employers and clients browsing your profile will see these recommendations, as will the connections of those who have recommended you.

- Linkedin recommendations are known for being overly positive and therefore not especially exciting. Focus requests for recommendations on people who can talk best about your skills, such as ex bosses and customers.

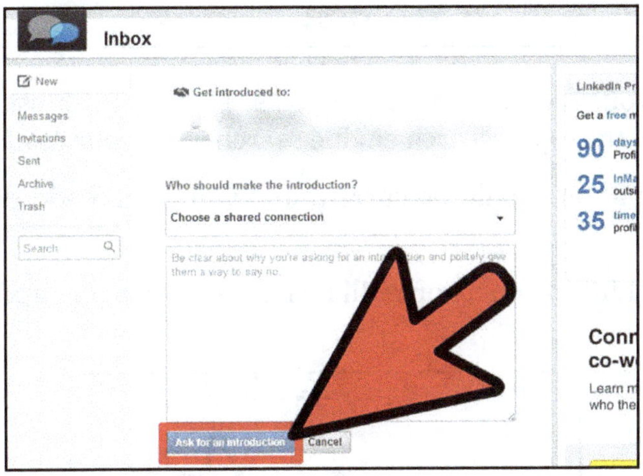

2. Ask for introductions. Asking for an introduction to a person from a connection you already know if a fast and friendly way to grow your network. On the free version of LinkedIn, you have 5 free introduction requests.

- If you browse the connections of one of your connections, you may invite them to become your connections. Only do this if you know the person professionally. You may also ask your connections to introduce you by sending your profile and a note to someone in their networks.

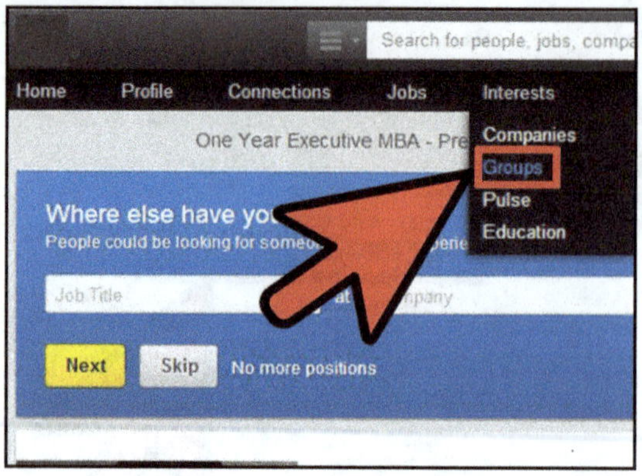

3. Join and participate in LinkedIn groups. You can increase your network and your visibility by starting and contributing to discussions. Local groups will inform you of networking activities and events.

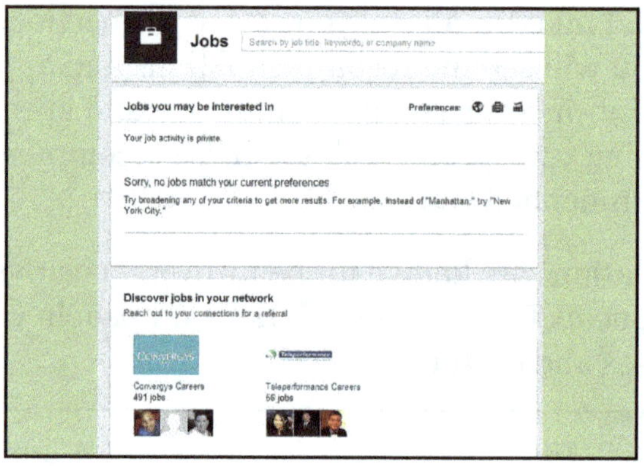

4. Maintain and update your profile on a regular basis. This is your most visible professional profile. It will usually rank at the top of search engine searches for your name.

- All of your information should be current and you should add occasional updates in the space provided.
- Members of your LinkedIn network will be notified when you update your profile or add a new contact.

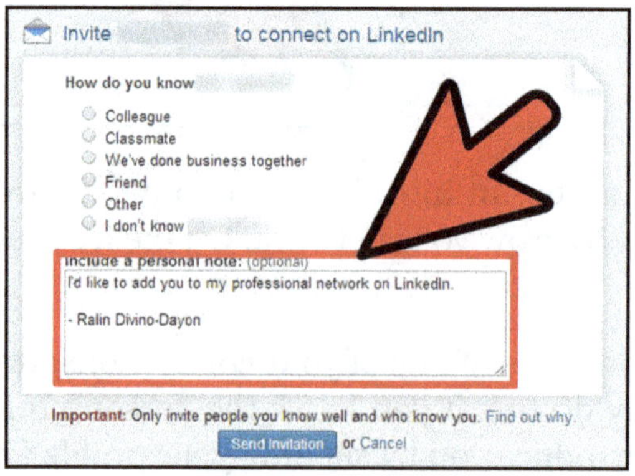

5. Continue to build your network on a regular basis, adding new connections with a personal note

of invitation. A good rule of thumb is to only add those connections who you could envision giving you a good recommendation. Think twice before adding connections who aren't too fond of you or any of your companies or businesses.

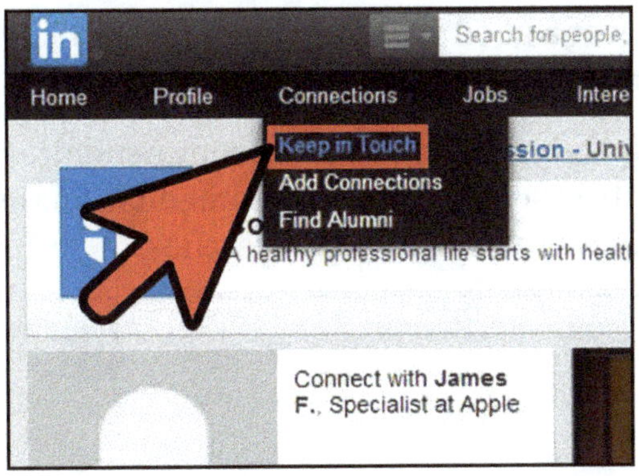

6. Stay in contact with your connections. Respond to their updates by sending them notes of congratulations on a new position or achievement. The most important connections to nurture are the ones from previous jobs, or other people you haven't spoken to in years.

Method 3. Finding a Job

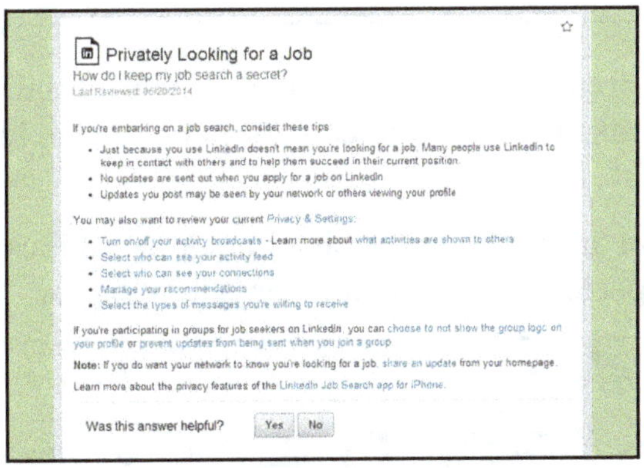

1. Know when LinkedIn can help you find a job. LinkedIn is at its best when you know exactly what you want to do, and just need to find the right people to talk to.

2. Make sure your LinkedIn profile is accurate, updated, and showing you in the best light. Spend

the most time making sure your profile has a concrete list of your achievements and notes the special skills, qualifications, publications and such that you have. If you have been quoted in the press, have a patent, or have a similar "wow" in your background, state it on your profile.

- Lying on a resume is never a good idea, but it is worse in LinkedIn. Potential employers can use your own LinkedIn connections to check up on you.
- Do not worry too much about filling out the recommendations and skills on your LinkedIn profile. Employers pretty much discount recommendations as being sappy and always positive. The skills are only useful for keyword searches.

3. Know that an up-to-date profile can bring the jobs to you. Building out your profile with the right skills can on occasion make highly qualified jobs come to you, instead of the usual other way around.

- It is still unlikely to get hit up out of the blue for a job, but it can happen. It mostly happens to people who have specific skills an employer is looking for.

4. Find jobs posted on LinkedIn. You can simply go to the Jobs tab on LinkedIn to find jobs that may fit your preferences.

- LinkedIn job postings are helpful, and you should look for them. Compared to free message boards, they tend to have higher quality jobs, and it is very unlikely that you would find anything unsavory or dangerous. Still, they are "just a job board."

- LinkedIn searching is best if you have a specific skill that an employer is hiring for. You may find an employer looking for someone exactly like you.

5. Consider signing up for LinkedIn Job Seeker premium. Job seeker premium is best for helping you find specific people and/or specific companies. It costs between USD$20 - USD$50 per month.

- Job seeker premium lets you see the names of people at companies you might be interested in. Better yet, it lets you contact them directly via LinkedIn messaging (known as In Mail.)
- LinkedIn gives you only a few of these premium messages a month, so it is useful if you know exactly what you are looking for.
- The other benefits of Job Seeker premium are not as helpful. Getting a badge as a Featured Applicant can actually be counterproductive, since recruiters might see it as you being desperate. So, again, better if you are looking for a specific position rather than just looking around.

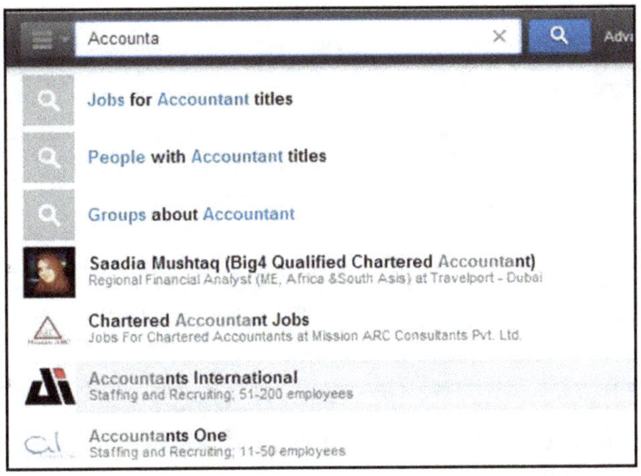

6. Use LinkedIn differently for jobs that are less specific. If you are looking for a job where there are a large number of people with similar skills (example: sales, office manager, CPA), you may find LinkedIn less effective.

- For these kinds of less specific jobs, the key to using LinkedIn is to target specific companies you might want to work for, or use it to find people in your network to contact.

Method 4. Recruiting

1. Know what kind of candidates can best be found via LinkedIn. LinkedIn is very good at helping you:

- Find candidates with very specific skill sets.
- Target people from specific companies.
- Reach out to people who are not currently looking for a job. (Passive job seekers.).
- Hit up contacts of contacts. It is good for helping find friends of current employees.

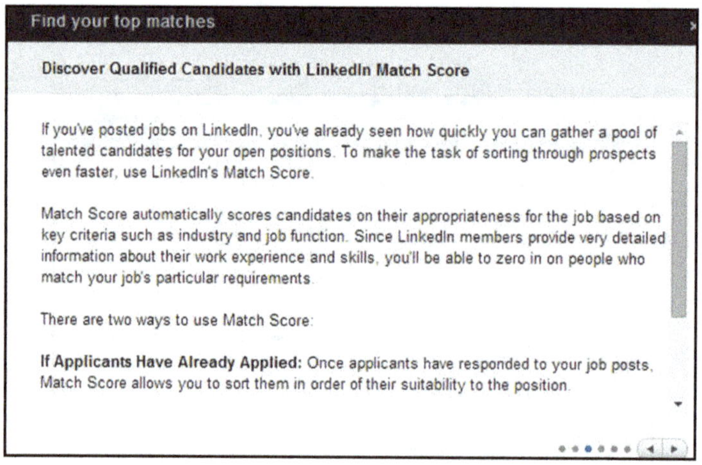

2. Know what kinds of candidates for which LinkedIn doesn't work as well. You won't do as well using LinkedIn to find people with:

- Very general skills.
- New college graduates
- Hourly employees

3. Ensure your company profile is set up and looks good. When you contact someone via LinkedIn, it will be natural for them to check out your company profile first thing, so you want them to find the information there helpful and putting the company in the best light.

- Search LinkedIn to see your current company profile. For example, the XYZ entry is here: https://www.linkedin.com/company/XYZ. Look at the "Careers" section in particular.
- If the company profile is not to your liking, ask the right person at your company to update it. Your marketing people may have specific thoughts as to the content, so you want to keep them in the loop.
- If there is no company profile, set it up from the Companies>Add a Company. You can then follow the prompts to verify your identity and fill out the sections for Overview, Careers, Product Pages, Employees and Statistics. Obviously, the part you want to flesh out is the "Careers" section.

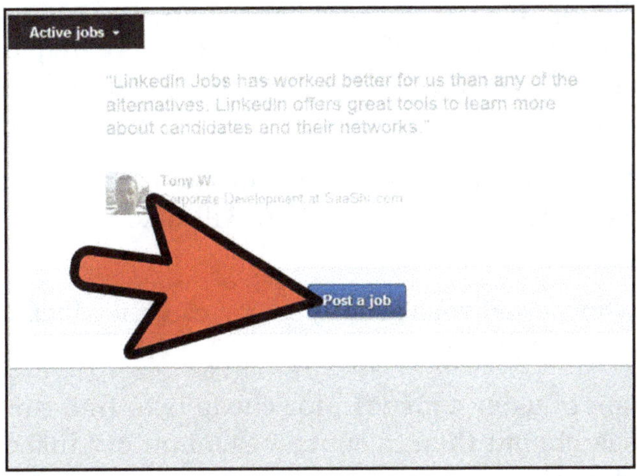

4. Post a job on LinkedIn. You can simply pay to list a job on LinkedIn without a recruiter account. It is not cheap, but will get you applicants. The quality of the applicants will be somewhat better than what you can find on Craigslist.

- Similar to Craigslist, a job posting will be not as effective to recruit people in very high demand.

- It will be effective if you have a specific skill set that lends itself to keyword search. As an example, if you want to hire a copy-editor in Sydney, you will find people can find you easily and apply. You have to ask yourself if you will get too many applicants (Salesperson in London) or no applicants (actuary in Marfa, Texas.)

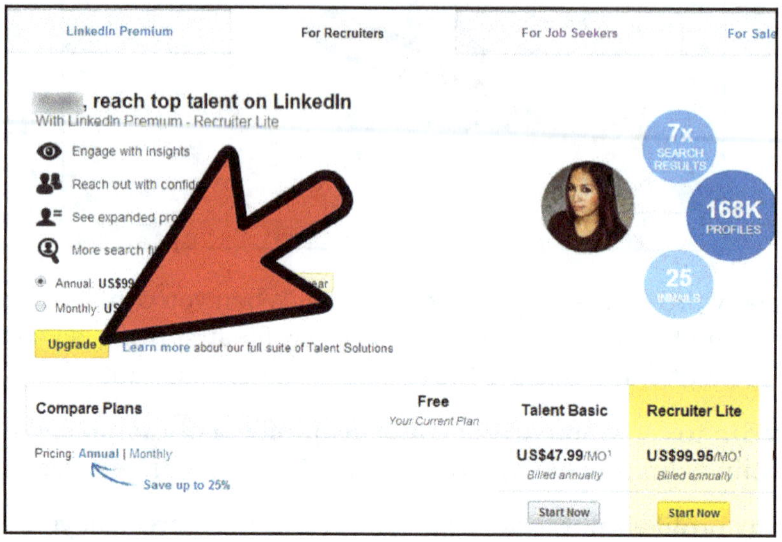

5. Sign up for a LinkedIn Recruiter Account. Recruiter accounts are very effective if you are trying to reach out to specific people. They are rather unmatched if you are trying to find people who are not currently looking for a job.

- Recruiter accounts are expensive. The most powerful version approaches USD$10,000 per year.
- You can find just the right person you are looking for, and contact them with a "LinkedIn InMail." InMails are opened most of the time; much more frequently than regular emails. Some people don't check their LinkedIn, though, so you probably want to follow with a regular email or phone call.
- Reaching out to people who are not looking for a job can be amazingly effective in finding highly qualified candidates. Naturally, it will take longer, but you may find better people.
- You also will see who viewed your profile, so you can tell which candidates are interested and you can follow up with them.
- The hillbilly version of using LinkedIn for cheap is to find the person you are looking for on LinkedIn search, but then to contact them off of LinkedIn. LinkedIn is making that harder by hiding the family names of the people you are searching for. With a recruiter account, you see the person's full name and can contact them directly with an In Mail.

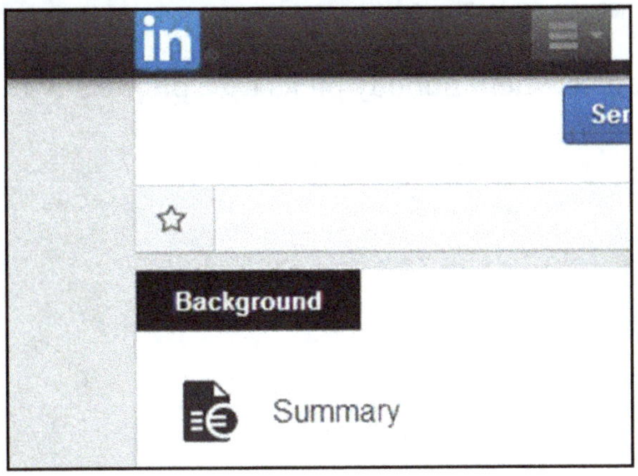

6. Know that LinkedIn is very effective in background checks. You will be amazed how quickly you can find people who know any candidate.

- Check up on the references your candidate provided, to ensure they are who they are who the candidate said they are.
- Find "backdoor" references using LinkedIn. Search for people with similar jobs at the company your job candidate came from, and you can find and reach out to people who can give you the true scoop about him or her.
- Ignore the recommendations about your candidate on LinkedIn. They are useless; in fact, glowing recommendations mean nothing more than the candidate has been trying to get good recommendations.
- The skills and expertise section is rarely helpful. It can be inaccurate, it might give you clues only if the candidate is stressing a skillset they don't really have.

Method 5. Getting Sales Leads

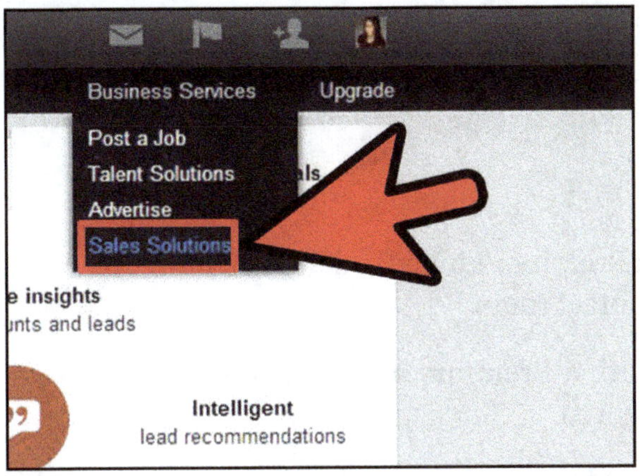

1. Know that LinkedIn is very powerful in getting sales leads. In particular, it can help you if you:

- Belong to a company that is not well known
- Can't always find the right person at a large company to sell to

- Are looking for leads for big ticket items
- Are selling to companies where nobody picks up a phone any more.

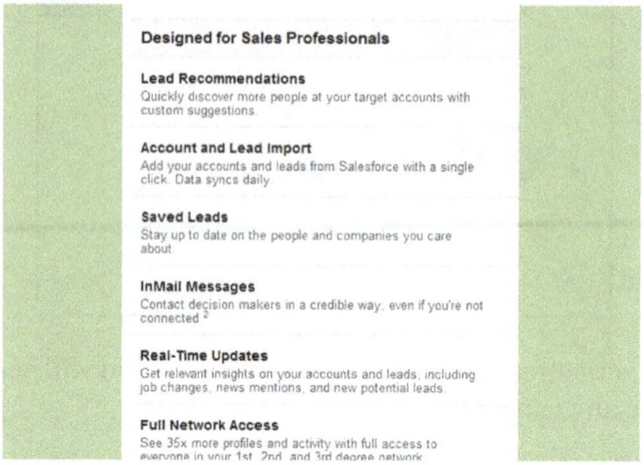

2. Know when LinkedIn cannot help you.

- LinkedIn selling is somewhat limited if you are selling to individuals.
- LinkedIn is great for finding leads. But if you are already in contact with the right people at prospect companies, it won't be very helpful.

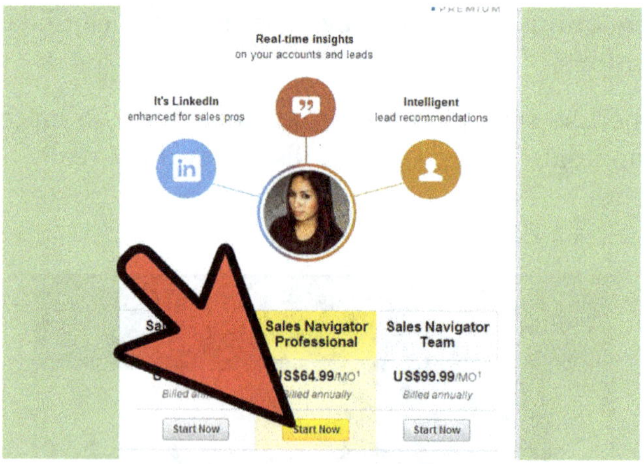

3. Consider signing up for a Premium LinkedIn sales account. The Premium accounts will help you find the right buyers and contact them.

- When you search with a Premium account, you will be able to read the full name of the people you find in search.
- Premium account holders can also send a limited number of "LinkedIn InMails" directly to the sales prospects they find. They are "guaranteed opened," meaning, if the person you are trying to contact does not open the message in seven days, your credit is refunded and you get to try with someone else.
- Sales accounts cost USD$ a few hundred to USD$1000 per year.

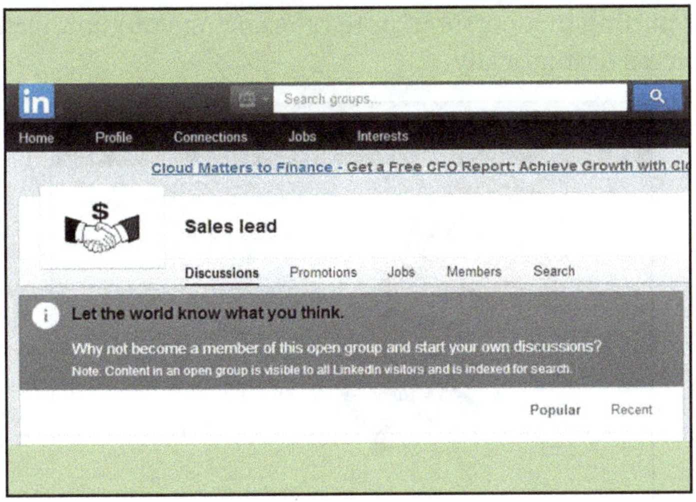

4. Determine the job titles of your sales prospects, so that you can search for them. LinkedIn search is pretty user friendly, but it still takes a bit of practice to get the right people to come back on the search.

- You probably already know who the economic buyers for your product are, but you may not know what their job titles are.
- For example, if you want to set up meetings with materials managers of food manufacturing companies, you simply set your search filter to show you people in food manufacturing with title material manager.
- You may need to specify additional keywords to get the exact list of people you are looking for.

5. Contact your prospects via LinkedIn InMails. InMails are messages sent via LinkedIn to the prospect you want to contact.

- Consider hand crafting the message to the prospect. LinkedIn only gives you a limited number of InMails, and charges you for them, so you want to make each one count. LinkedIn fits the VITO letter model a lot more than the smile and dial model.

- Remember that putting in a personal note referencing your connection to the prospect increases your success dramatically.

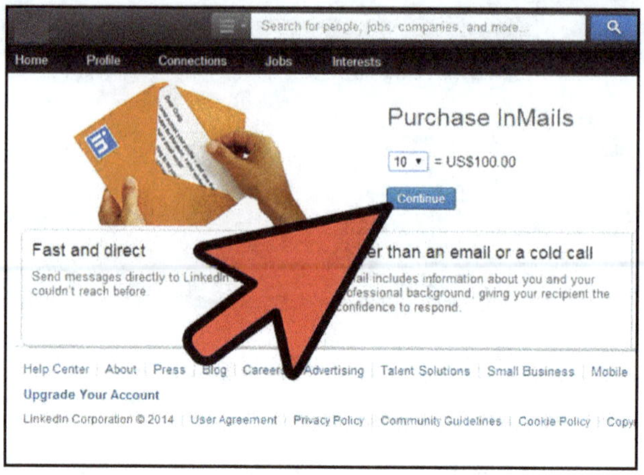

6. Don't waste your InMails. Since you only have a limited number of InMails, you may want to use other ways of contacting prospects that you can find without LinkedIn. You can try:

- Guessing their email address.
- Using a lead database.
- Phone call.
- Facebook messages. Facebook also charges for premium emails, but sometimes it is pretty cheap.

7. Use LinkedIn for reference selling. LinkedIn lets you see the contacts of your contacts, some of which could be sales prospects.

- Make a list of your happy/reference customers who might introduce you to their friends.
- Add these customers as connections on LinkedIn.
- Browse your customers' connections. You will find some connections that could also be sales prospects for you.

- You can approach these new prospects in several ways. You can hit them with an InMail, do a LinkedIn introduction request (which does not count against your InMail quota), contact them offline, or ask your customer for an introduction.
- Note that adding your customers as your connections can have risks. A clever competitor sales rep might be able to see who you are connected to unless you set your privacy correctly. You can avoid this by hiding your connections.

Method 6. Building your Personal Brand

1. Appear on Google and other searches. LinkedIn displays how often your profile appears in search, and what people are looking for when they find you.

- By adding more details about what you are doing, you can directly see how many more people are finding you online.

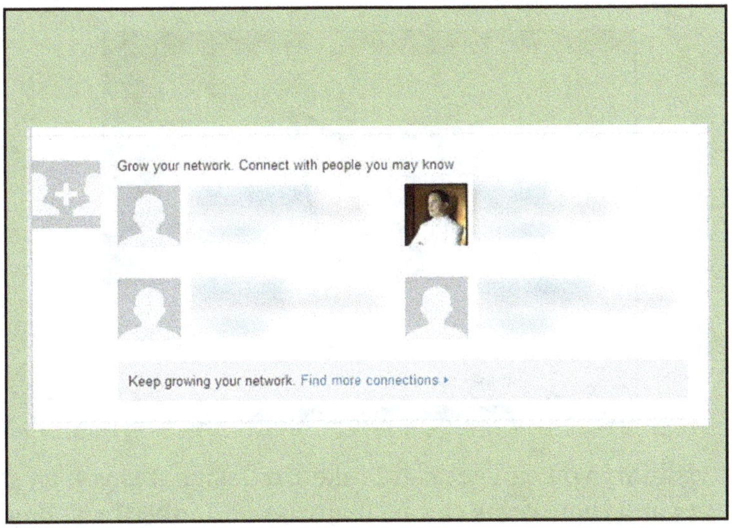

2. Don't add people you don't know, but continue to build out your contacts. The more contacts you add, the more people will see your updates.

3. Post updates to your LinkedIn contacts periodically. They tend not to be commented on like a Facebook post, but they are widely read. Use the same caveats as in any social media posting.

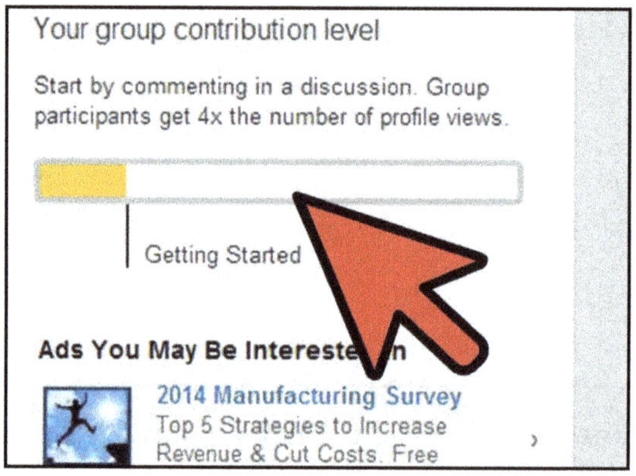

4. Contribute to the right LinkedIn groups. The most important posts you can make to spread your personal brand are to LinkedIn groups that consist of professionals like yourself. They are most likely to be interested in what you post, and take action (should you want them to).

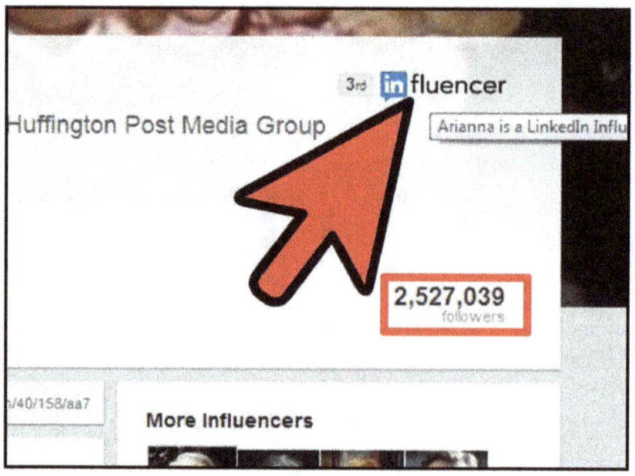

5. Know that the most visibility you can get is if LinkedIn designates you as an "Influencer." Influencers can have followers and their posts can be featured on LinkedIn Today.

- Influencers also can write mini blog posts that include images, which also boosts your readership.

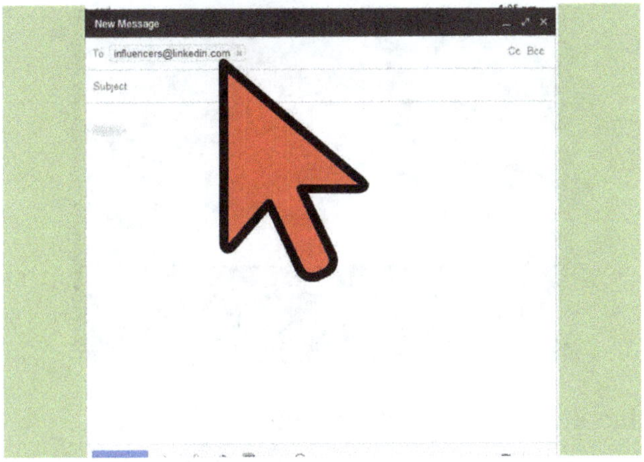

6. LinkedIn's criteria for becoming an influence has been changing, and is currently officially closed.

- There are ways to show LinkedIn that you are an influencer. You can tie your personal blog to LinkedIn so LinkedIn knows your readership carries over to LinkedIn.

How to use Tumblr

Tumblr is a social media platform that encourages creative text- and image-based posts, community engagement, and general entertainment.

Part 1. Creating an Account

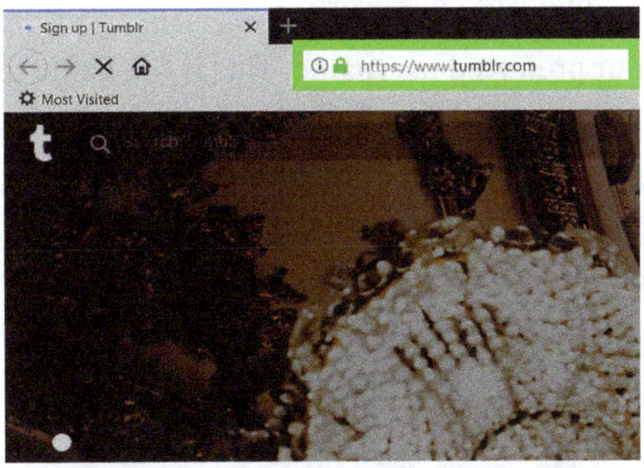

1. Open Tumblr. Go to https://www.tumblr.com/ in your preferred web browser to open the Tumblr website.

- On mobile, tap the Tumblr app icon, which resembles a white "t" on a dark-blue background.
- If you haven't yet downloaded the Tumblr app on mobile, you can do so for both iPhone and Android platforms.

2. Select Get started. It's the blue button in the middle of the page.

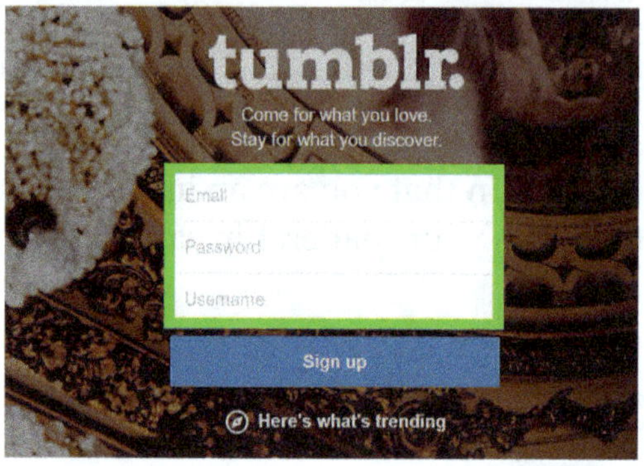

3. Enter your account information. Fill out the following fields:

- Email - Enter your preferred email address. You'll have to verify this email address later, so make sure that you have access to it.
- Password - Enter your preferred password.
- Username - Enter your preferred username. This is the name that other people will see for your account.
    - On desktop, Tumblr will also generate a list of usernames from which you can choose.
    - You may have to try a few different usernames, since some usernames related to you preferred one may already be taken.

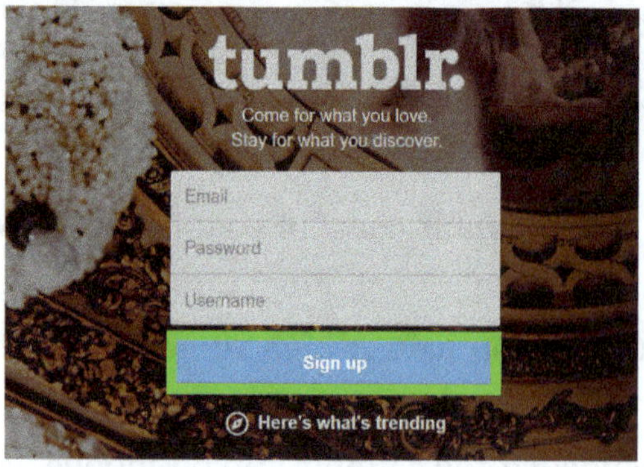

4. Click Sign up. It's at the bottom of the page.

- On mobile, tap Next in the top-right corner.

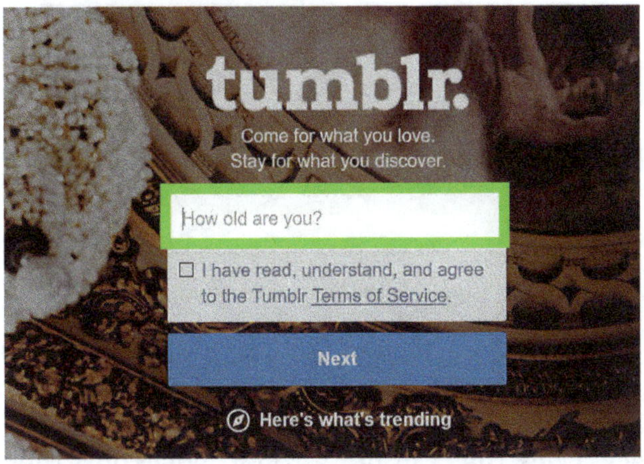

5. Enter your age. Type your current age into the text field in the middle of the page.

6. Check the "I have read..." box. This indicates that you agree to Tumblr's terms of use and community guidelines.

- Skip this step on mobile.

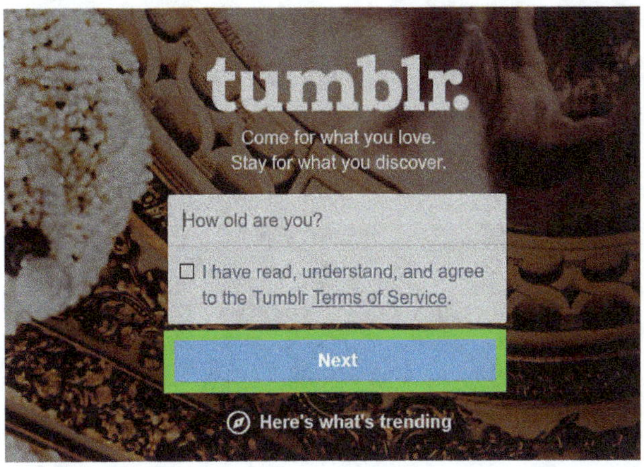

7. Click Next. It's a blue button below the "I have read..." checkbox.

- On mobile, tap Next in the top-right corner instead.

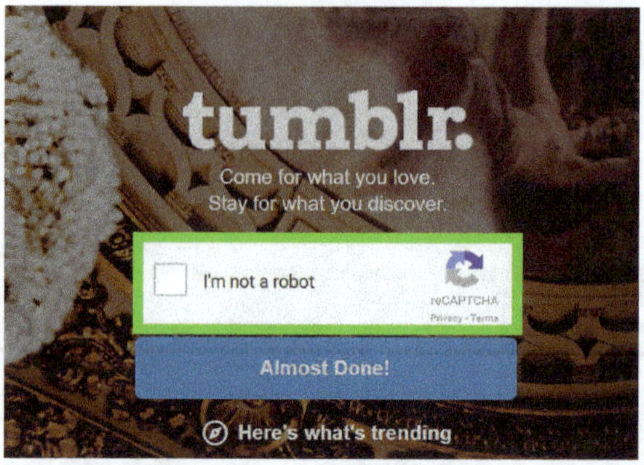

8. Complete the spam check. Click the "I'm not a robot" checkbox, then follow the on-screen instructions. You'll usually have to pick instances of a specific item (e.g., a car) out of a series of related pictures. Once you complete this step, you'll automatically be taken to the next one.

- Skip this step on mobile.

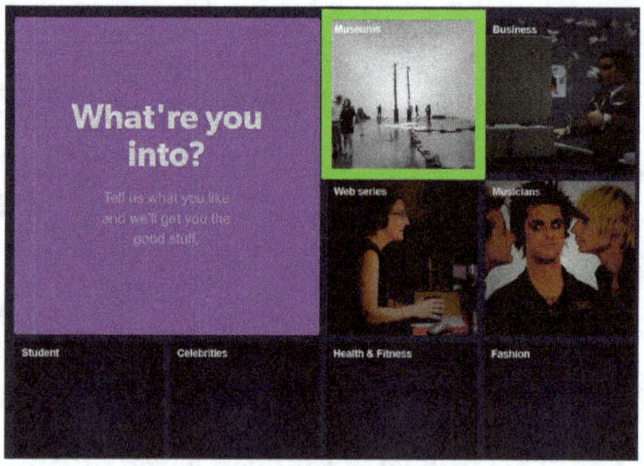

9. Select interests. Click or tap at least 5 categories of content that you'd like to see on your Tumblr page, then click or tap Next in the top-right corner of the page or screen.

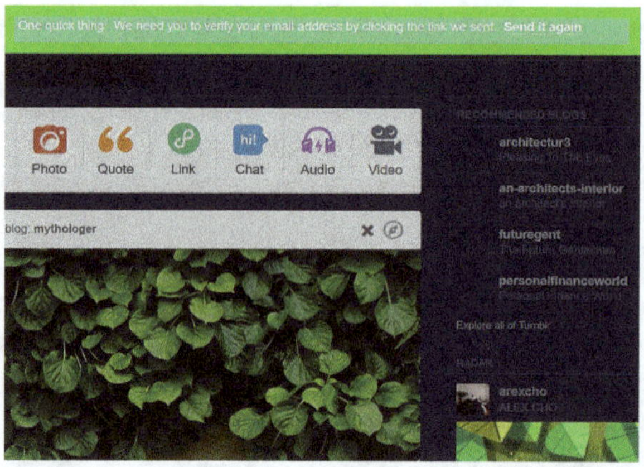

10. Verify your email address. The last step in creating your Tumblr account is verifying your email. To do so:

- Open your Tumblr email address' inbox.
- Select the "Verify your email address" email from Tumblr.
- Select the This is me! button in the body of the email.
- Check the "I'm not a robot" box, complete another spam check, click Verify Email, and click or, skip to your dashboard (desktop only).

Part 2. Interacting with Posts

1. Review the dashboard. At any time, you can select the house-shaped "Home" button on the Tumblr page (or at the bottom of your screen on mobile) to return to your dashboard, which is where all of the content from your blog and any blogs you follow will appear.

2. Find a post that you want to interact with. Scroll through your dashboard until you find a post that you want to like, reblog, or send in a message.

3. Like a post. If you like a post's content, you can click or tap the heart-shaped icon below the post to "like" it. This will also add the post to your profile's "Likes" section so that you can find it later if you please.

4. Reblog a post. To add the post to your blog, click or tap the rectangular arrow-shaped icon below the post (to the left of the "like" button), then click Reblog (desktop) or tap Post.

- You can add a comment to the post before reblogging it. To do so, click or tap the text box below the post, then add your commentary.
    1. You can also schedule a reblogged post for later by clicking next to Reblog (or by tapping in the upper-right corner), selecting the Schedule option, entering or selecting a post date and time, and selecting Schedule again.
    2. To add a reblogged post to your queue, click next to Reblog (or tap ☐ in the upper-right corner), select Add to queue, and select Queue.

5. Send a post in a direct message. You can forward a post to another person by selecting the paper

plane-shaped icon below the post, entering a username in the text box at the top of the message window, and then selecting the paper plane-shaped icon again.

- Like reblogging, you can add your own commentary to the message by selecting the text box below the post and entering your text before sending the message.

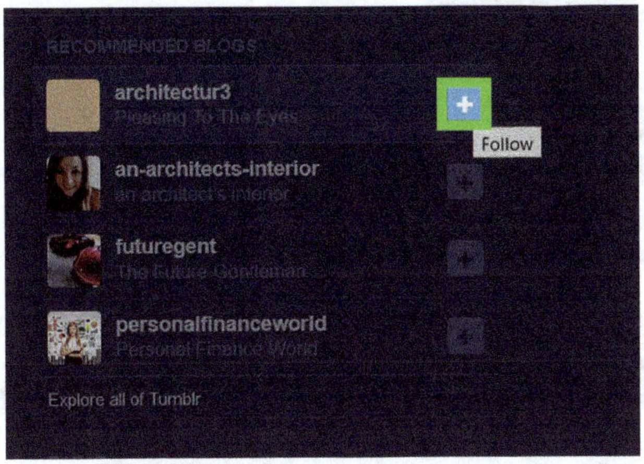

6. Follow a post's creator. Select the profile picture of the person who created a post, then select Follow to add them to your "Following" list. Content from people who you follow will appear in your dashboard.

- If you have someone specific whom you want to follow, you can search for them by clicking the text field on the dashboard (or by tapping the magnifying glass icon on mobile) and entering their name, selecting their name in the drop-down menu, and selecting Follow.

Part 3. Viewing your Content

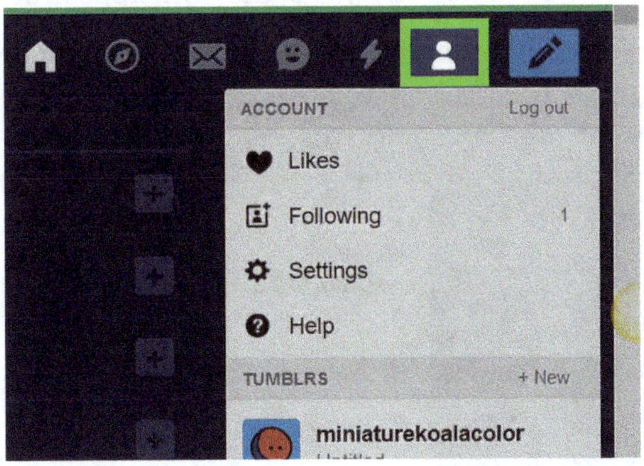

1. Open the profile menu. Click or tap the person-shaped silhouette icon in the upper-right side of the page (desktop) or in the bottom-right corner of the screen (mobile). On desktop, a drop-down menu will appear.

- This will take you to your profile's "POSTS" section on mobile.

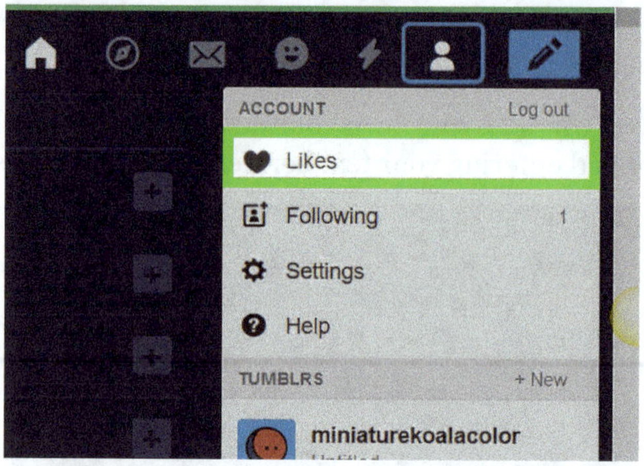

2. Select Likes. It's at the top of the drop-down menu (desktop) or below your blog's title (mobile).

3. Review your liked posts. If you've liked any posts, they will appear here.

- You can remove liked posts by tapping the heart icon on them here.

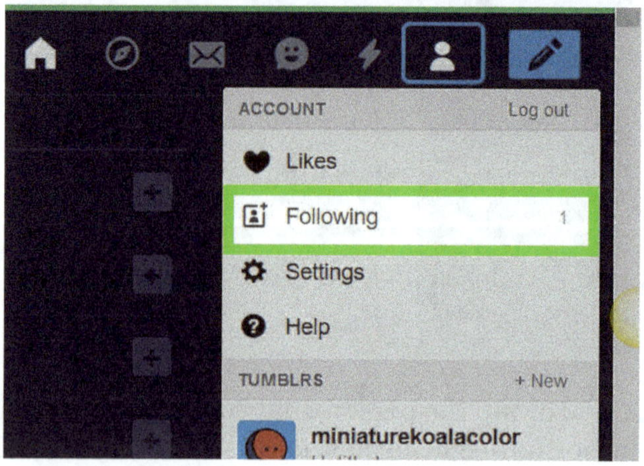

4. View the people who you're following. Open the profile menu again, then select Following. You can see a list of the people who you follow here.

- On mobile, just tap FOLLOWING to the right of the LIKES tab.
- You can unfollow users by clicking Unfollow to the right of a profile (desktop), or by tapping a profile, tapping the person-shaped icon in the top-right corner, and tapping Unfollow in the resulting menu.

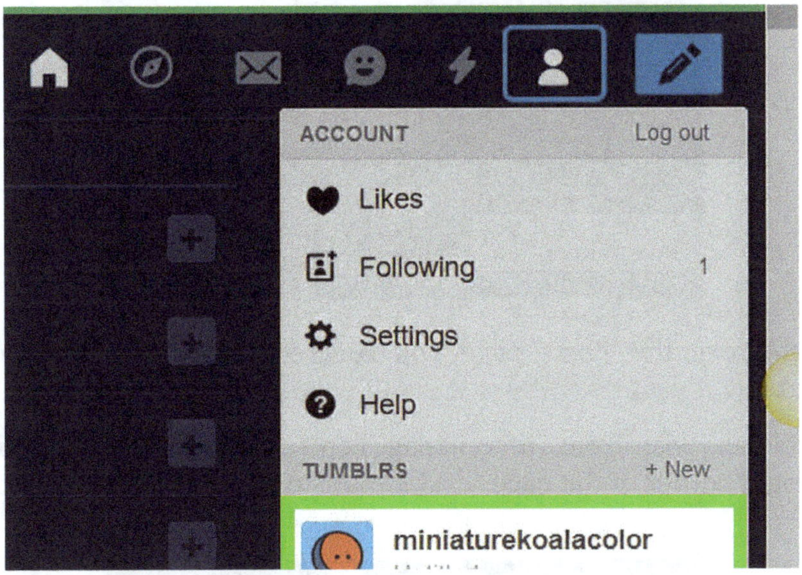

5. Go to your profile's "Posts" section. Open the profile menu, then click your username in the drop-down menu.

- On mobile, tap POSTS on the far-left side of the page.

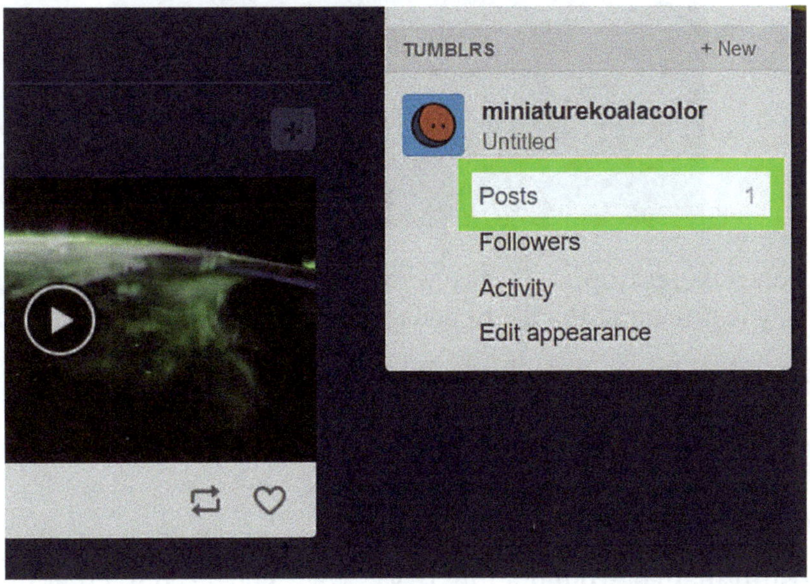

6. Review your content. This is where you'll see any posts that you've created. If you haven't created any posts, this will be a blank page.

Part 4. Creating a Post

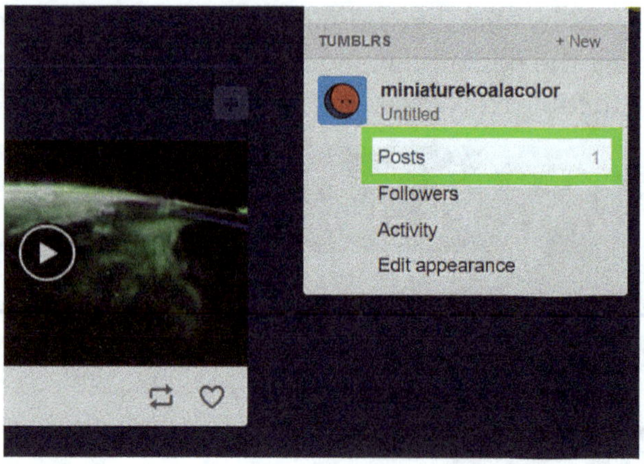

1. Make sure that you're on the "Posts" page. You can create a post here, or you can create a post from the dashboard.

- You can also make posts from different pages on Tumblr as well by selecting the pencil icon in the top-right corner of the page (desktop) or in the middle of the bottom of the screen (mobile).

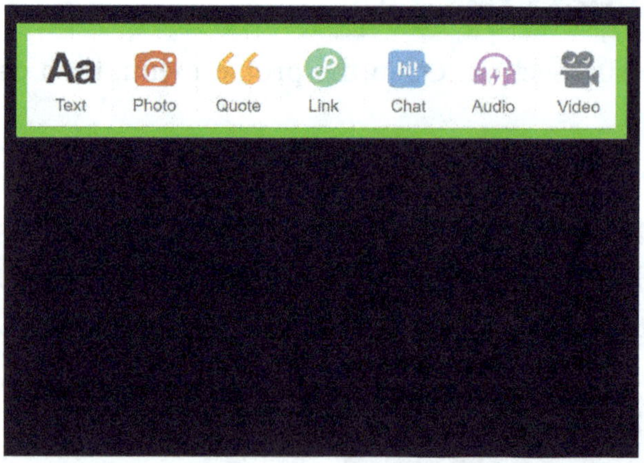

2. Select a type of post. On desktop, you'll see seven different colored post options near the top of the page; on mobile, you must first tap the pencil icon at the bottom of the page. The post types are as follows:

- Text - A text-only post.
- Photo - A photo (and possibly text) post.
- Quote - A quote and source post.
- Link - A post formatted around a link (e.g., "www.google.com") that opens to a different site.
- Chat - A post formatted for two or more chat recipients.
- Audio - An audio recording (e.g., music or a podcast).

- Video - A video post.
- GIF (mobile only) - A dynamic photo post.

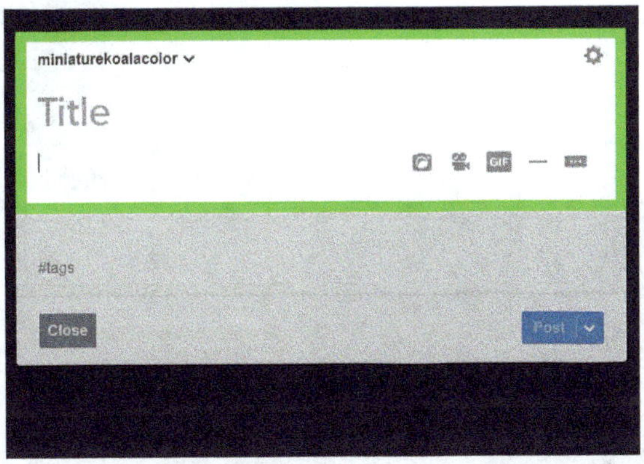

3. Create your post. Depending on the type of post that you select, the process for doing so will vary:
    - Text - Enter a title in the "Title" box, then enter the post's text in the "Your text here" box.
    - Photo - Select a photo upload option, select a photo, and enter a caption (optional). On mobile, you will have to allow Tumblr access to your camera and photos.
    - Quote - Enter your quote in the "Quote" box, then enter the quote's source in the "Source" box.
    - Link - Enter the link's title (mobile only), enter the link's web address, and add a caption (optional; mobile only).
    - Chat - Type in a recipient's name followed by a colon (e.g., "Mom:"), enter their dialogue, start a new line, and repeat.
    - Audio - Enter a song or audio clip's name, select it, and add a caption (optional).
    - Video - Select a video upload option, select a video, click the "This is my original work" switch (desktop only), and add a caption (optional).
    - GIF (mobile only) - Select a video to turn into a GIF, tap Next, add text and then tap Next, and tap Next one last time.

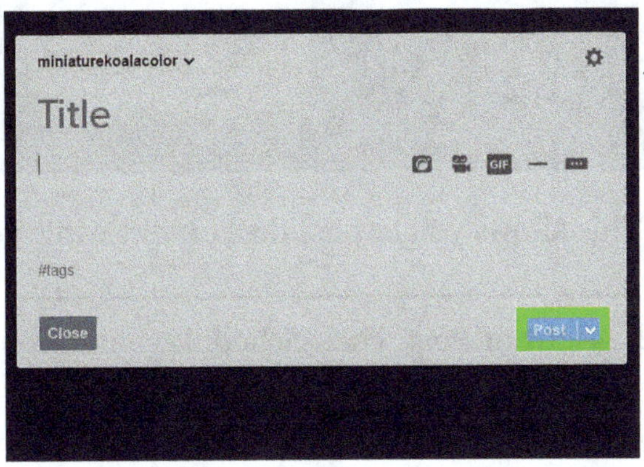

4. Post your content. Click or tap post at the bottom or in the top-right corner of the post to add it

to your blog. Your post will also appear on your dashboard and on the dashboards of anyone who follows you.

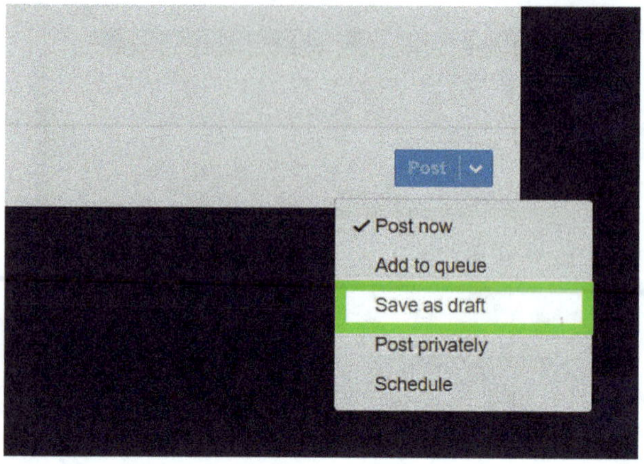

5. Save a post as a draft. You can save a draft of a post to continue working on it later from the "Drafts" section of your profile. Instead of selecting Post, do the following:

- Desktop - Click to the right of Post, click Save as draft, and click Save draft in the bottom-right corner of the post. You can find drafts on desktop by clicking the Drafts tab on the "Posts" page.
- Mobile - Tap the gear-shaped icon in the top-right corner of the post, tap Save as draft in the drop-down menu, and tap Save as draft in the top-right corner of the screen. You can find drafts on mobile by tapping the gear-shaped icon in the top-right corner of the "Posts" page and then tapping Drafts.

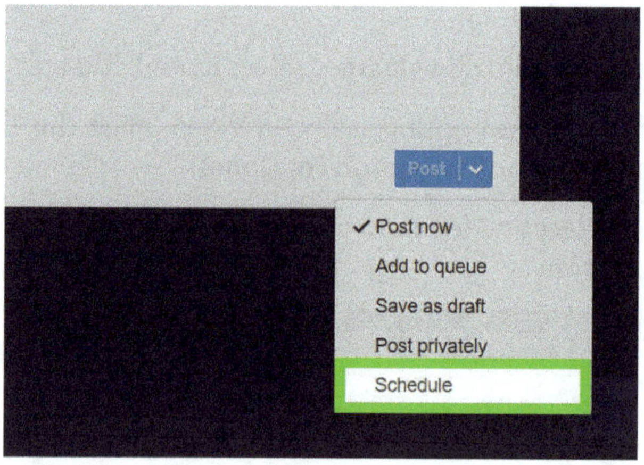

6. Schedule a post for later. This allows you to post the content while you're away from your Tumblr account. To do so:

- Desktop - Click to the right of Post, click Schedule, enter your preferred time, and click Schedule.
- Mobile - Tap the gear-shaped icon at the top of the post, tap Schedule, select a time, and tap Schedule.

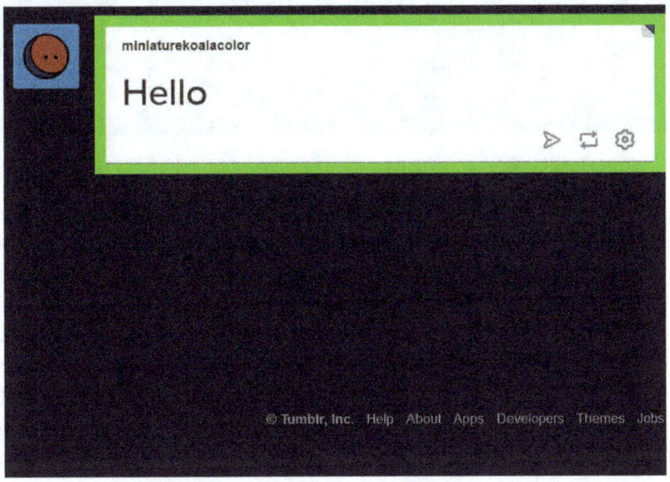

7. Review your posts. Return to the "Posts" section to see all of the posts that you have created.
    - You can delete posts from here by selecting the gear-shaped icon (or trash icon) below a post and then selecting Delete when prompted.

Permissions

All chapters in this book are published with permission under the Creative Commons Attribution Share Alike License or equivalent. Every chapter published in this book has been scrutinized by our experts. Their significance has been extensively debated. The topics covered herein carry significant information for a comprehensive understanding. They may even be implemented as practical applications or may be referred to as a beginning point for further studies.

We would like to thank the editorial team for lending their expertise to make the book truly unique. They have played a crucial role in the development of this book. Without their invaluable contributions this book wouldn't have been possible. They have made vital efforts to compile up to date information on the varied aspects of this subject to make this book a valuable addition to the collection of many professionals and students.

This book was conceptualized with the vision of imparting up-to-date and integrated information in this field. To ensure the same, a matchless editorial board was set up. Every individual on the board went through rigorous rounds of assessment to prove their worth. After which they invested a large part of their time researching and compiling the most relevant data for our readers.

The editorial board has been involved in producing this book since its inception. They have spent rigorous hours researching and exploring the diverse topics which have resulted in the successful publishing of this book. They have passed on their knowledge of decades through this book. To expedite this challenging task, the publisher supported the team at every step. A small team of assistant editors was also appointed to further simplify the editing procedure and attain best results for the readers.

Apart from the editorial board, the designing team has also invested a significant amount of their time in understanding the subject and creating the most relevant covers. They scrutinized every image to scout for the most suitable representation of the subject and create an appropriate cover for the book.

The publishing team has been an ardent support to the editorial, designing and production team. Their endless efforts to recruit the best for this project, has resulted in the accomplishment of this book. They are a veteran in the field of academics and their pool of knowledge is as vast as their experience in printing. Their expertise and guidance has proved useful at every step. Their uncompromising quality standards have made this book an exceptional effort. Their encouragement from time to time has been an inspiration for everyone.

The publisher and the editorial board hope that this book will prove to be a valuable piece of knowledge for students, practitioners and scholars across the globe.

Index

www.ingramcontent.com/pod-product-compliance
Lightning Source LLC
LaVergne TN
LVHW080647210926
848485LV00003B/338